CW01560562

Contents

Articles

References

Article Licenses

Lana Del Rey

This article is about the singer. For her debut studio album, see Lana Del Ray (album). For her first extended play, see Lana Del Rey (EP).

Lana Del Rey	
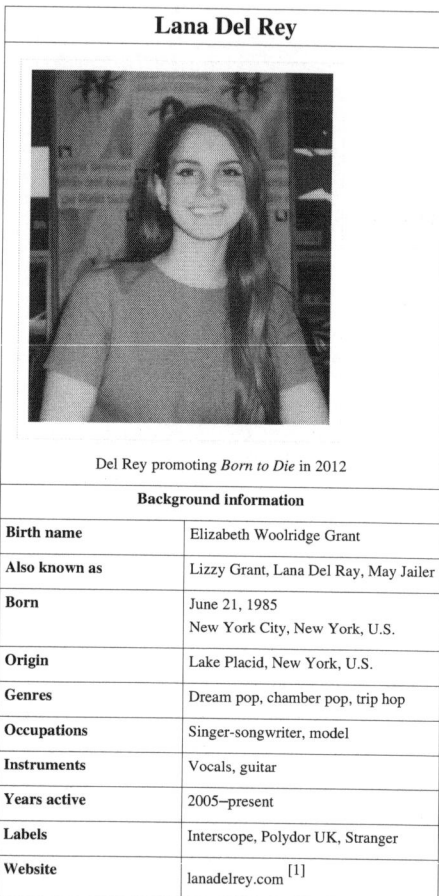 Del Rey promoting *Born to Die* in 2012	
Background information	
Birth name	Elizabeth Woolridge Grant
Also known as	Lizzy Grant, Lana Del Ray, May Jailer
Born	June 21, 1985 New York City, New York, U.S.
Origin	Lake Placid, New York, U.S.
Genres	Dream pop, chamber pop, trip hop
Occupations	Singer-songwriter, model
Instruments	Vocals, guitar
Years active	2005–present
Labels	Interscope, Polydor UK, Stranger
Website	lanadelrey.com [1]

Elizabeth Woolridge Grant (born June 21, 1985),[2] known by her stage name **Lana Del Rey**, is an American singer-songwriter. Del Rey started songwriting at the age of 18 and signed her first recording contract with 5 Points Records in 2007, releasing her first digital album *Lana Del Ray* in January 2010. Del Rey bought herself out of the contract with 5 Points Records in April 2010. She signed a joint contract with Interscope, Polydor, and Stranger Records in July 2011.

Del Rey released her second studio album *Born to Die* in January 2012. It debuted at number two on the U.S. *Billboard* 200, and was the fifth best-selling album of 2012. A remix of its fifth single "Summertime Sadness", produced by Cedric Gervais, became her highest-charting track on the U.S. *Billboard* Hot 100 after peaking at number six in the country. Del Rey released her third extended play *Paradise* that November; three of its tracks were featured in her short film *Tropico*, which was premiered in December. Her third studio album *Ultraviolence* was released in June 2014 and debuted as number one on the *Billboard* 200.

Del Rey's music has been noted for its cinematic sound and its references to various aspects of pop culture, particularly that of the 1950s and 1960s Americana. The singer has described herself as a "self-styled gangsta Nancy Sinatra". Musically, she draws influence from what she deems to be the masters of each genre, including Elvis Presley, Amy Winehouse, Janis Joplin, Nirvana, Eminem, Bruce Springsteen, and Britney Spears, as well as from poetry and film noir.[3]

Early life

"I loved church. I loved the mysticism, the idea of something bigger, the idea of a divine plan. For me, the concept of religion transitioned into a really healthy idea of God--I don't have the traditional views of a conservative Catholic, but my imagination was opened within the big blue-and-gold cathedral walls. I liked the idea of being looked after."

—Del Rey on the Catholic Church

Lana Del Rey was born Elizabeth Woolridge Grant in New York City on June 21, 1985, to former Grey Group copywriter turned entrepreneur, Rob Grant, and former Grey account executive, Pat Grant. She is of Scottish descent. She has a sister, Caroline (born 1988/1989), and a brother, Charlie (born 1993/1994). Del Rey grew up in Lake Placid, New York until age 15,[4] when she was sent to Kent School, a boarding school in Connecticut, for three years to deal with her alcohol dependence.[5] Before that, she attended a Catholic elementary school. Around age 18, she moved to The Bronx to attend Fordham University, studying a branch of philosophy known as metaphysics because "it bridged the gap between God and science. I was interested in God and how technology could bring us closer to finding out where we came from and why." She said, "that was when my musical experience began. I kind of found people for myself." She stayed in the Bronx for four years and Brooklyn for another four years. While enrolled in university, Del Rey helped paint and rebuild houses on an Indian reservation "across the country".

She began singing in the church choir when she was a child, where she was the cantor. After her uncle taught her how to play the guitar when she was 18, she "realized [that she] could probably write a million songs with those six chords," and she began performing in nightclubs around the city under various names such as Sparkle Jump Rope Queen and Lizzy Grant and the Phenomena. "I was always singing, but didn't plan on pursuing it seriously. When I got to New York City when I was 18, I started playing in clubs in Brooklyn—I have good friends and devoted fans on the underground scene, but we were playing for each other at that point—and that was it."

Career

2005–10: Career beginnings, *Kill Kill*, and *Lana Del Ray*

Main articles: Sirens (May Jailer album), Kill Kill and Lana Del Ray (album)

"I wanted to be part of a high-class scene of musicians. It was half-inspired because I didn't have many friends, and I was hoping that I would meet people and fall in love and start a community around me, the way they used to do in the '60s."

—Del Rey explaining why she went into the music industry.

On April 25, 2005, a seven-track compact disc was registered under Elizabeth Woolridge Grant with the United States Copyright Office. The application title was "Rock Me Stable" with another title "Young Like Me" also listed. The track titles are currently unknown. Between 2005 and 2006, the album *Sirens* was recorded under the name "May Jailer" and leaked in May 2012.

"Kill Kill"

"Kill Kill" combines electronica and blues rock elements, over Marilyn Monroe inspired vocals. One of Del Rey's earlier tracks, it differs from her current style in that it is jazzier and less-melancholic.

At her first performance in 2006 for the Williamsburg Live Songwriting Competition, Del Rey met Van Wilson, an A&R rep for 5 Points Records, an independent label owned by David Nichtern. In 2007, Del Rey signed a record contract for $10,000 with 5 Points Records while still a senior at Fordham University and moved into Manhattan Mobile Home Park, a trailer park in North Bergen, New Jersey, and subsequently began working with producer David Kahne, with whom she released her first three-track EP titled *Kill Kill* in October 2008. She explained that "David asked to work with me only a day after he got my demo. He is known as a producer with a lot of integrity and who had an interest in making music that wasn't just pop." Her album, however, was shelved, causing her to shift her focus. Instead, she began to work in community service. "Homeless outreach, drug, and alcohol rehabilitation—that's been my life for the past five years," she told *Vogue UK* in 2012. Her debut full-length album, titled *Lana Del Ray*, was released in January 2010. Her father, Robert Grant, helped with the marketing of the album, which was available for purchase on iTunes for a brief period before being withdrawn. David Kahne, who produced Grant and previous label owner David Nichtern have both stated that Grant bought the rights back from her label, 5 Points, as she wanted it out of circulation to "...stifle future opportunities to distribute it—an echo of rumors that the action was part of a calculated strategy. Del Rey met her current managers, Ben Mawson and Ed Millett, three months after *Lana Del Ray* and they helped her to get out of her contract with 5 Points Records, where, in her opinion, "nothing was happening." Shortly after, she moved to London, England and moved in with Mawson "for a few years." About choosing her stage name, she has said: "I wanted a name I could shape the music towards. I was going to Miami quite a lot at the time, speaking a lot of Spanish with my friends from Cuba - Lana Del Rey reminded us of the glamour of the seaside. It sounded gorgeous coming off the tip of the tongue. She has said that her lawyers and managers made up the name Lana Del Rey and persuaded her to adopt the stage name. On September 1, 2010, Del Rey was featured by Mando Diao in their MTV Unplugged concert at Union Film-Studios in Berlin.[6]

2011–13: *Born to Die, Paradise,* and *Tropico*

Main articles: Born to Die (Lana Del Rey album), Paradise (Lana Del Rey EP) and Tropico (film)

After uploading a few of her tracks to her YouTube channel, Del Rey was discovered and signed by Stranger Records to release her debut single "Video Games". She told *The Observer*, "I just put that song online a few months ago because it was my favourite. To be honest, it wasn't going to be the single but people have really responded to it." The song earned her a Q award for "Next Big Thing" in October 2011 and an Ivor Novello for "Best Contemporary Song" in 2012. The same month, she signed a joint deal with Interscope Records and Polydor to work on her second studio album *Born to Die*. Del Rey built anticipation to the album by doing a number of live appearances, such as promotional concerts at the Bowery Ballroom and at the Chateau Marmont, and with performances at television shows such as *De Wereld Draait Door*, and *Later... with Jools Holland*. Del Rey also performed two songs from the album on *Saturday Night Live* on January 14, 2012 and received a negative response from critics and the general public. Del Rey's performance was defended by the evening program's guest host, actor Daniel Radcliffe, despite not having seen her performance. She had earlier defended her spot on the program, saying: "I'm a good musician [...] I have been singing for a long time, and I think that [*SNL* creator] Lorne Michaels knows that [...] it's not a fluke decision." The following week on SNL, Kristen Wiig impersonated Del Rey where she humorously defended herself during Weekend Update. When asked how long she was able to enjoy her success before she started receiving backlash, Del Rey said "I never felt any of the enjoyment. It was all bad, all of it."

Del Rey performing at the Bowery Ballroom in 2011

Born to Die was officially released on January 31, 2012 worldwide, and reached number one in 11 countries, though critical reaction was divided. The same week, Del Rey said that she bought back the rights to her 2010 debut album, and had plans to re-release it in the summer of 2012 under Interscope Records and Polydor. Contrary to Del Rey's press statement, her previous record label and producer David Kahne have both stated that she bought the rights to the album when she and the label parted company, due to the offer of a new deal, in April 2010. *Born to Die* sold 3.4 million copies in 2012, making it the fifth-best-selling album of 2012. In the United States, *Born to Die* charted on the *Billboard* 200 album chart well into 2012, lingering at number 76, after 36 weeks on the chart.

In an interview with RTVE on June 15, 2012, Del Rey announced she has been working on a new album due in November; in an interview with Tim Blackwell for Nova FM in Melbourne, Australia, Del Rey added that her upcoming November release would not be a new album, but more like an EP.

Mid-September saw the official announcement of *Paradise*'s lead single, "Ride". On September 19, 2012, the music video for "Blue Velvet" was released through H&M. One day later, on September 20, "Blue Velvet" became available for purchase as a promotional single. "Ride" became available for purchase on September 25, 2013. The music video for "Ride" was premiered at the Aero Theatre in Santa Monica, California on October 10, 2012. Some critics panned the video as pro-prostitution and antifeminist, the latter being a word attributed to Del Rey's work since "Video Games".

Del Rey's *Paradise Edition* of *Born to Die* was set to be released on November 12. With the release of her third EP, *Paradise*, Del Rey spawned her second top 10 album in the United States, debuting at number 10 on the *Billboard* 200 with 67,000 copies sold in its first week. At the 2012 MTV Europe Music Awards, Del Rey received nominations in the categories Best Alternative, Best Push, and Best New Act. Winning Best Alternative, Del Rey presented the award for Best Female to Taylor Swift.

At the 2013 BRIT Awards, she won the award for International Female Solo Artist, making it her second BRIT Award to date. Del Rey's win surprised critics who highly anticipated Taylor Swift to win the award. In March 2013, Del Rey recited Walt Whitman's poem "Song of Myself" for the French fashion magazine, L'Officiel Paris.

Del Rey's seventh single, "Dark Paradise", was released as a single in Germany, Austria, and Switzerland on March 1, 2013. Del Rey won the ECHO Awards for Best International Newcomer and Best International Pop/Rock Artist on March 21, 2013. A music video for Del Rey's cover of Leonard Cohen's "Chelsea Hotel #2" was released on March 27, 2013. The following month, in April 2013, another self-produced video was released; it showed Del Rey and her boyfriend, Barrie-James O'Neil, covering "Summer Wine", by Lee Hazlewood. "Burning Desire" became available for purchase as a stand-alone download on March 19, 2013 as the second promotional single from *Paradise*; its music

Del Rey performing at Planeta Terra Festival in 2013

video was premiered the previous month on Valentine's Day of 2013. Together with the film's director, co-writer, and co-producer Baz Luhrmann, Del Rey penned the original song "Young and Beautiful" for the soundtrack of the 2013 film adaptation of *The Great Gatsby*. Following the song's release, it peaked at 22 on the *Billboard* Hot 100, making it Del Rey's highest peak on the chart. However, shortly after its release to contemporary hit radio, the label prematurely pulled it and decided to send a different song to that format; on July 2, 2013, a Cedric Gervais remix of

Del Rey's "Summertime Sadness" was sent there; a sleeper hit, the song proved to be a success, surpassing "Young and Beautiful", reaching number 6 and becoming her first American top ten hit. The remix won the Grammy Award for Best Remixed Recording, Non-Classical in 2013.

Alongside *Paradise*, Del Rey announced plans to launch a short film titled *Tropico*. *Tropico* was filmed in late June 2013 and directed by Anthony Mandler. On November 22, 2013, an official trailer for *Tropico* was released; at the end of the trailer, it was announced that the film would be uploaded to Del Rey's official VEVO account on December 5, 2013. The short film premiered on December 4 at Cinerama Dome in Hollywood, California. Before showing the film, Del Rey told the audience "I really just wanted us all to be together so I could try and visually close out my chapter before I release the new record, *Ultraviolence*." Journalists identified the phrase from the Anthony Burgess' dystopian novella *A Clockwork Orange* (1962), but reports were conflicting as to whether or not the title was stylized as one or two words. On December 6, 2013, an EP, also titled *Tropico*, was made available for purchase via iTunes; it includes the film itself along with the three aforementioned songs.

2014: *Ultraviolence*

Main article: Ultraviolence (album)

On January 23, 2014, it was announced that Del Rey would be covering the song "Once Upon a Dream" (from the 1959 film *Sleeping Beauty*) for the 2014 dark fantasy film *Maleficent*. The single was released on January 26. On February 20, Del Rey posted a picture of herself and Dan Auerbach on Twitter with the caption "Me and Dan Auerbach are excited to present you Ultraviolence". Del Rey and Auerbach were rumoured to be working together at Auerbach's Easy Eye Sound recording studio in Nashville, Tennessee in January and he was said to be producing her upcoming album. In March, Rufus Wainwright revealed in an interview that he was currently working with Del Rey. The first single of *Ultraviolence*, "West Coast", was released on April 14. On May 23, Del Rey performed three songs at Kim Kardashian and Kanye West's pre-wedding celebration at the Palace of Versailles. West had previously played Del Rey's "Young & Beautiful" during his proposal to Kardashian in October 2013. "Shades of Cool", the second single, was released on May 26, 2014. The third single and title track, "Ultraviolence", was released on June 4. June 8 saw the release of the fourth single, "Brooklyn Baby". *Ultraviolence* was released on June 13, 2014, and debuted at number one in twelve countries, including the United States and United Kingdom. The album sold 880,000 copies in its first week, worldwide. Del Rey described her third studio album as being "more stripped down but still cinematic and dark." A *Rolling Stone* article revealed that Del Rey would be a guest on Brian Wilson's forthcoming studio album.

Artistry

Lana Del Rey performing "Body Electric" at Irving Plaza in 2012

Musical style

She has been described as a "self-styled gangsta Nancy Sinatra" and "Lolita lost in the hood" and her music has been noted for its cinematic sound and its references to various aspects of pop culture, particularly that of 1950s and '60s Americana. *Rolling Stone* noted that Del Rey enjoys playing the role of lounge singer. Del Rey has also been called "a torch singer of the internet era" and "the anti-Gaga." Born Lizzy Grant, Del Rey has attributed her work to various stage names including Lana Rey Del Mar, Sparkle Jump Rope Queen, and May Jailer. Settling on Lana Del Rey, the singer claims she selected the name because it was beautiful. First mention of the name Lana Del Rey came from her Spanish-speaking Cuban friends. Following in the shadow of artists like Prince and David Bowie, Del Rey chose her musical identity because it "reminded [her] of the glamour of the seaside. It sounded gorgeous coming off the tip of the tongue."

Del Rey has stylized her musical sound as "Hollywood sadcore". *Time* said the solid core of her sound was "movie music", with a fairy-dusting of harp and an ominous timpani, laid out over-top a hip hop vocal cadence. Her vocal style has been likened to rap. Of *Born to Die*, indie music journal *Drowned in Sound* wrote, "She likes that whole hip hop thing though, has this whole swagger thing going that not many girls like her got," adding that it sounded like a poppier Bond soundtrack. In "National Anthem", "Off to the Races," and "Diet Mountain Dew", Del Rey employs this alternative rapping technique. Under the stage name Lizzy Grant, she called her music "Hawaiian glam metal", while the work of her May Jailer project was acoustic. Attributed to many genres, Del Rey's sound has been primarily linked to indie and baroque pop and experiments with hip hop and trip hop genres.

Lyrically, "Born to Die" was described as sad. Del Rey elaborates: "I'm not sad, I'm happy. I feel like I'm happy because I'm at peace with the way that things are... I did have a darker filter on sometimes, but that slowly lifted through doing a lot of different things. And finding true love is something that really did inspire me, lyrically. Because I felt so much the same for so much of my life and then when you find someone exciting, you don't know that you could actually feel differently than you did before. I was inspired."

Voice and timbre

"Million Dollar Man"

"Million Dollar Man", from the album *Born to Die*, demonstrates Del Rey's contralto range that transitions to high timbres with great ease.

Problems playing this file? See media help.

Del Rey possesses an expansive contralto vocal range, which has been described as captivating and highly emotive, being able to transcend from sounding high and girlish in her timbre, down to a low and jazzy sound with great ease, although both these areas of the voice can be conflicting in the contrast of their sound, polarizing opinion. When recording in the studio Del Rey is known for vocal multi-layering, double tracking and overlays which, as it has been noted, is difficult for her to replicate within a live setting, especially with the lack of backing singers to fill out the original vocal style. Contemporary music critics have called her voice "smoky", "gravely", and reminiscent of

Marilyn Monroe.

Del Rey stated the use of her lower vocals on the tracks from *Born to Die*, claiming that "people weren't taking me very seriously, so I lowered my voice, believing that it would help me stand out. Now I sing quite low... well, for a female anyway." "I sing low now, but my voice used to be a lot higher. Because of the way I look, I needed something to ground the entire project. Otherwise I think people would assume I was some airhead singer. Well, I don't think... I know. I've sung one way, and sung another, and I've seen what people are drawn to", she said on the topic.

Influences

Lana Del Rey performing in Cologne in 2011

Amongst her musical influences, Del Rey cites several contemporary artists such as Elvis Presley, Antony and the Johnsons, Frank Sinatra, Amy Winehouse and Eminem. "[I really] just like the masters of every genre", she told BBC radio presenter Jo Whiley. Her favorite artists include Bob Dylan, Frank Sinatra, Jeff Buckley and Leonard Cohen. She covered Cohen's "Chelsea Hotel #2" in 2013. She also cited "strong female characters" such as Courtney Love, Stevie Nicks, and Joni Mitchell as inspirational.

Janis Joplin's live version of "Summertime" from the *Cheap Thrills* compilation album is one of Del Rey's favorite songs. Del Rey has also cited "Time of the Season" by The Zombies and "Hotel California" by The Eagles as favorites and inspirations. Her favorite films, *The Godfather*, *The Godfather Part II*, and *American Beauty* have also inspired her musical style. Inspired by poetry, Del Rey cites Walt Whitman and Allen Ginsberg as instrumental to her songwriting. Specifically, she enjoys the chapbook "Leaves of Grass" by Whitman and the poem "Howl" by Ginsberg. Her song, "Body Electric" from her third EP, *Paradise*, alludes to Whitman in the lyric, "Whitman is my daddy". The song's chorus of "I sing the body electric" is a direct reference to his poem "I Sing The Body Electric". She recited Whitman's poem "Song of Myself" for the French fashion magazine, L'Officiel Paris. Before becoming a singer, Del Rey wanted to be a poet. As a child, her father wrote country songs for personal enjoyment, while her mother was interested in singing; the former introduced her to The Beach Boys, while the latter was a fan of Carly Simon.

Other ventures

On January 4, 2012, it was reported she had signed a deal with NEXT Model Management agency. H&M confirmed that Del Rey would be modeling and recording a cover version of the popular 1950s prom anthem "Blue Velvet" for their 2012 Autumn Campaign. H&M's 2012 Winter campaign, featuring Lana Del Rey, was released on October 12. This is the second H&M campaign Lana Del Rey is featured in. On August 22, 2012, executives announced that Del Rey would endorse their new Jaguar F-Type which was unveiled by Del Rey at the Paris Motor Show in September 2012. Adrian Hallmark, Jaguar's global brand director, explained their choice, saying Del Rey had "a unique blend of authenticity and modernity."

The song "Burning Desire", which was initially available for immediate digital download upon pre-ordering Del Rey's third EP, Paradise, was later made available for purchase on Amazon.com and 7digital as a stand-alone download on March 19, 2013, one month after its music video hit YouTube. The song serves as the title track to a 13 minute promotional short film for the Jaguar F-Type, called *Desire*. The film, directed by Adam Smith, was produced by Ridley Scott and stars Damian Lewis.

In 2010, Del Rey also acted in a short film called *Poolside*, which she made with several friends on a reported budget of $400.

Personal life

Del Rey stated that she suffered from alcoholism at a young age. At the age of 15, she was sent to Kent School, a boarding school in Connecticut, for three years to get sober. Del Rey has been sober since 2004. In September 2012, she told *GQ*:

> I was a big drinker at the time. I would drink every day. I would drink alone. I thought the whole concept was so fucking cool. A great deal of what I wrote on *Born To Die* is about these wilderness years. When I write about the thing that I've lost I feel like I'm writing about alcohol because that was the first love of my life. My parents were worried, I was worried. I knew it was a problem when I liked it more than I liked doing anything else. I was like, 'I'm fucked. I am totally fucked'. Like, at first it's fine and you think you have a dark side – it's exciting – and then you realise the dark side wins every time if you decide to indulge in it. It's also a completely different way of living when you know that...a different species of person. It was the worst thing that ever happened to me.

She was in a relationship with Kassidy ex-member Barrie-James O'Neill from August 2011 until June 2014. Previously, Del Rey was in a relationship with alternative rock and antifolk musician, Steven Mertens, who produced her debut album, *Lana Del Ray*, before it was re-recorded by David Kahne. She was also in a seven-year long on-again, off-again relationship with the head of a record label, who was a great inspiration to her and whom she calls the love of her life. She met him in her early twenties when she was trying to have her debut album released by a major label, and they are still close. Del Rey lives near Hancock Park in Koreatown, Los Angeles, with her siblings, Caroline and Charlie. Del Rey is Roman Catholic.

Having been labeled as antifeminist multiple times in the past, Del Rey dismissed feminism in June 2014, telling *The Fader*: "For me, the issue of feminism is just not an interesting concept. I'm more interested in, you know, SpaceX and Tesla, what's going to happen with our intergalactic possibilities. Whenever people bring up feminism, I'm like, god. I'm just not really that interested." She also defended herself against the accusations of antifeminism, saying "For me, a true feminist is someone who is a woman who does exactly what she wants. If my choice is to, I don't know, be with a lot of men, or if I enjoy a really physical relationship, I don't think that's necessarily being anti-feminist. For me the argument of feminism never really should have come into the picture. Because I don't know too much about the history of feminism, and so I'm not really a relevant person to bring into the conversation. Everything I was writing was so autobiographical, it could really only be a personal analysis."

Del Rey's left hand is tattooed with the letter "M", referencing her grandmother, Madeleine, and the word "paradise". Her right hand is tattooed with the phrase "trust no one". She also has the phrase "die young" tattooed on her right ring finger. Another tattoo on her right arm says, "Whitman Nabokov". Most recently, she had "Nina & Billie" tattooed across her chest. She is a supporter of the English Premier League team Liverpool and Scottish Premier League side Celtic.

Discography

Main article: Lana Del Rey discography

- *Lana Del Ray* (2010)
- *Born to Die* (2012)
- *Ultraviolence* (2014)

Filmography

Films			
Year	Film	Role	Notes
2010	*Poolside*	Lisa	Short film
2013	*Tropico*	Eve	

Awards and nominations

Main article: List of awards and nominations received by Lana Del Rey

Del Rey's work has earned her numerous awards and nominations; she has won the Q Award for "Best New Thing", a *GQ* Award for "Woman of the Year", two BRIT Award for "International Breakthrough Act" and "International Pop Female Solo Artist", and an EMA for "Best Alternative Act". In 2013, she received her first Grammy nominations at the 56th Annual Grammy Awards. These nominations include Best Pop Vocal Album for *Paradise* and Best Song Written for Visual Media for "Young and Beautiful".

References

[1] http://lanadelrey.com

[2] ; ;

[3] Kaufman, Gil. (February 2, 2012) Lana Del Rey 'Compelled' By Britney Spears - Music, Celebrity, Artist News (http://www.mtv.com/news/articles/1678375/lana-del-rey-britney-spears.jhtml). MTV.com. Retrieved on May 12, 2013.

- [a] "Yeah, I grew up in Lake Placid, New York until I was fifteen, and then I went to boarding school for three years in Connecticut. Then I moved to the Bronx when I was almost eighteen."
- [b] "That was my focus since I moved to the Bronx when I was eighteen."
- [c] "Well, I lived in the Bronx for four years. I lived in Brooklyn for like four years after that. I always consider myself to have a serious street side, even when I was in high school. I mean, I was pretty crazy. Everyone I knew was really crazy.
- [d] "I did move into a trailer park when I made my first record. I got ten grand from Five Points Records and moved into Manhattan Mobile Home in New Jersey."

[5] Lana Del Rey Goes Nude in GQ's Men of the Year Issue (http://theblemish.com/2012/09/lana-del-rey-goes-nude-in-gqs-men-of-the-year-issue/). theblemish.com. Retrieved September 8, 2012

[6] "INTERVIEW MIT MANDO DIAO" (http://hitparade.ch/interview.asp?id=443). hitparade.ch. Retrieved August 27, 2012

External links

- Official website (http://LanaDelRey.com)
- Lana Del Rey (http://www.discogs.com/artist/Lana+Del+Rey) discography at Discogs
- Lana Del Rey (http://Last.FM/music/Lana+Del+Rey) statistics and tagging at Last.FM
- Lana Del Rey (http://www.imdb.com/name/nm4787894/) at the Internet Movie Database
- Lana Del Rey (https://twitter.com/LanaDelRey) on Twitter
- Lana Del Rey (http://MusicTea.org/music/lanadelrey) discography at MusicTea

Ultraviolence (album)

Ultraviolence	
Studio album by Lana Del Rey	
Released	June 13, 2014
Recorded	2013–14; Easy Eye Sound (Nashville); The Bridge (Glendale); Electric Lady Studios (New York City); Echo Studio (Los Angeles); The Church Studios (London); The Green Building (Santa Monica)
Genre	Dream pop
Length	51:24
Label	• Interscope • Polydor
Producer	• Dan Auerbach • Lana Del Rey • Paul Epworth • Lee Foster • Daniel Heath • Greg Kurstin • Rick Nowels • Blake Stranathan
Lana Del Rey chronology	
• *Tropico* • *Ultraviolence* • (2013) • (2014)	
Alternative cover	
Urban Outfitters-exclusive vinyl version cover	
Singles from *Ultraviolence*	

1. "West Coast"
   Released: April 14, 2014
2. "Shades of Cool"
   Released: May 26, 2014
3. "Ultraviolence"
   Released: June 4, 2014
4. "Brooklyn Baby"
   Released: June 8, 2014	

Ultraviolence is the third studio album by American singer-songwriter Lana Del Rey, released on June 13, 2014 by Interscope and Polydor Records. Despite originally dismissing the possibility of releasing another record after her major-label debut *Born to Die* (2012), Del Rey began planning its follow-up in 2013. Production continued into 2014, at which time she heavily collaborated with Dan Auerbach to revamp what she initially considered to be the completed record. The project saw additional contributions from producers including Paul Epworth, Greg Kurstin, and Rick Nowels.

Ultraviolence received positive reviews from contemporary music critics, who commended its cohesiveness and overall production. It debuted at number one on the U.S. *Billboard* 200 with first-week sales of 182,000 copies, becoming Del Rey's first number-one album on the chart and the best-selling debut week of her career. As of July 2014, it has sold more than one million copies worldwide. *Ultraviolence* was preceded by the digital release of four singles, "West Coast", "Shades of Cool", "Ultraviolence", and "Brooklyn Baby".

Background and production

After the release of *Born to Die* in 2012, Del Rey dismissed the idea of releasing another album, because she had "already said everything [she] wanted to say." However, by February 2013, Del Rey had started work on an album saying, "It's a little more stripped down but still cinematic and dark. I've been working on it really slowly but I love everything I've done. I've been writing in Santa Monica and I know what the record sounds like. Now I just have to finish it. Musically I've worked with the same three guys." She mentioned that one of the songs off the album would be called "Black Beauty". When the demo version leaked in July, Del Rey stated "I do feel discouraged, yeah. I don't really know what to put on the record. But I guess I could just put them on and see what happens. Each time I write... I'll never write a song if I don't think it's going to be perfect for the record." She also stated that she was writing "low-key and stripped back" songs and was working with Dan Heath, her boyfriend Barrie-James O'Neill and that she wanted to work with Lou Reed.

In October, Del Rey said about the prospect of a new album, "When people ask me about it, I just have to be honest — I really don't know. I don't want to say, 'Yeah, definitely — the next one's better than this one,' because I don't really hear a next one. My muse is very fickle. She only comes to me sometimes, which is annoying."

By January 2014, Del Rey and Dan Auerbach were rumoured to be working together at Auerbach's Easy Eye Sound recording studio in Nashville, Tennessee and he was said to be producing her upcoming album.

Del Rey and Auerbach were initially scheduled to work together for three days but ended up spending two weeks on recording a full album. On February 20, Del Rey posted a picture of herself and Auerbach on Twitter with the caption "Me and Dan Auerbach are excited to present you Ultraviolence". About working with Del Rey, Auerbach later said "She impressed me every day. There were moments when she was fighting me. I could sense that maybe she didn't want to have anybody think she wasn't in control because I'm sure it's really hard to be a woman in the music business. So we bumped heads a little bit, but at the end of the day we were dancing to the songs." The artist stated that the album draws inspiration from the West Coast, as well as from Brooklyn, New York. In addition, it also features heavy guitars and jazz tones. Del Rey also stated that the inclusion of Auerbach was last-minute. The two had met in New York when she believed that the record was finished. On the release of *Ultraviolence*, she reaffirmed her earlier reluctance to make another album, saying "I mean, I still feel that way, but with this album I felt less like I had to chronicle my journeys and more like I could just recount snippets in my recent past that felt exhilarating to me."

Release and artwork

During the premiere of her short film *Tropico* on December 4, 2013, Del Rey explained to the audience that "I really just wanted us all to be together so I could try and visually close out my chapter [of her second studio album *Born to Die* (2012) and third extended play *Paradise* (2012)] before I release the new record, *Ultraviolence*." Journalists identified the phrase from Anthony Burgess' dystopian novella *A Clockwork Orange* (1962), although initial reports were conflicting as to whether or not the title would be stylized as the one-word "Ultraviolence" or two-word "Ultra Violence". In February 2014, she mentioned the possibility of releasing the record on May 1, although during her concert in Montreal on May 5 stated that the project would be released the following month.

On May 8, Del Rey announced the track listings for the 11-track standard version and 14-track deluxe version of *Ultraviolence*. Its black-and-white album artwork depicts Del Rey dressed in a sheer white T-shirt and a white strapless bra while leaning against her Mercedes-Benz 380SL; the title "Ultraviolence" is positioned beneath her image in an all-capitalized typeface, similar to the covers for *Born to Die* and *Paradise*. The artwork was unveiled on May 14, along with the confirmation that the record itself would be released on June 17 in the United States. It was made available through the traditional CD, digital download, and vinyl formats, and was additionally distrubuted in a multi-piece box set; it covers the title "Ultraviolence" in black foil, includes the deluxe record on compact disc and on a two-piece vinyl collection, and is packaged with four photo art cards. Clothing retailer Urban Outfitters offers an exclusive vinyl version of the standard version of *Ultraviolence*, and features an alternate cover which depicts a close-up of Del Rey's knee in torn jeans as she holds a loose strand of fabric from the torn denim.

Composition

"Shades of Cool", was described by Consequence of Sound as "a slow and slightly gloomy ballad marked by reverberated guitars, slight atmospherics, and Del Rey's vocals that alternate between a hushed whisper and ephemeral wailing." The song consists of "a chiming guitar, slow-burn bass line, and swelling orchestra" which surround Del Rey's vocals. Del Rey said that she wrote "Brooklyn Baby" with Lou Reed in mind. She was supposed to work with him and flew to New York City to meet him, but he died the day she arrived. He is referenced in the line "And my boyfriend's in a band/ He plays guitar while I sing Lou Reed". In the title track, "Ultraviolence", Del Rey directly references The Crystals' "He Hit Me (and It Felt Like a Kiss)" in the chorus, which she had also heard a rendition of by Hole.[1]

	"West Coast" "The tempo [of the song] shifts frequently, the instrumentation is jagged, and Lana's voice skips between breathy franticness and slurred, drugged-out ecstasy."
Problems playing this file? See media help.	

"West Coast" is a mid-tempo song with a pop and soft rock verse and a surf rock slow-tempo chorus. Musically, its composition is built around reggae drum fills, blues-influenced guitar riffs, and draws influences from indie rock music.

"Sad Girl" was written about being "the other woman" in an affair. Del Rey wrote "Money Power Glory" as a reaction to her rise to fame. About writing it, she says, "I was in more of a sardonic mood. Like, if all that I was actually going to be allowed to have by the media was money, loads of money, then fuck it... What I actually wanted was something quiet and simple: a writer's community and respect."

"Fucked My Way Up to the Top" was written about an undisclosed female singer who, at first, mocked her for her supposedly unauthentic style, but then "stole and copied it" and became successful with it. Asked about the meaning of the song, Del Rey said "It's commentary, like, "I know what you think of me," and I'm alluding to that. You know, I have slept with a lot of guys in the industry, but none of them helped me get my record deals. Which is annoying."

Singles and promotion

Del Rey premiered "West Coast" as part of her set at the Coachella music festival on April 13, 2014. "West Coast" was serviced as *Ultraviolence*'s lead single the next day. Its music video was released on May 7 and directed by Vincent Haycock. "Shades of Cool" was released as the second single on May 26. A music video was directed by Jake Nava and released on June 17. The third single and title track, "Ultraviolence", was released on June 4 and was followed by the fourth single, "Brooklyn Baby", four days later.

Prior to the album release, Del Rey announced a North American concert tour, as well as performances at several European festivals. Del Rey received attention for taking a "less is more" approach to promoting the album. She did not promote the album with television performances or interviews, instead relying on a couple of print interviews, music videos, and social media.

Critical reception

Professional ratings	
Aggregate scores	
Source	Rating
Metacritic	75/100
Review scores	
Source	Rating
AllMusic	★ ★ ★ ★ ★
Billboard	83/100
Clash	7/10
Consequence of Sound	A
Entertainment Weekly	A
The Guardian	★ ★ ★ ★ ★
Los Angeles Times	★ ★ ★ ★
New York Daily News	★ ★ ★ ★ ★
Pitchfork	7.1/10
Rolling Stone	★ ★ ★ ★ ★

Ultraviolence received positive reviews upon its release. According to Metacritic, which assigns a normalized rating out of 100 to reviews from mainstream critics, the album held a score of 75/100 based on 31 reviews—indicating "generally favorable reviews"—following its release.

European media

The Guardian writer Alexis Petridis wrote that "Every chorus clicks, the melodies are uniformly beautiful, and they soar and swoop, the better to demonstrate Del Rey's increased confidence in her voice. It's all so well done that the fact that the whole album proceeds at the same, somnambulant pace scarcely matters". Tony Clayton-Lea of *The Irish Times* noted, "What seems certain is that whatever she really is, or whatever she does in her chosen milieu, Del Ray [*sic*] is the best at it." Mike Diver for Clash Music commented, "For all its lows-inspired highs, *Ultraviolence* is not quite the complete picture. It goes so far as to reflect, albeit perhaps coincidentally, this era: black and white, the colour has to come from the performance, not the film it's captured on." The critic gave a bottom line for Del Rey—"A bruised beauty, just short of classic status..." At the *The Independent* the album scored 3 out of 5 and critic Hugh Montgomery felt, "Ultraviolence is more of the same, but less. There is quasi-transgressive mixture of hopeless passivity and coquettish sexuality running through songs."

US media

Jim Farber of *New York Daily News* wrote, "Ultimately, she's milking classic male fantasies of the sad Marilyn Monroe, the babe in distress who can only be saved by you - and your dollars." Kyle Anderson of *Entertainment Weekly* wrote about Del Rey's aesthetic, stating, "Kubrick would have loved Del Rey — a highly stylized vixen who romanticizes fatalism to near-pornographic levels, creating fantastically decadent moments of film-noir melodrama. It's an aesthetic that demands total commitment from both artist and listener, and it would be difficult to buy into if she didn't deliver such fully realized cinema." He also added, "*Ultraviolence* masterfully melds those elements, and completes the redemption narrative of a singer whose breakout-to-backlash arc on 2012's *Born to Die* made her a cautionary tale of music-industry hype." Caryn Ganz for *Rolling Stone* gave a positive review, commenting the album "is a melancholy crawl through doomed romance, incorrigible addictions, blown American dreams," although she also wrote " [it] wraps desire, violence and sadness into a tight bundle that Del Rey doesn't always seem sure how to unpack." Justin Charity of *Complex magazine* noted, "*Ultraviolence* is a blues affair, with moody innuendo spilling bloody and bold as the opening sequence to a vintage Bond saga." The critic also called it 'intimate', 'drunk driven'.

Commercial performance

On June 18, 2014, *Billboard* estimated that *Ultraviolence* would sell approximately 175-180,000 copies in first-week United States sales. The album debuted at number-one on the *Billboard* 200, with sales of 182,000, making it Del Rey's first number-one album in the United States and her best sales week yet. The album declined to number four the following week, selling another 44,000 copies, meaning that, after two weeks, "Ultraviolence" has sold over 220,000 copies in the US alone. Overall, *Ultraviolence* debuted at number one in twelve countries, including the United Kingdom making it her second consecutive album to reach number one following *Born To Die*. The album sold 880,000 copies in its first week, worldwide. *Ultraviolence* was certified Gold in Canada on June 25, and Silver in the United Kingdom, two days later. As of July 2014, *Ultraviolence* has sold more than one million copies worldwide.

Track listing

Ultraviolence – Standard edition

No.	Title	Writer(s)	Producer(s)	Length
1.	"Cruel World"	• Lana Del Rey • Blake Stranathan	Dan Auerbach	6:39
2.	"Ultraviolence"	• Del Rey • Daniel Heath	Auerbach	4:11
3.	"Shades of Cool"	• Del Rey • Rick Nowels	Auerbach	5:42
4.	"Brooklyn Baby"	• Del Rey • Barrie O'Neill	Auerbach	5:51
5.	"West Coast"	• Del Rey • Nowels	Auerbach	4:16
6.	"Sad Girl"	• Del Rey • Nowels	• Auerbach • Nowels[a]	5:17
7.	"Pretty When You Cry"	• Stranathan • Del Rey	• Del Rey • Stranathan • Lee Foster	3:54
8.	"Money Power Glory"	• Del Rey • Greg Kurstin	Kurstin	4:30
9.	"Fucked My Way Up to the Top"	• Del Rey • Heath	Auerbach	3:32
10.	"Old Money"	• Del Rey • Heath • Robbie Fitzsimmons	Heath	4:31
11.	"The Other Woman"	Jessie Mae Robinson	Auerbach	3:01
Total length:				**51:24**

Ultraviolence – Austrian, German, and Swiss edition (bonus track)									
No.	Title	Writer(s)	Producer(s)	Length					
12.	"West Coast" (radio mix)	• Del Rey • Nowels	Nowels	3:47					
Total length:				55:11					

Ultraviolence – Deluxe edition (bonus tracks)				
No.	Title	Writer(s)	Producer(s)	Length
12.	"Black Beauty"	• Del Rey • Nowels	• Paul Epworth • Nowels[a]	5:14
13.	"Guns and Roses"	• Del Rey • Nowels	• Del Rey • Nowels • Foster	4:30
14.	"Florida Kilos"	• Del Rey • Auerbach • Harmony Korine	Auerbach	4:14
Total length:				65:22

Ultraviolence – iTunes Store edition (bonus track)								
No.	Title	Writer(s)	Length					
15.	"Is This Happiness"	• Del Rey • Nowels	3:44					
Total length:			69:06					

Ultraviolence – Japanese, Spotify, and Target edition (bonus track)								
No.	Title	Writer(s)	Length					
15.	"Flipside"	• Del Rey • Stranathan	5:10					
Total length:			70:32					

Ultraviolence – Fnac edition (bonus disc)				
No.	Title	Writer(s)	Producer(s)	Length
1.	"Flipside"	• Del Rey • Stranathan	• Del Rey • Stranathan	5:11
Total length:				70:33

Ultraviolence – Japanese iTunes Store edition (bonus tracks)								
No.	Title	Writer(s)	Length					
15.	"Is This Happiness"	• Del Rey • Nowels	3:44					
16.	"Flipside"	• Del Rey • Stranathan	5:10					
Total length:			74:16					

Notes

• ^[a] signifies a vocal producer

Credits and personnel

Credits adapted from the liner notes of *Ultraviolence*.

Performance credits

• Lana Del Rey – vocals (all tracks); background vocals (tracks 2, 5)
• Dan Auerbach – background vocals (track 14)
• Seth Kaufman – background vocals (tracks 4, 14)
• Alfreda McCrary Lee – background vocals (track 2)
• Ann McCrary – background vocals (track 2)
• Regina McCrary – background vocals (track 2)

Instruments

• Dan Auerbach – claps (track 1); electric guitar (tracks 1, 2, 3, 4, 5, 6, 9, 14); shaker, 12–string acoustic guitar (track 5); synthesizer (tracks 5, 6, 11, 14)
• Collin Dupuis – drum programming (tracks 2, 3, 9, 14); synthesizer (track 6)
• Brian Griffin – drums (tracks 6, 13)
• Ed Harcourt – piano (track 12)
• Tom Herbert – bass guitar (track 12)
• Seth Kaufman – synthesizer, claps (track 1); electric guitar (tracks 2, 4, 6, 9); omnichord (track 3); percussion (track 4)
• Nikolaj Torp Larsen – philicorda, mellotron (track 12)
• Leon Michaels – claps (track 1); synthesizer (tracks 1, 2, 9, 11, 14); piano (tracks 2, 9); mellotron (tracks 1, 2, 3, 4, 6, 9, 11, 14); tambourine, percussion, tenor saxophone (track 4, 11)
• Nick Movshon – claps (track 1); bass guitar (tracks 1, 2, 3, 5, 9); upright bass (track 4); drums (tracks 4, 5, 6, 11, 14)
• Rick Nowels – piano (track 12)
• Russ Pahl – pedal steel guitar (tracks 1, 2, 4, 9, 11); electric guitar (tracks 3, 14); acoustic guitar (tracks 4, 6)
• Blake Stranathan – guitar (tracks 7, 13)
• Pablo Tato – guitar (track 12)
• Leo Taylor – drums (track 12)
• Kenny Vaughan – electric guitar (tracks 1, 2, 3, 9, 11); acoustic guitar (track 4); synthesizer, mellotron (track 6)
• Maximilian Weissenfeldt – claps (track 1); drums (tracks 1, 2, 3, 4, 5, 9)

Technical and production

• Dan Auerbach – production (tracks 1, 2, 3, 4, 5, 6, 9, 11, 14); mixing (tracks 2, 14)
• Julian Burg – additional engineering (track 8)
• Vira Byramji – assistant engineer (track 13)
• John Davis – mastering (all tracks)
• Lana Del Rey – production (tracks 7, 13)

- Collin Dupuis – engineering (tracks 1, 2, 3, 4, 5, 6, 9, 11, 14); mixing (tracks 2, 14)
- Paul Epworth – production (track 12)
- Lee Foster – production (tracks 7, 13)
- Milton Gutiérrez – engineering (track 10)
- Daniel Heath – production, arrangement (track 10)
- Phil Joly – engineering (track 7); tracking engineer, mixing (track 13)
- Greg Kurstin – production, mixing (track 8)
- Neil Krug – photography
- Mat Maitland – design
- Matthew McGaughey – orchestration (track 10)
- Kieron Menzies – vocal engineering (tracks 6, 12)
- Rick Nowels – vocal production (tracks 6, 12); production (track 13)
- Alex Pasco – additional engineering (track 8)
- Robert Orton – mixing (tracks 1, 3, 4, 6, 7, 9, 10, 11, 12)
- Myan Soffia – additional photography
- Blake Stranathan – production (track 6)
- Matt Wiggins – engineering (track 12)
- Andy Zisakis – assistant engineer (track 10)

Charts

Chart (2014)	Peak position
Argentinian Albums (CAPIF)[2]	4
Australian Albums (ARIA)[3]	1
Austrian Albums (Ö3 Austria)[4]	5
Belgian Albums (Ultratop Flanders)[5]	1
Belgian Albums (Ultratop Wallonia)[6]	1
Canadian Albums (*Billboard*)[7]	1
Croatian Foreign Albums (IFPI)[8]	7
Czech Albums (ČNS IFPI)[9]	4
Danish Albums (Hitlisten)[10]	1
Dutch Albums (MegaCharts)[11]	5
Finnish Albums (Suomen virallinen lista)[12]	1
French Albums (SNEP)[13]	2
German Albums (Official Top 100)[14]	3
Greek Albums (IFPI)	1
Hungarian Albums (MAHASZ)[15]	6
Irish Albums (IRMA)[16]	2
Italian Albums (FIMI)	2

Japanese Albums (Oricon)	50
Korean Albums (GAON)[17]	28
Mexican Albums (AMPROFON)	3
New Zealand Albums (Recorded Music NZ)[18]	1
Norwegian Albums (VG-lista)[19]	1
Polish Albums (ZPAV)[20]	1
Portuguese Albums (AFP)[21]	3
Scottish Albums (OCC)[22]	1
Spanish Albums (PROMUSICAE)[23]	1
Swedish Albums (Sverigetopplistan)[24]	6
Swiss Albums (Schweizer Hitparade)[25]	2
Taiwanese Western Albums (G-Music)	7
UK Albums (OCC)[26]	1
US *Billboard* 200[27]	1
US Digital Albums (*Billboard*)[28]	2
US Top Tastemaker Albums (*Billboard*)[29]	1

Certifications

Region	Certification	Sales/shipments
Canada (Music Canada)[30]	Gold	40,000^
United Kingdom (BPI)[31]	Silver	60,000^

*sales figures based on certification alone
^shipments figures based on certification alone
xunspecified figures based on certification alone

Release history

Country	Date	Edition	Format(s)	Label
Germany	June 13, 2014	• Standard • Deluxe • Super deluxe	• CD • LP • digital download	Universal
Netherlands		• Standard • Deluxe		Polydor
Switzerland				Universal
France	June 16, 2014	• Standard • Deluxe • Super deluxe		
United Kingdom		• Standard • Deluxe		Polydor
Italy		• Standard • Deluxe • Super deluxe		
Canada	June 17, 2014	• Standard • Deluxe		Universal
Mexico		• Deluxe	• CD • digital download	Interscope
Spain		• Standard • Deluxe • Super deluxe	• CD • LP • digital download	Universal
United States		• Standard • Deluxe		Interscope
Japan	June 18, 2014			

References

[1] Del Rey, Lana. Interview with Laura Leishman. France. May 2014 (https://www.youtube.com/watch?v=J12fT4Lk0P4)

[2] " Lana Del Rey – Ultraviolence" (http://adminlic.capif.org.ar/sis_resultados_rankings_web.aspx). Argentinian Albums. CAPIF. On **Fecha**, select *{{{date}}}* to see the correspondent chart. Retrieved June 30, 2014.

[3] " Lana Del Rey – Ultraviolence" (http://www.australian-charts.com/showitem.asp?interpret=Lana+Del+Rey&titel=Ultraviolence& cat=a). Australiancharts.com. Hung Medien. Retrieved June 21, 2014.

[4] " Lana Del Rey - Ultraviolence" (http://austriancharts.at/showitem.asp?interpret=Lana+Del+Rey&titel=Ultraviolence&cat=a) (in German). Austriancharts.at. Hung Medien. Retrieved June 26, 2014.

[5] " Lana Del Rey – Ultraviolence" (http://www.ultratop.be/nl/showitem.asp?interpret=Lana+Del+Rey&titel=Ultraviolence&cat=a) (in Dutch). Ultratop.be. Hung Medien. Retrieved June 27, 2014.

[6] " Lana Del Rey – Ultraviolence" (http://www.ultratop.be/fr/showitem.asp?interpret=Lana+Del+Rey&titel=Ultraviolence&cat=a) (in French). Ultratop.be. Hung Medien. Retrieved June 27, 2014.

[7] " Lana Del Rey Album & Song Chart History" (http://www.billboard.com/artist/306420/Lana+Del+Rey/chart?f=309) *Billboard* Canadian Albums Chart for Lana Del Rey. Prometheus Global Media. Retrieved June 27, 2014.

[8] " Top Stranih [Top Foreign]" (http://www.hdu-toplista.com/index.php?what=arhiva&w=details&id=1354) (In Croatian). Top Foreign Albums. Hrvatska Diskografska Udruga. Retrieved June 26, 2014.

[9] " Top 50 Prodejnf" (http://www.ifpicr.cz/hitparada/index.php?a=hitparada&hitparada=14). Czech Albums. ČNS IFPI. **Note**: On the chart page, select **201426** on the field besides the word "Zobrazit", and then click over the word to retrieve the correct chart data. Retrieved July 1, 2014.

[10] " Lana Del Rey – Ultraviolence" (http://www.danishcharts.com/showitem.asp?interpret=Lana+Del+Rey&titel=Ultraviolence&cat=a). Danishcharts.com. Hung Medien. Retrieved June 20, 2014.

[11] " Lana Del Rey – Ultraviolence" (http://www.dutchcharts.nl/showitem.asp?interpret=Lana+Del+Rey&titel=Ultraviolence&cat=a) (in Dutch). Dutchcharts.nl. Hung Medien. Retrieved June 20, 2014.

[12] " Lana Del Rey: Ultraviolence" (http://www.ifpi.fi/tilastot/virallinen-lista/artistit/Lana+Del+Rey/Ultraviolence) (in Finnish). Musiikkituottajat – IFPI Finland. Retrieved June 22, 2014.

[13] " Lana Del Rey – Ultraviolence" (http://www.lescharts.com/showitem.asp?interpret=Lana+Del+Rey&titel=Ultraviolence&cat=a). Lescharts.com. Hung Medien. Retrieved June 27, 2014.

[14] " Lana Del Rey – Ultraviolence" (http://www.officialcharts.de/album.asp?artist=Lana+Del+Rey&title=Ultraviolence&cat=a&
country=de). Officialcharts.de. GfK Entertainment. Retrieved July 3, 2014.

[15] " Archívum – Slágerlisták – MAHASZ – Magyar Hangfelvétel-kiadók Szövetsége" (http://www.mahasz.hu/?menu=slagerlistak&
menu2=archivum&lista=top40&ev=2014&het=25&submit_=Keresés). Mahasz.hu. LightMedia. Retrieved June 26, 2014.

[16] " GFK Chart-Track" (http://www.chart-track.co.uk/index.jsp?c=p/musicvideo/music/archive/index_test.jsp&ct=240002&arch=t&
lyr=2014&year=2014&week=25). Chart-Track.co.uk. GFK Chart-Track. IRMA. Retrieved June 20, 2014.

[17] "South Korea GAON Albums Chart" (http://gaonchart.co.kr/digital_chart/album.php). On the page, select year "2014" and then
"2014.06.15~2014.06.21" to obtain the corresponding chart. Korean Charts. GAON. Retrieved June 26, 2014.

[18] " Lana Del Rey – Ultraviolence" (http://www.charts.org.nz/showitem.asp?interpret=Lana+Del+Rey&titel=Ultraviolence&cat=a).
Charts.org.nz. Hung Medien. Retrieved June 22, 2014.

[19] " Lana Del Rey – Ultraviolence" (http://www.norwegiancharts.com/showitem.asp?interpret=Lana+Del+Rey&titel=Ultraviolence&
cat=a). Norwegiancharts.com. Hung Medien. Retrieved June 29, 2014.

[20] " Oficjalna lista sprzedaży :: OLIS - Official Retail Sales Chart" (http://olis.onyx.pl/listy/index.asp?idlisty=870&lang=en). OLiS. Polish
Society of the Phonographic Industry. Retrieved June 27, 2014.

[21] " Lana Del Rey – Ultraviolence" (http://www.portuguesecharts.com/showitem.asp?interpret=Lana+Del+Rey&titel=Ultraviolence&
cat=a). Portuguesecharts.com. Hung Medien. Retrieved June 29, 2014.

[22] "2014-06-28 Top 40 Scottish Albums Archive UNIQ-nowiki-0-6d9da8360ebd6116-QINU Official Charts" (http://www.officialcharts.
com/archive-chart/_/23/2014-06-28). UK Albums Chart. The Official Charts Company. Retrieved June 22, 2014.

[23] " Lana Del Rey – Ultraviolence" (http://www.spanishcharts.com/showitem.asp?interpret=Lana+Del+Rey&titel=Ultraviolence&
cat=a). Spanishcharts.com. Hung Medien. Retrieved June 30, 2014.

[24] " Lana Del Rey – Ultraviolence" (http://www.swedishcharts.com/showitem.asp?interpret=Lana+Del+Rey&titel=Ultraviolence&
cat=a). Swedishcharts.com. Hung Medien. Retrieved June 20, 2014.

[25] " Lana Del Rey – Ultraviolence" (http://www.swisscharts.com/showitem.asp?interpret=Lana+Del+Rey&titel=Ultraviolence&cat=a).
Swisscharts.com. Hung Medien. Retrieved June 25, 2014.

[26] "2014-06-28 Top 40 Official UK Albums Archive UNIQ-nowiki-1-6d9da8360ebd6116-QINU Official Charts" (http://www.officialcharts.
com/archive-chart/_/3/2014-06-28). UK Albums Chart. The Official Charts Company. Retrieved June 22, 2014.

[27] "Lana Del Rey Album & Song Chart History" (http://www.billboard.com/artist/306420/Lana+Del+Rey/chart?f=305) Billboard 200
for Lana Del Rey. Prometheus Global Media. Retrieved June 29, 2014.

[28] " Album & Song Chart History" (http://www.billboard.com/artist/306420/Lana+Del+Rey/chart?f=400) Billboard Digital Albums for
Lana Del Rey. Prometheus Global Media. Retrieved June 29, 2014.

[29] " Lana Del Rey Album & Song Chart History" (http://www.billboard.com/artist/306420/Lana+Del+Rey/chart?f=407) Billboard Top
Tastemaker Albums for Lana Del Rey. Prometheus Global Media. Retrieved June 29, 2014.

[30] "Canadian album certifications – Lana Del Rey – Ultraviolence" (http://www.musiccanada.com/gold-platinum/#!/
gp_search="Ultraviolence" "Lana+Del+Rey"). Music Canada. Retrieved June 30, 2014.

[31] "British album certifications – Lana Del Rey – Ultraviolence" (http://www.bpi.co.uk/certified-awards.aspx). British Phonographic
Industry. Retrieved June 27, 2014. Enter Ultraviolence in the field Search. Select Title in the field Search by. Select album in the field By
Format. Click Go

Tropico (film)

Tropico	
Film poster	
Directed by	Anthony Mandler
Produced by	Heather Heller
Written by	Lana Del Rey
Starring	Lana Del Rey Shaun Ross
Music by	Lana Del Rey
Cinematography	David Devlin
Edited by	Jeff Selis
Release date(s)	• December 4, 2013 (Hollywood, California) December 5, 2013 (VEVO)
Running time	27 minutes
Country	United States
Language	English

Tropico is a short film "based on the Biblical story of sin and redemption", starring Lana Del Rey as Eve and Shaun Ross as Adam. Directed by Anthony Mandler, the film premiered at the Cinerama Dome in Hollywood, California on December 4, 2013 before being uploaded to Del Rey's official VEVO account the following day. It features the songs "Body Electric", "Gods & Monsters", and "Bel Air", all taken from Del Rey's 2012 EP, *Paradise*. An EP of the same name was also released that same month to the iTunes Store; it includes the film itself along with the three aforementioned songs.

Production and release

Tropico was filmed in late June 2013; it was directed by Anthony Mandler, who also directed Del Rey's previous music videos for "National Anthem" and "Ride". Via social media platforms, Del Rey released several promotional images for the film, one depicting Del Rey in a mantilla as Mary, Mother of Jesus and another with Del Rey holding a snake and posing as Eve, the biblical wife of Adam from Genesis. In August 2013, Del Rey announced on Twitter that the film would have two premieres: one at the Hollywood Forever Cemetery in Los Angeles and one in an unspecified location in New York; she referred to the short film as a "farewell". Critics noted that this contradicted other claims by Del Rey that she would release a third studio album, with a demo of the song "Black Beauty" leaking online. On November 22, 2013, an official trailer for *Tropico* was released; at the end of the trailer, it was announced that the film would be uploaded to Del Rey's official VEVO account on December 5, 2013. On December 3, 2013, Del Rey's official website announced that the film will premiere at the Cinerama Dome in Hollywood, California, prior to its VEVO release.[1] Prior to playing the movie, Del Rey announced the title of her upcoming third album and explained to the audience what she meant when she said that the film is a "farewell", stating: "I really just wanted us all to be together so I could try and visually close out my [Born to Die/Paradise] chapter[s] before I release the new record, *Ultraviolence*".

Synopsis

Chapter I – *Body Electric*

The movie starts out with the original Adam (Shaun Ross) and Eve (Lana Del Rey) in the Garden of Eden. God (portrayed by a John Wayne character), Jesus, Marilyn Monroe, and Elvis Presley are all present with Adam and Eve – as "Body Electric" begins to play. The whole movie is intercut with scenes of Del Rey playing Jesus' mother Mary. At the end of the song, Eve – tempted by the snake – decides to disobey God and eats an apple from Tree of Knowledge of Good and Evil. After she eats it, thunder strikes, symbolizing God's wrath. Adam then decides to eat from the apple as well. As a result of this, all humanity subsequently inherits sin, pain, and spiritual death. They are furthermore cast out of the garden and thus never get the chance to eat from the Tree of Life, which would have made their bodies immortal. God could not allow imperfect human beings to become immortal unless they had gone through a process of repentance and purification first.

Chapter II – *Gods & Monsters*

Del Rey then starts to recite Walt Whitman's "I Sing the Body Electric" as time flash forwards to a modern-day Adam and Eve living in Los Angeles; Del Rey works as a stripper while Ross is a gang member who also works as a clerk at a convenience store during the day. In this segment – "Gods & Monsters" begins to play. After the song ends, Del Rey recites Allen Ginsberg's "Howl" as a group of wealthy middle aged men are seen surprising their friend on his birthday by bringing him two strippers. A couple of minutes after the strippers enter the room, Ross and his gang suddenly show up with guns in hand and steal all their money.

Chapter III – *Bel Air*

God appears and begins to narrate John Mitchum's poem "Why I Love America" ("You ask me why I love her? Well, give me time. I'll explain. Have you seen a Kansas sunset, or an Arizona rain?"). Following this narration, Del Rey and Ross decide to repent from their sins in order to become Born again Christians. They then get in their car and end up driving to a country-side wheat field – as "Bel Air" begins to play in the sunset. Coincidentally, God decides to end the world right then and there and thus the Rapture occurs, resulting in Del Rey and Ross being "ascended up in the clouds" to meet "the Lord in the air" (1 Thessalonians 4:17), as flying saucers appear in the sky.

Tropico (EP)

Tropico	
EP by Lana Del Rey	
Released	December 6, 2013
Genre	• Alternative rock • baroque pop • indie pop
Label	• Polydor • Interscope
Lana Del Rey chronology	
• *Born to Die – The Paradise Edition* • (2012)	• *Tropico* Ultraviolence • (2013) (2014)

Tropico is a 2013 EP by Lana Del Rey named after the short film of the same name, also starring Del Rey. The EP includes the film itself along with the three *Paradise* songs featured in it: "Body Electric", "Gods & Monsters", and "Bel Air".[2]

Track listing

No.	Title	Writer(s)	Producer(s)	Length
1.	"Body Electric"	• Lana Del Rey • Rick Nowels	• Nowels • Dan Heath	3:53
2.	"Gods & Monsters"	• Lana Del Rey • Tim Larcombe	• Larcombe • Emile Haynie	3:57
3.	"Bel Air"	• Lana Del Rey • Heath	Heath	3:57
4.	"Tropico"	Lana Del Rey	Anthony Mandler (Director)	27:00

Reception

Upon release, *Tropico* received mixed to positive reviews from critics. Jason Lipshutz of *Billboard* called the film "a work of overflowing, era-traversing passion" and called the climax of the film "pure bliss". *Under the Gun* took issue with the "somewhat nonsensical" narration throughout the film but said as a whole the film was "certainly something special." Similarly, Jimmy So of *The Daily Beast* also criticized the film's narration and compared it to "a campy arthouse movie" and described Del Rey's videos to this point as being "starved of creativity." In contrast, James Caterino of *Examiner* gave the film a 5-star review writing "The imagery is breathtaking and the voice-over narration so jam-packed with poetic prose that it sears into the soul... She is an artistic force who never fails to fascinate—and to make us feel." In a slightly more critical but equally optimistic review, Sal Cinquemani of *Slant* added "It's obvious from the big bang that opens the film that Del Rey and Mandler have zero interest in subtlety, but interestingly, Del Rey doesn't position herself among the film's icons of Americana the way, say, Kanye West or Lady Gaga might. Instead, her work continues to serve as both a tribute to an imagined past and a critique of contemporary pop culture." In an essay for *Fader Magazine*, Duncan Cooper highlights the questions she posits in her film: "she seems to be provoking conversation about that other form of power (or contesting power): the fist, the gun."[3] He goes on to say: "This is Lana at her most modern, her most relatable. As the olden-times god is gone, we're alone, but we hold the power of art within ourselves. We just have to figure out how to use it: after we abandon religion's comforting narrative."

References

[1] http://www.lanadelrey.com/news/tropico-premier

[2] https://itunes.apple.com/us/album/tropico-single/id767753025

[3] Duncan Cooper, "Why Did Lana Del Rey Make a 30-Minute Video About God, and What Does It Mean for Me?" (http://www.thefader.com/2013/12/06/why-did-lana-del-rey-make-a-30-minute-video-about-god-and-what-does-it-mean-for-me/#ixzz2uqTwI8xq), *Fader Magazine* (Online), December 6, 2013. Retrieved March 2, 2014

External links

- *Tropico* (http://www.imdb.com/title/tt3384034/?ref_=nm_flmg_act_1) at The Internet Movie Database
- "Tropico" (Short Film) (Explicit) (https://www.youtube.com/watch?v=VwuHOQLSpEg) on YouTube

Lana Del Ray (album)

Not to be confused with Lana Del Rey (EP).

Lana Del Ray		
Studio album by Lana Del Ray		
Released	January 4, 2010	
Recorded	2008	
Length	47:23	
Label	5 Points	
Producer	David Kahne	
Lana Del Ray chronology		
Kill Kill (2008)	*Lana Del Ray* (2010)	*Lana Del Rey* (2012)

Lana Del Ray is the debut studio album by American singer-songwriter Lana Del Rey, released through the independent record label 5 Points Records in 2010 when she was known as Lana Del Ray.

The album was released digitally through iTunes, but was eventually pulled from online retailers soon after it was released because, according to Del Rey, the label was unable to fund it. Del Rey ultimately bought back the rights to the album, whose title uses an alternate spelling of the singer's stage name, "Del Rey" being spelled "Del Ray" instead. After releasing *Born to Die* (2012) under her stage name Lana Del Rey, she expressed that she eventually wanted to re-release the album.

Recording and history

"Kill Kill"

"Kill Kill combines electronica and blues rock elements, over Marilyn Monroe inspired vocals. The lyrics were composed solely by Del Rey and were called "dark", "poetic," and "elegant".

Problems playing this file? See media help.

The album was produced by major music producer David Kahne, who recorded the album with Del Rey over a period of three months, in 2008. Prior to the release of the album, Del Rey released an EP titled *Kill Kill* to iTunes in October 2008, which featured the tracks "Kill Kill", "Gramma", and "Yayo". "Yayo" would later be re-recorded, released again, on the "Paradise Edition" of *Born to Die* Del Rey stated that Kahne "is known as a producer with a lot of integrity and who had an interest in making music that wasn't just pop." Her father, Robert Grant, helped with the marketing of the album, which was available for purchase on iTunes for a brief period before being withdrawn. According to David Kahne, who produced Grant and Label owner David Nichtern, Grant bought the rights back from her label, 5 Points, as she wanted it out of circulation. In an interview with David Nichtern he stated "Her and her new manager came in and said 'We want to get this off the market. We're going for a completely new deal. We'll buy you out of the deal.' So we made a separation agreement." In January 2012, upon the release of her major-label album, *Born to Die*, Del Rey stated to the BBC that she recently bought back the rights of the album and was planning on re-releasing it in the Summer of 2012. In May 2012, she announced that the album would not be re-released that summer. Del Rey did however re-record and re-release "Yayo" on her *Paradise* EP.

Track listing

No.	Title	Writer(s)	Producer	Length
1.	"Kill Kill"	Elizabeth Grant	David Kahne	3:57
2.	"Queen of the Gas Station"	• Grant • Kahne	Kahne	3:04
3.	"Oh Say Can You See"	Grant	Kahne	3:40
4.	"Gramma (Blue Ribbon Sparkler Trailer Heaven)"	• Grant • Kahne	Kahne	3:55
5.	"For K, Pt. 2"	Grant	Kahne	3:24
6.	"Jump"	Grant	Kahne	2:50
7.	"Mermaid Motel"	Grant	Kahne	3:59
8.	"Raise Me Up (Mississippi South)"	Grant	Kahne	4:22
9.	"Pawn Shop Blues"	• Grant • Kahne	Kahne	3:26
10.	"Brite Lites"	Grant	Kahne	2:57
11.	"Put Me in a Movie"	Grant	Kahne	3:13
12.	"Smarty"	• Grant • Kahne	Kahne	2:49
13.	"Yayo"	Grant	Kahne	5:45
Total length:				47:23

References

Born to Die (Lana Del Rey album)

Born to Die	
Studio album by Lana Del Rey	
Released	January 27, 2012
Recorded	2010–11
Genre	• Baroque pop • trip hop
Length	49:28
Label	• Polydor • Interscope
Producer	• Patrik Berger • Jeff Bhasker • Chris Braide • Emile Haynie • Justin Parker • Rick Nowels • Robopop • Al Shux
Lana Del Rey chronology	
• *Lana Del Rey* • *Born to Die* • *Paradise* • (2012) • (2012) • (2012)	
Singles from *Born to Die*	

• "Video Games"
  Released: October 17, 2011
• "Born to Die"
  Released: December 30, 2011
• "Off to the Races"
  Released: January 6, 2012
• "Carmen"
  Released: January 26, 2012[1]
• "Blue Jeans"
  Released: April 6, 2012
• "Summertime Sadness"
  Released: June 22, 2012
• "National Anthem"
  Released: July 6, 2012
• "Dark Paradise"
  Released: March 1, 2013	

Born to Die is the second studio album by American singer-songwriter Lana Del Rey. It was released on January 27, 2012 by Interscope Records, Polydor Records, and Stranger Records. Del Rey collaborated with producers including Patrik Berger, Jeff Bhasker, Chris Braide, Emile Haynie, Justin Parker, Rick Nowels, Robopop, and Al Shux to achieve her desired sound. Their efforts resulted in a primarily baroque pop record, which sees additional influences from alternative hip hop and trip hop music. Contemporary music critics were divided in their opinions of *Born to Die*; some commended its distinctive production, while its repetitiveness and melodramatic tendencies were a recurring complaint. The record debuted at number two on the U.S. *Billboard* 200 with first-week sales of 77,000 copies; it was later certified platinum by the Recording Industry Association of America (RIAA) after moving one million units. *Born to Die* reached the peak position on eleven international record charts, and has sold more than four million copies worldwide as of July 2014.

After attaining online success after its initial premiere on June 29, 2011, "Video Games" was released as the lead single from *Born to Die* on October 17, 2011; it peaked at number 91 on the U.S. *Billboard* Hot 100. Its follow-up singles "Born to Die", "Off to the Races", "Blue Jeans", "Summertime Sadness", "National Anthem", and "Dark Paradise" performed sporadically across *Billboard* component charts and international record charts. "Summertime Sadness" was re-released on July 11, 2013 after being remixed by Cedric Gervais, and became Del Rey's highest-charting single in the United States after reaching number six on the *Billboard* Hot 100. Del Rey additionally promoted *Born to Die* with several televised performances, including a widely-criticized appearance on *Saturday Night Live*. It was reissued on November 9, 2012 as an expanded version subtitled *The Paradise Edition*, which was packaged with her third extended play *Paradise* (2012).

Background and development

In 2007, Elizabeth "Lizzy" Grant signed a recording contract with the independent record label 5 Point Records, and began planning for her debut studio album. However, after hiring new management services, taking an interest in adopting the stage name Lana Del Ray, and a perceived lack of motivation during production, she found herself in conflict with the record label and her producer David Kahne. The final product *Lana Del Ray* was digitally released in January 2010, although her stage name was respelled Lana Del Rey shortly after its launch. Grant was successfully bought out of her recording contract upon the request of her manager; consequently, *Lana Del Ray* was pulled out of circulation before physical versions were produced.

After settling with her current stage name, Del Rey signed a recording contract with Stranger Records in June 2011, and released the track "Video Games". Initially, she had released the song because it was her "favorite" and had no intentions of releasing it as a single, although the video went viral on YouTube after its premiere. During an appearance on the French television series *Taratata* in November 2011, Del Rey announced that her second studio album would be titled *Born to Die*.

The cover for *Born to Die* was photographed by Nicole Nodland, while Del Rey and David Bowden oversaw the overall direction for its packaging. On behalf of *Complex*, Dale Eisinger ranked the cover eighth on their list of "The 50 Best Pop Album Covers of the Past Five Years", commending its usage of the typeface Steelfish and speaking favorably of the "ominous" feeling it evoked, which she credited to "the shadows or whatever the shapes in the background are [and] how properly Lana can affect her detached and still-flawless persona to a simple gaze." Its track listing was announced on January 9, 2012, while the record itself was released on January 31 in the United States; it became her major-label debut after securing a distribution arrangement with Interscope Records.

Composition

	"National Anthem" A 22-second sample of the song's chorus, features Del Rey incorporating a Jessica Rabbit persona over a "lush-strings-meet-hard-beats" background.
Problems playing this file? See media help.	

In regards to the use of her lower vocals on the tracks, she stated that "people weren't taking me very seriously, so I lowered my voice, believing that it would help me stand out. Now I sing quite low... well, for a female anyway." The singer's first singles, "Video Games" and "Born to Die" were described variously as "quasi-cabaret balladry",[2] "woozy and sometimes soporific soundtrack soul",[3] and "pop".[4] Her own description of her music is "Hollywood sadcore".[5] Tim Lee of musicOMH noted the songs are extremely similar, commenting that "her (alleged) agents clearly having stumbled upon a formula with which they can (allegedly) print money and (allegedly) further consign Lana's secretive, (allegedly) real debut LP to the annals of history. You didn't hear it from us, right?" Del Rey has once been described as a "gangsta Nancy Sinatra", though she cites Britney Spears, Elvis Presley and Antony and the Johnsons as her musical influences. When asked about her musical style, the singer stated:

> "I would have loved to be part of the indie community. But I wasn't. I was looking for a community, I don't even know any people who are musicians. I never met that indie popular indie, whoever the fuck that is. Who IS indie? First of all, I can't really get my head around what indie music is. Because if you've heard of it, it's sort of pop music, right? Because it's, like, popular? Or is it just that it's not on the radio? It's not like I was in an indie community and then I blew up. It's like, I was living on the street and I'm not — like, for real, you know what I'm saying?"

The third track, "Blue Jeans", was influenced by hip hop and has a minimalist beat that recalls songs by Timbaland. "Off to the Races" has been lyrically described as "a freak show of inappropriate co-dependency", with a chorus that recalls Sheryl Crow's "down and out drunken loner persona" in her 1994 single "Leaving Las Vegas". Pryia Elan of *NME* noted the track "almost falls under the weight of this persona. There's none of 'Video Games" measured, piano-led reflection. Instead the psychosexual rumblings of the lyrics and the dual voices she uses off set the comparatively simple musical shades on display."

"Off to the Races", "National Anthem", and "Diet Mountain Dew" employ an alternative rap technique that was described as almost "chatty". "Million Dollar Man" was likened to a sedated Fiona Apple. Musically compared to soundtracks for James Bond films, *Born to Die* contains trip hop beats and a cinematic sound reminiscent of the 1950s. Thematically, *Born to Die* circulates around sex and drugs, with Del Rey playing a Lolita-esque persona. Bill Lamb, a reviewer at About.com, wrote that "National Anthem" "[seems] lost in a messy blend of money, sex, and corporate greed, but it is the rousing yet graceful arrangement that solidifies the song's point of view as a clever critique of a society that is just as messy as these words." "National Anthem", Lamb says, fits into the lyrical structure of *Born to Die* in that the theme, as a whole, is that of a "bitter, albeit narcotized, criticism of all of the wealth and emotional artifice Lana Del Rey is accused of embracing." Vocally, *NME* observed that Del Rey sings like a "perfect mannequin" on "National Anthem", criticizing the track for baldly revisiting the beat-driven chorus of "Born to Die". Del Rey recorded a demo of a song called "Ghetto Baby" in 2012, but the song was cut from the album and given to Cheryl Cole who recorded it for third studio album *A Million Lights*.

Singles

"I feel like "Video Games" and "Blue Jeans" and "Born to Die" are all like part of a trilogy; I had met this guy and I was really struck by him visually and when it became clear that we couldn't be together anymore, I just knew in my heart that I would still honor that relationship for a long time...It was just more about living in the memories of the best of the past and just honoring that time."

"Video Games" was released as Del Rey's debut single on October 10, 2011. The song received mostly positive reviews from contemporary critics, who praised Del Rey's vocals and considered it as one of the best songs of 2011. "Video Games" attained worldwide success, reaching number one in Germany and top-ten positions in Austria, Belgium, Czech Republic, France, Netherlands, Ireland, Poland, Scotland, Switzerland and the United Kingdom. An accompanying music video was directed and edited by Del Rey, assembled from video clips of skateboarders, cartoons, shots from old movies, and paparazzi footage of Paz de la Huerta falling down while intoxicated. The music video was considered as the one that propelled the singer's online popularity. The second single and title track, "Born to Die", was released as a digital download on December 30, 2011. The music video for it leaked on December 14, 2011, and was based on a concept created by the singer, while being directed by Yoann Lemoine. The music video received generally favorable reviews from contemporary critics.

Del Rey announced "Blue Jeans" as the third single from the album following "Video Games" and "Born to Die". It was officially released on April 6, 2012. An accompanying music video, directed by Yoann Lemoine, premiered around the web on March 19, 2012. The song "National Anthem" was announced as the fourth single and was released on July 9, 2012. The music video for "National Anthem" was released on June 27, 2012. "Summertime Sadness" was released as the fifth single on June 22, 2012. The official music video for "Summertime Sadness" was released on July 20, 2012. "Dark Paradise" was also released as the sixth and last single on March 1, 2013 only in Germany, Switzerland, Austria and Poland.

Due to strong digital downloads following the album's release "Radio" charted at number 67 in France. Also, "Without You" debuted at number 121 in the UK. "Off to the Races" was released as a promotional single in The Netherlands on January 6, 2012. A music video, directed by Del Rey, was released on December 22, 2011. "Carmen" was released as a promotional single in Germany, Austria, and Switzerland on January 26, 2012. On February 27, 2012, Del Rey revealed through her Facebook that the video for the song "Carmen" was shot and would be finished being edited that day. The video for "Carmen" was released on April 21, 2012.

Promotion

Del Rey's song "Video Games" was featured for the first time on prime spot on The CW's *Ringer* on September 28, 2011 during a pivotal scene, propelling Del Rey into the mainstream. Del Rey also promoted the album with performances in a number of live appearances, including for MTV Push, and at the Bowery Ballroom, where, according to Eliot Glazer of *New York*, "the polarizing indie hipstress brought her 'gangsta Nancy Sinatra' swagu." Matthew Perpetua of *Rolling Stone* commented that, despite Del Rey being nervous and anxious while performing her songs live, the singer "sang with considerable confidence, though her transitions from husky, come-hither sexuality to bratty, girlish petulance could be rather jarring." Del Rey also performed "Video Games" on Dutch television program *De Wereld Draait Door*, on British music television show *Later... with Jools Holland*, and on an intimate show at Chateau Marmont in Los Angeles, California. Del Rey also gave several interviews for newspapers and online magazines such as The Quietus, *The Observer*, and Pitchfork Media, while creating her own music videos for several tracks such as "Blue Jeans" and

Del Rey performing during a promotional concert held in Amsterdam, 2011.

"Off to the Races". On January 14, 2012, Del Rey appeared on *Saturday Night Live* to perform "Blue Jeans" and "Video Games". Her performance soon came under scrutiny, and was even criticized by NBC anchor Brian Williams, who referred to the performance as "the worst in SNL history". Hosts Andy Samberg and Daniel Radcliffe quickly came to her defence, with the latter stating the criticism towards her was less about the performance and more about "her past and her family". *Ringer* played another Del Rey song "Blue Jeans" on February 14, 2012 during the last scene of episode 13.

Critical reception

Professional ratings	
Aggregate scores	
Source	Rating
Metacritic	(61/100)
Review scores	
Source	Rating
Allmusic	★ ★ ★ ★ ★
Entertainment Weekly	C+
The Guardian	★ ★ ★ ★ ★
The Independent	★ ★ ★ ★ ★
Los Angeles Times	mixed
The New York Times	negative
The Observer	★ ★ ★ ★ ★
Paste Magazine	6.4/10
Pitchfork Media	5.5/10
Rolling Stone	★ ★ ★ ★ ★
Slant Magazine	★ ★ ★ ★ ★

Born to Die received polarized reviews from music critics. At Metacritic, which assigns a weighted mean rating out of 100 to reviews from mainstream critics, the album received an average score of 61, based on 38 reviews, which indicates "generally favorable reviews". Jaime Gill of BBC Music commented that the album "isn't perfect", criticizing the production of songs such as "Dark Paradise". However, Gill concluded that *Born to Die* is the most distinctive debut album since Glasvegas's eponymous disc released in 2008. Slant Magazine writer Sal Cinquemani gave the album 4 out of 5 stars, and commented that several tracks had their production changed for the album, making tracks such as "National Anthem" and "This is What Makes Us Girls" less "radio-friendly". Cinquemani stated that, "ironically, the album's sole weakness is the strength of its immaculate production, which can be a bit overwhelming over the course of 12 tracks." Alexis Petridis of *The Guardian* also graded it 4 out of 5 stars, saying that *Born to Die* is "beautifully turned pop music, which is more than enough", with most melodies "constructed magnificently", while also stating that Del Rey "doesn't have the lyrical equipment to develop a persona throughout the album." Greg Kot of the *Chicago Tribune* gave a negative review, and highly criticized the repetitive production.

Rob Sheffield of *Rolling Stone* declared that the lyrics, with their "pop-trash perversity", were the strength of the album but that Del Rey had a voice that was "pinched and prim" and that she "wasn't ready to make an album yet". Sheffield rated the album 2 out of 5 and concluded, "given her chic image, it's a surprise how dull, dreary and pop-starved *Born to Die* is". Allmusic gave the album two-and-a-half out of five, saying "There is a chasm that separates 'Video Games' from the other material and performances on the album, which aims for exactly the same target—sultry, sexy, wasted—but with none of the same lyrical grace, emotional power, or sympathetic productions... an intriguing start, but Del Rey is going to have to hit the books if she wants to stay as successful as her career promised early on". Sputnikmusic disliked the album, saying "The worst thing about *Born to Die* is that even its great songs contain problems" *The Observer*'s Kitty Empire rated the album 3 out of 5 stars, and said that, unlike pop singers Lady Gaga and Katy Perry and their "hedonic outpourings", "Lana Del Rey's partying is fuelled by a knowing sadness, and sung in that laconic, hypnotic voice, which ultimately saves this thoroughly dissolute, feminist nightmare of a record for the romantics among us."

The A.V. Club panned the album, calling it "Shallow and overwrought, with periodic echoes of Kesha's Valley Girl aloofness, the album lives down to the harshest preconceptions against pop music." Randall Roberts of *Los Angeles Times* also noted that the singer's vocals have "so much potential and yet [are] unrefined", and said that despite having stand out tracks like "Summertime Sadness" and "Dark Paradise", listening to the album "has become tiring and woozy, like if you'd taken a half-dozen Ambiens when you'd put the record on – and now you're getting very, very sleepy." Pitchfork's Lindsay Zoladz gave the album 5.5/10, and commented: "The album's point of view—if you could call it that—feels awkward and out of date... [it] never allows tension or complexity into the mix, and its take on female sexuality ends up feeling thoroughly tame. For all of its coos about love and devotion, it's the album equivalent of a faked orgasm—a collection of torch songs with no fire." *NME* gave a positive review, giving the album 8/10 and saying "Although it's not quite the perfect pop record 'Video Games' might have led us to wish for, *Born To Die* still marks the arrival of a fresh—and refreshingly self-aware—sensibility in pop."

Accolades

Publication	Accolade	Year	Rank
The Hype Machine	Top Ten Albums of 2012	2012	#2[6]
Spinner	Spinner's 50 Best Albums of 2012	2012	#45[7]
Gigwise	Gigwise's Top 50 Albums of 2012	2012	#42[8]
NME	NME's 50 Best Albums Of 2012	2012	#45[9]
NME	101 Albums To Hear Before You Die	2014	#87[10]
FACT	FACT Magazine's 50 Best Albums of 2012	2012	#19[11]
The Fly	The Fly's Top 50 Albums of 2012	2012	#11
The Guardian	The Guardian's Best Albums of 2012	2012	#17
Uncut	Uncut's Top 75 Albums of 2012	2012	#51
Drowned in Sound	Drowned in Sound's 50 Favorite Albums of 2012	2012	#40

Commercial performance

Born to Die was a commercial success. In the United Kingdom, it sold 50,000 copies on its first day of release. It debuted at number one on the UK Albums Chart and sold 116,745 copies. By accumulating digital sales of 50,007, the album became the fifth album ever to sell upwards of 50,000 downloads in a single week. *Born to Die* remained at the summit of the chart in its second week, selling an additional 60,000 copies. As of November 2013, the album had sold over 836,000 copies in the UK. On the week-ending July 27, 2013 the album rose twenty positions to number 50, re-entering the Top 50. In France, the LP debuted at number one on the French Albums Chart with sales of 48,791, whose 16,968 digital copies. The album remained at the top position the following week with 23,888 copies sold. As of June 2014, it has sold over 500,000 copies in France. In New Zealand, the album debuted and peaked at number two on the charts, spending forty-weeks in the chart. After the conjunction of *Born to Die – The Paradise Edition*, the album charted at number six.[12] "Born to Die" is the fifty-seventh best selling album of all time in that country.

In the United States, the album attained first-week sales of 77,000 copies, subsequently debuting at number two on the *Billboard* 200, behind Adele's *21*, and shipped over 500,000 units in the country by January 2013, getting Gold certification. On the week ending August 31, 2013, though the album was over its 80th week on the chart, it re-entered the Top 20. As of June 2014, *Born to Die* has sold 1,100,000 copies in the United States, and has been certified platinum by the RIAA. In Italy, the album debuted at number five. The week after, it fell to number nine. In the first two weeks, the album has sold 6,271 copies. As of June 2012, the album has sold in Italy 24,372 copies. After the re-release in November 2012, the album jumped from 27 to 14. The LP has since been certified Gold. Following an iTunes discount, the album re-entered the iTunes Top 10 and jumped from 57 to 31 on the Italian Charts on the week-ending April 28, 2013. On the week-ending June 2, 2013, the album spent its seventieth week on the chart and fell ten spots to number 46. According to the International Federation of the Phonographic Industry (IFPI), *Born to Die* was the fifth global best-selling album of 2012 with sales of 3.4 million copies. As of July 2014, *Born to Die* has sold 4.79 million copies worldwide.

Track listing

Credits adapted from the liner notes of *Born to Die*.

Born to Die – **Standard version**

No.	Title	Writer(s)	Producer(s)	Length
1.	"Born to Die"	• Lana Del Rey • Justin Parker	• Emile Haynie • Parker[b]	4:46
2.	"Off to the Races"	• Del Rey • Tim Larcombe	• Patrik Berger • Haynie	5:00
3.	"Blue Jeans"	• Del Rey • Haynie • Dan Heath	Haynie	3:30
4.	"Video Games"	• Del Rey • Parker	Robopop	4:42
5.	"Diet Mountain Dew"	• Del Rey • Mike Daly	• Haynie • Jeff Bhasker[a] • Daly[b]	3:43
6.	"National Anthem"	• Del Rey • Parker • The Nexus	• Haynie • Bhasker[c] • David Sneddon[b] • James Bauer-Mein[b]	3:51
7.	"Dark Paradise"	• Del Rey • Rick Nowels	• Haynie • Nowels[a]	4:03
8.	"Radio"	• Del Rey • Parker	• Haynie • Parker[c]	3:34
9.	"Carmen"	• Del Rey • Parker	• Haynie • Bhasker[c] • Parker[b]	4:08
10.	"Million Dollar Man"	• Del Rey • Chris Braide	• Haynie • Braide	3:51
11.	"Summertime Sadness"	• Del Rey • Nowels	• Haynie • Nowels[a]	4:25
12.	"This Is What Makes Us Girls"	• Del Rey • Larcombe • Jim Irvin	• Al Shux • Haynie	3:58
Total length:				**49:28**

Born to Die – Deluxe version (bonus tracks)

No.	Title	Writer(s)	Producer(s)	Length
13.	"Without You"	• Del Rey • Skarbek	Haynie	3:49
14.	"Lolita"	• Del Rey • Howe • Robinson	• Haynie • Howe[a]	3:40
15.	"Lucky Ones"	• Del Rey • Nowels	• Haynie • Nowels[a]	3:45
Total length:				**60:40**

Born to Die – North American iTunes Store and Japanese versions (bonus track)

No.	Title	Writer(s)	Producer(s)	Length					
13.	"Video Games" (Joy Orbison Remix)	• Del Rey • Parker	• Robopop • Orbison[d]	4:59					

Born to Die – Target version (bonus tracks)

No.	Title	Writer(s)	Producer(s)	Length
13.	"Without You"	• Del Rey • Sacha Skarbek	Haynie	3:49
14.	"Lolita"	• Del Rey • Liam Howe • Hannah Robinson	• Haynie • Howe[a]	3:40
Total length:				**56:51**

Born to Die – French standard version (bonus track)

No.	Title	Length
13.	"Born to Die" (Woodkid & The Shoes Remix)	7:32

Born to Die – French deluxe version (bonus track)

No.	Title	Length							
16.	"Video Games" (White Lies C-Mix)	7:32							

Notes

- [a] signifies a co-producer
- [b] signifies a vocal producer
- [c] signifies an additional producer
- [d] signifies a remixer

Credits and personnel

Credits adapted from the liner notes of *Born to Die*.

Performance credits

- Lana Del Rey - vocals (all tracks)
- Emilie Bauer-Mein - backing vocals (track 6)
- James Bauer-Mein - backing vocals (track 6)
- Lenha Labelle - French vocals (track 9)
- David Sneddon - backing vocals (track 6)
- Hannah Robinson - backing vocals (track 14)
- Maria Vidal - additional vocals (tracks 7, 15)

Instruments

- Patrik Berger - guitar, bass guitar, percussion, synthesizer, sampler, drum programming (track 2)
- Jeff Bhasker - guitar (tracks 1, 5, 6); keyboards (track 5); additional keyboards (track 6, 9); additional strings (track 9)
- Chris Braide - guitar, acoustic piano, strings, drum programming (track 10)
- Pelle Hansen - cello (track 2)
- Emile Haynie - drums (tracks 1, 2, 3, 5, 6, 7, 8, 10, 11, 12, 13, 15); keyboards (tracks 1, 2, 6, 7, 8, 9, 11, 13, 15); additional keyboards (tracks 2, 5, 10, 12); guitar (tracks 3, 8, 9, 13, 15)
- Dan Heath - flute (track 11), additional strings (track 13)
- Erik Holm - viola (track 2)
- Liam Howe - additional keyboards, programming (track 14)
- Devrim Karaoglu - additional synthesizer, orchestral drums (track 7); additional pads (track 11)
- Brent Kolatalo - additional drums (track 5)
- Ken Lewis - additional vocal noises (track 1); additional drums (track 5)
- Rick Nowels - guitar (track 7); additional strings (track 11); keyboards (track 15)
- Dean Reid - pads (track 7)
- Al Shux - guitar, bass guitar, keyboards, programming (track 12)
- Sacha Skarbek - omnichord (track 13)
- Fredrik Syberg - violin (track 2)
- Patrick Warren - chamberlain strings (track 7); additional strings (track 11); guitar, keyboards (tracks 11, 15); strings, secondary strings (track 15)

Technical and production

- Carl Bagge - string arrangements (track 2)
- Patrik Berger - production (track 2)
- Jeff Bhasker - co-production (track 5), additional production (tracks 6, 9)
- Chris Braide - production (track 10)
- Lorenzo Cosi - engineering (track 13)
- Mike Daly - vocal production (track 5)
- John Davis - mastering (all tracks)
- Duncan Fuller - mixing assistant (tracks 1, 2, 3, 8, 10, 11, 13)
- Chris Galland - mixing assistant (tracks 5, 6, 7, 12, 15)
- Larry Gold - string arrangements, conductor (tracks 1, 5, 6, 7, 8, 9, 11, 12, 13, 15)
- Dan Grech-Marguerat - mixing (tracks 1, 2, 3, 8, 10, 11, 13, 14)
- Emile Haynie - production (tracks 1, 2, 3, 5, 6, 7, 8, 9, 10, 11, 12, 13, 14, 15)
- Dan Heath - string arrangements, conductor (tracks 3, 6)
- Liam Howe - co-production (track 14)
- Brent Kolatalo - additional recording (track 1)

- Erik Madrid - mixing assistant (tracks 5, 6, 7, 12, 15)
- Manny Marroquin - mixing (tracks 5, 6, 7, 12, 15)
- Kieron Menzies - engineering (track 15)
- The Nexus - vocal production (track 6)
- Rick Nowels - co-production (tracks 7, 11, 15); vocal production (track 15)
- Justin Parker - vocal production (tracks 1, 9); additional production (track 8)
- Robopop - production, mixing (track 4)
- Al Shux - production, vocal production (track 12)
- Steve Tirpak - string assistant (tracks 1, 5, 6, 7, 8, 9, 11, 12, 13, 15)

Charts

Weekly charts

Chart (2012–13)	Peak position
Australian Albums (ARIA)[13]	1
Austrian Albums (Ö3 Austria)[14]	1
Belgian Albums (Ultratop Flanders)[15]	2
Belgian Albums (Ultratop Wallonia)[16]	2
Canadian Albums (*Billboard*)[17]	3
Czech Albums (ČNS IFPI)[18]	5
Danish Albums (Hitlisten)[19]	3
Dutch Albums (MegaCharts)[20]	2
Finnish Albums (Suomen virallinen lista)[21]	5
French Albums (SNEP)[22]	1
German Albums (Official Top 100)[23]	1
Greek Albums (IFPI)	1
Irish Albums (IRMA)[24]	1
Italian Albums (FIMI)[25]	5
Japanese Albums (Oricon)	50
New Zealand Albums (Recorded Music NZ)[26]	2
Norwegian Albums (VG-lista)[27]	1
Portuguese Albums (AFP)[28]	3
Scottish Albums (OCC)[29]	1
Spanish Albums (PROMUSICAE)[30]	7
Swedish Albums (Sverigetopplistan)[31]	2
Swiss Albums (Schweizer Hitparade)[32]	1

UK Albums (OCC)[33]	1
US Billboard 200[34]	2
US Top Alternative Albums (Billboard)[35]	1
US Digital Albums (Billboard)[36]	1
US Top Rock Albums (Billboard)[37]	1
US Top Tastemaker Albums (Billboard)[38]	15

Year-end charts

Chart (2012)	Position
Australian Albums (ARIA)[39]	14
Austrian Albums (Ö3 Austria)[40]	6
Belgian Albums (Ultratop Flanders)[41]	2
Belgian Albums (Ultratop Wallonia)[42]	8
Belgian Midprice Albums Chart (Ultratop Flanders)	14
Dutch Albums (MegaCharts)[43]	33
French Albums (SNEP)[44]	7
German Albums (Offizielle Top 100)[45]	4
Hungarian Albums (MAHASZ)[46]	72
Irish Albums (IRMA)[47]	6
Italian Albums (FIMI)[48]	37
Swiss Albums (Schweizer Hitparade)[49]	2
US Billboard 200[50]	70
US Top Alternative Albums (Billboard)[51]	14
US Top Rock Albums (Billboard)[52]	21

Chart (2013)	Position
Australian Albums (ARIA)[53]	76
Belgian Midprice Albums Chart (Ultratop Flanders)	2
Danish Albums (Hitlisten)[54]	59
Hungarian Albums (MAHASZ)[55]	61
Spanish Albums (PROMUSICAE)[56]	29
Swiss Albums (Schweizer Hitparade)[57]	29
US Billboard 200[58]	53

US Top Alternative Albums (*Billboard*)[59]	7
US Top Rock Albums (*Billboard*)[60]	10

Certifications

Region	Certification	Sales/shipments
Australia (ARIA)[61]	2× Platinum	140,000^
Austria (IFPI Austria)[62]	2× Platinum	40,000x
Belgium (BEA)[63]	Platinum	30,000*
Brazil (ABPD)[64]	2× Platinum	80,000*
Canada (Music Canada)[65]	Platinum	80,000^
Denmark (IFPI Denmark)[66]	Platinum	20,000^
France (SNEP)	Diamond	500,000*
Germany (BVMI)[67]	3× Platinum	600,000^
Greece (IFPI Greece)[68]	3× Gold	9,000^
Hungary (Mahasz)[69]	Gold	3,000x
Ireland (IRMA)[70]	2× Platinum	30,000x
Italy (FIMI)[71]	Platinum	60,000*
Mexico (AMPROFON)[72]	Platinum	60,000^
New Zealand (RMNZ)[73]	Platinum	15,000^
Norway (IFPI Norway)[74]	Gold	15,000*
Poland (ZPAV)[75]	Diamond	100,000*
Portugal (AFP)	2× Platinum	40,000x
Russia (NFPF)	Platinum	10,000*
Spain (PROMUSICAE)	Platinum	40,000^
Sweden (GLF)[76]	2× Platinum	80,000^
Switzerland (IFPI Switzerland)[77]	2× Platinum	60,000x
United Kingdom (BPI)[78]	3× Platinum	900,000
United States (RIAA)[79]	Platinum	1,000,000
Summaries		
Europe (IFPI)[80]	2× Platinum	2,000,000*

*sales figures based on certification alone
^shipments figures based on certification alone
xunspecified figures based on certification alone

Release history

Country	Date	Format	Ref.
Germany	January 27, 2012	• CD • digital download	
Ireland		• LP	
France	January 30, 2012	• CD • digital download	
United Kingdom		• CD • digital download • LP	
United States	January 31, 2012	• CD • digital download	
Australia	February 3, 2012	CD	
Japan	February 8, 2012	• CD • CD/DVD • digital download	
United States	February 21, 2012	LP	

References

[1] iTunes - Musik – „Carmen - Single" von Lana Del Rey (https://itunes.apple.com/de/album/carmen-single/id493132396)

[2] Perpetua, Matthew (2011) " Lana Del Rey to Appear on 'Saturday Night Live' (http://www.rollingstone.com/music/news/lana-del-rey-to-appear-on-saturday-night-live-20111219)", *Rolling Stone*, December 19, 2011, retrieved 2012-01-04

[3] Caramanica, Jon (2011) " Finally Taking the Stage, Direct From the Internet (http://www.nytimes.com/2011/12/08/arts/music/lana-del-rey-at-bowery-ballroom-review.html?_r=1)", *The New York Times*, December 11, 2011, retrieved 2012-01-04

[4] Ritchie, Kevin (2011) " Lana del Rey (http://www.nowtoronto.com/music/story.cfm?content=183939)", *Now*, retrieved 2012-01-04

[5] " Lana Del Rey, Scala, London/Wild Beasts, The Cathedral, Manchester (http://www.independent.co.uk/arts-entertainment/music/reviews/lana-del-rey-scala-london-wild-beasts-the-cathedral-manchester-6264811.html)", *The Independent*, November 20, 2011, retrieved 2012-01-04

[6] Hype Machine + Tumblr Music Blog Zeitgeist: Top... - Hype Tumblr (http://hypem.tumblr.com/post/38468735631#notes-container)

[7] Spinner's 50 Best Albums of 2012 (http://www.albumoftheyear.org/list/150-spinners-50-best-albums-of-2012.php)

[8] Gigwise's Top 50 Albums of 2012 (http://www.albumoftheyear.org/list/166-gigwises-top-50-albums-of-2012.php)

[9] NME's 50 Best Albums Of 2012 - Stereogum (http://stereogum.com/1208412/nmes-50-best-albums-of-2012/list/)

[10] 101 Albums To Hear Before You Die (http://www.nme.com/list/101-albums-to-hear-before-you-die/338322/article/339086#article)

[11] Lana Del Rey - Born To Die - Reviews & Ratings (http://www.albumoftheyear.org/album/3061-lana-del-rey-born-to-die.php)

[12] NZ Top 40 Albums Chart I The Official New Zealand Music Chart (http://nztop40.co.nz/chart/albums?chart=2098). Date: 19 November 2012.

[13] " Lana Del Rey – Born to Die" (http://www.australian-charts.com/showitem.asp?interpret=Lana+Del+Rey&titel=Born+to+Die&cat=a). Australiancharts.com. Hung Medien. Retrieved June 29, 2014.

[14] " Lana Del Rey - Born to Die" (http://austriancharts.at/showitem.asp?interpret=Lana+Del+Rey&titel=Born+to+Die&cat=a) (in German). Austriancharts.at. Hung Medien. Retrieved June 29, 2014.

[15] " Lana Del Rey – Born to Die" (http://www.ultratop.be/nl/showitem.asp?interpret=Lana+Del+Rey&titel=Born+to+Die&cat=a) (in Dutch). Ultratop.be. Hung Medien. Retrieved June 29, 2014.

[16] " Lana Del Rey – Born to Die" (http://www.ultratop.be/fr/showitem.asp?interpret=Lana+Del+Rey&titel=Born+to+Die&cat=a) (in French). Ultratop.be. Hung Medien. Retrieved June 29, 2014.

[17] " Lana Del Rey Album & Song Chart History" (http://www.billboard.com/artist/306420/Lana+Del+Rey/chart?f=309) *Billboard* Canadian Albums Chart for Lana Del Rey. Prometheus Global Media. Retrieved June 29, 2014.

[18] " Top 50 Prodejní" (http://www.ifpicr.cz/hitparada/index.php?a=hitparada&hitparada=14). Czech Albums. ČNS IFPI. **Note:** On the chart page, select **201206** on the field besides the word "Zobrazit", and then click over the word to retrieve the correct chart data. Retrieved June 29, 2014.

[19] " Lana Del Rey – Born to Die" (http://www.danishcharts.com/showitem.asp?interpret=Lana+Del+Rey&titel=Born+to+Die&cat=a). Danishcharts.com. Hung Medien. Retrieved June 29, 2014.

[20] " Lana Del Rey – Born to Die" (http://www.dutchcharts.nl/showitem.asp?interpret=Lana+Del+Rey&titel=Born+to+Die&cat=a) (in Dutch). Dutchcharts.nl. Hung Medien. Retrieved June 29, 2014.

[21] " Lana Del Rey: Born to Die" (http://www.ifpi.fi/tilastot/virallinen-lista/artistit/Lana+Del+Rey/Born+to+Die) (in Finnish). Musiikkituottajat – IFPI Finland. Retrieved June 29, 2014.

[22] " Lana Del Rey – Born to Die" (http://www.lescharts.com/showitem.asp?interpret=Lana+Del+Rey&titel=Born+to+Die&cat=a). Lescharts.com. Hung Medien. Retrieved June 29, 2014.

[23] " Lana Del Rey – Born to Die" (http://www.officialcharts.de/album.asp?artist=Lana+Del+Rey&title=Born+to+Die&cat=a& country=de). Officialcharts.de. GfK Entertainment. Retrieved June 29, 2014.

[24] " Lana Del Rey – Born to Die" (http://www.irishcharts.com/showitem.asp?interpret=Lana+Del+Rey&titel=Born+to+Die&cat=a). Irishcharts.com. Hung Medien. Retrieved June 29, 2014.

[25] " Lana Del Rey – Born to Die" (http://www.italiancharts.com/showitem.asp?interpret=Lana+Del+Rey&titel=Born+to+Die&cat=a). Italiancharts.com. Hung Medien. Retrieved June 29, 2014.

[26] " Lana Del Rey – Born to Die" (http://www.charts.org.nz/showitem.asp?interpret=Lana+Del+Rey&titel=Born+to+Die&cat=a). Charts.org.nz. Hung Medien. Retrieved June 29, 2014.

[27] " Lana Del Rey – Born to Die" (http://www.norwegiancharts.com/showitem.asp?interpret=Lana+Del+Rey&titel=Born+to+Die& cat=a). Norwegiancharts.com. Hung Medien. Retrieved June 29, 2014.

[28] " Lana Del Rey – Born to Die" (http://www.portuguesecharts.com/showitem.asp?interpret=Lana+Del+Rey&titel=Born+to+Die& cat=a). Portuguesecharts.com. Hung Medien. Retrieved June 29, 2014.

[29] "2012-02-11 Top 40 Scottish Albums Archive UNIQ-nowiki-0-6d9da8360ebd6116-QINU Official Charts" (http://www.officialcharts. com/archive-chart/_/23/2012-02-11). UK Albums Chart. The Official Charts Company. Retrieved June 29, 2014.

[30] " Lana Del Rey – Born to Die" (http://www.spanishcharts.com/showitem.asp?interpret=Lana+Del+Rey&titel=Born+to+Die&cat=a). Spanishcharts.com. Hung Medien. Retrieved June 29, 2014.

[31] " Lana Del Rey – Born to Die" (http://www.swedishcharts.com/showitem.asp?interpret=Lana+Del+Rey&titel=Born+to+Die& cat=a). Swedishcharts.com. Hung Medien. Retrieved June 29, 2014.

[32] " Lana Del Rey – Born to Die" (http://www.swisscharts.com/showitem.asp?interpret=Lana+Del+Rey&titel=Born+to+Die&cat=a). Swisscharts.com. Hung Medien. Retrieved June 29, 2014.

[33] "2012-02-11 Top 40 Official UK Albums Archive UNIQ-nowiki-1-6d9da8360ebd6116-QINU Official Charts" (http://www.officialcharts. com/archive-chart/_/3/2012-02-11). UK Albums Chart. The Official Charts Company. Retrieved June 29, 2014.

[34] "Lana Del Rey Album & Song Chart History" (http://www.billboard.com/artist/306420/Lana+Del+Rey/chart?f=305) *Billboard* 200 for Lana Del Rey. Prometheus Global Media. Retrieved June 29, 2014.

[35] " Lana Del Rey Album & Song Chart History" (http://www.billboard.com/artist/306420/Lana+Del+Rey/chart?f=794) *Billboard* Top Alternative Albums for Lana Del Rey. Prometheus Global Media. Retrieved June 29, 2014.

[36] " Album & Song Chart History" (http://www.billboard.com/artist/306420/Lana+Del+Rey/chart?f=400) *Billboard* Digital Albums for Lana Del Rey. Prometheus Global Media. Retrieved June 29, 2014.

[37] " Lana Del Rey Album & Song Chart History" (http://www.billboard.com/artist/306420/Lana+Del+Rey/chart?f=408) *Billboard* Top Rock Albums for Lana Del Rey. Prometheus Global Media. Retrieved June 29, 2014.

[38] " Lana Del Rey Album & Song Chart History" (http://www.billboard.com/artist/306420/Lana+Del+Rey/chart?f=407) *Billboard* Top Tastemaker Albums for Lana Del Rey. Prometheus Global Media. Retrieved June 29, 2014.

[39] "ARIA Charts - End Of Year Charts - Top 100 Albums 2012" (http://www.aria.com.au/pages/ aria-charts-end-of-year-charts-top-100-albums-2012.htm). Austrian Record Industry Association. Retrieved June 29, 2014.

[40] "Jahreshitparade Alben 2012" (http://austriancharts.at/year.asp?id=2012&cat=a). *Austriancharts.at* (Hung Medien). Retrieved June 29, 2014.

[41] "Jaaroverzichten 2012" (http://www.ultratop.be/nl/annual.asp?year=2012&cat=a). *Ultratop.be* (Hung Medien). Retrieved June 29, 2014.

[42] "Raports Annuels 2012" (http://www.ultratop.be/fr/annual.asp?year=2012&cat=a). *Ultratop.be* (Hung Medien). Retrieved June 29, 2014.

[43] "Jaaroverzichten - Album 2012" (http://www.dutchcharts.nl/jaaroverzichten.asp?year=2012&cat=a). *Dutchcharts.nl* (Hung Medien). Retrieved June 29, 2014.

[44] "Quels sont les tops musicaux de l'année 2012 ?" (http://www.chartsinfrance.net/actualite/news-83546.html). *Chartsinfrance.net*. Retrieved June 29, 2014.

[45] "Die Jahres-Charts 2012" (http://www.einslive.de/musik/charts/jahres_charts_2012.jsp). *1LIVE* (Westdeutscher Rundfunk). Retrieved June 29, 2014.

[46] "Összesített album- és válogatáslemez-lista - eladási darabszám alapján - 2012" (http://zene.slagerlistak.hu/archivum/ eves-osszesitett-listak/album_db/2012). *Mahasz* (LightMedia). Retrieved June 29, 2014.

[47] "Best of 2012" (http://www.irma.ie/best2012.htm). Irish Recorded Music Association. Retrieved June 29, 2014.

[48] "Top 100 Album Combined - Classifica annuale (dal 2 Gennaio 2012 al 30 Dicembre 2012)" (http://www.webcitation.org/6DiKI87yH). *TV Sorrisi e Canzoni*. Retrieved June 29, 2014.

[49] "Schweizer Jahreshitparade 2012" (http://hitparade.ch/year.asp?key=2012). *Hitparade.ch* (Hung Medien). Retrieved June 29, 2014.

[50] "Billboard 200 Albums" (http://www.billboard.com/charts/year-end/2012/the-billboard-200?page=6&begin=61&order=position). *Billboard* (Prometheus Global Media). Retrieved June 29, 2014.

[51] "Alternative Albums: 2012 Year-End Charts" (http://www.billboard.com/charts/year-end/2012/top-alternative-albums?page=1& begin=11&order=position). *Billboard* (Prometheus Global Media). Retrieved June 29, 2014.

[52] "Rock Albums" (http://www.billboard.com/charts/year-end/2012/top-rock-albums?page=2&begin=21&order=position). *Billboard* (Prometheus Global Media). Retrieved June 29, 2014.

[53] "ARIA Charts - End Of Year Charts - Top 100 Albums 2013" (http://www.aria.com.au/pages/ aria-charts-end-of-year-charts-top-100-albums-2013.htm). *Austrian Record Industry Association*. Retrieved June 29, 2014.

[54] "Album Top-100 2013" (http://hitlisten.nu/aarslister.asp). *Hitlisten.nu* (IFPI Denmark). Retrieved June 29, 2014.

[55] "Összesített album- és válogatáslemez-lista - eladási darabszám alapján - 2013" (http://zene.slagerlistak.hu/archivum/ eves-osszesitett-listak/album_db/2013). *Mahasz* (LightMedia). Retrieved June 29, 2014.

[56] "Annual Charts" (http://www.promusicae.es/estaticos/view/23-annual-charts). Productores de Música de España. Retrieved June 29, 2014.

[57] "Schweizer Jahreshitparade 2013" (http://hitparade.ch/year.asp?key=2013). *Hitparade.ch* (Hung Medien). Retrieved June 29, 2014.

[58] "Billboard 200 Albums" (http://www.billboard.com/charts/year-end/2013/the-billboard-200?page=5). *Billboard* (Prometheus Global Media). Retrieved June 29, 2014.

[59] "Alternative Albums: 2013 Year-End Charts" (http://www.billboard.com/charts/year-end/2013/top-alternative-albums). *Billboard* (Prometheus Global Media). Retrieved June 29, 2014.

[60] "Rock Albums" (http://www.billboard.com/charts/year-end/2013/top-rock-albums). *Billboard* (Prometheus Global Media). Retrieved June 29, 2014.

[61] "ARIA Charts – Accreditations – 2012 Albums" (http://www.aria.com.au/pages/httpwww.aria.com.aupagesALBUMaccreds2012. htm). Australian Recording Industry Association.

[62] "Austrian album certifications – Lana Del Rey – Born To Die" (http://www.ifpi.at/?section=goldplatin) (in German). IFPI Austria. *Enter* Lana Del Rey *in the field* Interpret. *Enter* Born To Die *in the field* Titel. *Select* album *in the field* Format. *Click* Suchen

[63] "Ultratop - Goud en Platina - 2012" (http://www.ultratop.be/nl/certifications.asp?year=2012). Ultratop & Hung Medien / hitparade.ch.

[64] "Brazilian album certifications – Lana Del Rey – Born To Die" (http://abpd.org.br/certificados_interna.asp?sArtista=Lana+Del+Rey& tmidia=1) (in Portuguese). Associação Brasileira dos Produtores de Discos. Retrieved 2013-10-15.

[65] "Canadian album certifications – Lana Del Rey – Born To Die" (http://www.musiccanada.com/gold-platinum/#!/gp_search="Born+ To+Die" "Lana+Del+Rey"). Music Canada.

[66] "Danish album certifications – Lana Del Rey – Born To Die" (http://www.hitlisterne.dk/default.asp?w=34&y=2013&list=a40). IFPI Denmark.

[67] "Gold-/Platin-Datenbank (Lana Del Rey; 'Born To Die')" (http://www.musikindustrie.de/gold_platin_datenbank/?action=suche& strTitel=Born+To+Die&strInterpret=Lana+Del+Rey&strTtArt=alben&strAwards=checked) (in German). Bundesverband Musikindustrie.

[68] "Greek album certifications – Lana Del Rey – Born To Die" (http://replay.waybackmachine.org/*/http://www.ifpi.gr/chart01.htm) (in Greek). IFPI Greece.

[69] "Adatbázis – Arany- és platinalemezek – 2013" (http://www.mahasz.hu/?menu=arany_es_platinalemezek&menu2=adatbazis& ev=2013) (in Hungarian). Mahasz.

[70] "Irish album certifications – Lana Del Ray – Born To Die" (http://www.irishcharts.ie/awards/multi_platinum12.htm). Irish Recorded Music Association.

[71] *Note: To retrieve the certifications, 1) type in Del Rey in the box of "Artista", 2) select "--" in the box of "Seleziona settimana e anno", 3) select "Album e Compilation" in the box of "Scegli la sezione" then click on "Avvia la Ricerca"*

[72] "Certificaciones —" (https://www.facebook.com/CertificacionesAmprofon/photos_stream) (in Spanish). Asociación Mexicana de Productores de Fonogramas y Videogramas. January 21, 2014. Retrieved January 21, 2014.

[73] "New Zealand album certifications – Lana Del Rey – Born To Die" (http://nztop40.co.nz/chart/albums?chart=2273). Recording Industry Association of New Zealand.

[74] "Norwegian album certifications – Lana Del Rey – Born To Die" (http://www.ifpi.no/sok/lst_trofeer_sok.asp?type=artist) (in Norwegian). IFPI Norway.

[75] "Polish album certifications – Lana Del Rey – Born To Die" (http://www.zpav.pl/rankingi/wyroznienia/diamentowe/index.php) (in Polish). Polish Producers of Audio and Video (ZPAV).

[76] "Guld- och Platinacertifikat – År 2014" (http://www.ifpi.se/wp-content/uploads/) (PDF) (in Swedish). IFPI Sweden.

[77] "The Official Swiss Charts and Music Community: Awards (Lana Del Rey; 'Born To Die')" (http://www.swisscharts.com/ search_certifications.asp?search=Lana+Del+Rey+Born+To+Die). Hung Medien.

[78] "British album certifications – Lana Del Rey – Born To Die" (http://www.bpi.co.uk/certified-awards.aspx). British Phonographic Industry. *Enter* Born To Die *in the field* Search. *Select* Title *in the field* Search by. *Select* album *in the field* By Format. *Click* Go

[79] "American album certifications – Lana Del Rey – Born To Die" (http://www.riaa.com/goldandplatinumdata.php?artist="Born+To+ Die"). Recording Industry Association of America. *If necessary, click* Advanced, *then click* Format, *then select* Album, *then click* SEARCH

[80] "IFPI Platinum Europe Awards – 2013" (http://www.ifpi.org/content/section_news/plat2013.html). International Federation of the Phonographic Industry.

Paradise (Lana Del Rey EP)

Paradise	
EP by Lana Del Rey	
Released	November 9, 2012
Recorded	2012
Length	33:07
Label	• Polydor • Interscope
Producer	• DK • Emile Haynie • Dan Heath • Tim Larcombe • Rick Nowels • Rick Rubin
Lana Del Rey chronology	
• *Born to Die* • (2012)	• *Paradise* • *Born to Die – The Paradise Edition* • (2012) • (2012)
Singles from *Paradise*	

1. "Blue Velvet"
    Released: September 20, 2012
2. "Ride"
    Released: September 25, 2012
3. "Burning Desire"
    Released: March 13, 2013	

Paradise is the second extended play (EP) and second major release by American singer-songwriter Lana Del Rey; it was released on November 9, 2012 by Universal Music. It is additionally packaged with the reissue of her second studio album *Born to Die* (2012), titled *Born to Die - The Paradise Edition*. Del Rey enlisted collaborators including producers Rick Nowels, Justin Parker, and Rick Rubin.

Upon its release, *Paradise* received generally favorable reviews from music critics. The extended play debuted at number 10 on the US *Billboard* 200 with first-week sales of 67,000 copies. It also debuted at number 10 on the Canadian Albums Chart and peaked within the top-five of various other *Billboard* charts. Charting across Europe, the extended play became a top-ten hit in Flanders and Poland, charting within the top twenty in Wallonia and the Netherlands.

The EP's lead single was the ballad "Ride" which became a modest hit in the United States, Switzerland, Ireland, and France and reached the top 10 in Russia and Belgium. "Blue Velvet", a cover of the popular 1950s track, and "Burning Desire" were released as follow-up singles. Music videos for "Ride", "Blue Velvet", "Bel Air", and "Burning Desire" were posted to VEVO and YouTube to help promote the EP.

In December 2013, Del Rey released the Anthony Mandler-directed *Tropico*, a short film that includes the songs "Body Electric", "Gods & Monsters", and "Bel Air". That same month, an EP of the same name was made available for purchase on iTunes, containing the film along with the three aforementioned songs. In 2014, the EP was nominated for Best Pop Vocal Album at the 56th Annual Grammy Awards.

Background

	**"Ride"**
	"Ride" serves as the EP's first single.
	"Blue Velvet"
	"Blue Velvet", inspired by David Lynch's eponymously titled film, is a cover of the popular 1950s song by The Clovers.

Problems playing these files? See media help.

In an interview with *RTVE* on June 15, 2012, Del Rey announced that she had been working on a new album due in November, and that five tracks had already been written, two of them being "Young and Beautiful"Wikipedia:Citation needed and "Gods and Monsters",Wikipedia:Citation needed and another track titled "Body Electric", which was performed and announced as one of her songs at the BBC Radio1's Hackney Weekend.Wikipedia:Citation needed In an interview with Tim Blackwell for Nova FM in Melbourne, Australia, Del Rey added that her upcoming November release would not be a new album, but more like an EP, which she described as the Paradise Edition of *Born to Die*.Wikipedia:Citation needed Del Rey stated that the new release would have around seven new songs.Wikipedia:Citation needed

Del Rey's *Paradise* was released on November 12, 2012 in the UK and one day later in the US. The album's re-release, titled *Born to Die - The Paradise Edition*, was available to pre-order offering an immediate download of "Burning Desire" in some countries. The nine tracks were issued as a stand-alone CD or vinyl LP titled *Paradise*, in a two-disc set including the original *Born to Die* album tracks, as well as in a deluxe box set which will include both albums, a remix CD including eight remixes of songs from *Born to Die*, a DVD with six music videos and a two-track vinyl 7" of "Blue Velvet".

Promotion

On the day of "Ride"'s release as the EP's first single, Del Rey uploaded a teaser trailer to video-hosting website YouTube, that contained snippets of each track on The Paradise Edition. To promote the album, two singles were released, a cover version of "Blue Velvet" and the original "Burning Desire". "Blue Velvet was used in a television commercial for H&M, as a part of a promotional endeavor. "Burning Desire", the album's third single, was used to promote the Jaguar F-Type model. At a promotional concert, Del Rey sang the song, wearing red lipstick, because the model features a built-in lipstick holder. Unlike in the US where it was released as an extended play, *Paradise* was released in the United Kingdom as a re-release of *Born to Die*. The song serves as the soundtrack for a short film called "Desire", directed by Ridley Scott and starring Damian Lewis. A promotional video for "Burning Desire" appeared online on Valentine's Day of 2013, featuring Del Rey as her usual lounge singer persona, interspersed with snippets of the Jaguar F-Type. Directed by Ridley Scott, the video was filmed in the Rivoli Ballroom in London's South end.

On November 30, 2012, Del Rey was a musical guest on *Later... with Jools Holland* and performed her latest single "Ride".

Singles

On September 13, 2012, the lead single of the *Paradise* was confirmed to be "Ride", the accompanying music video being shot in Las Vegas, Nevada. It was eventually released for purchase on September 25, 2012. On October 10, Del Rey premiered the music video for "Ride" at the Aero Theatre in Santa Monica, California. On October 12, the music video for "Ride" was released online. Del Rey portrays a prostitute in the video, which the NME described as "not exactly empowering," and said might be seen as "anti-feminist". To further solicit the single and album, an EP was released containing remixes of "Ride". Contributing artists include SOHN, MJ Cole, Eli Escobar, 14TH remix, Wes James, and James Lavelle & Charlie May.

Del Rey appearing in a photoshoot for the Jaguar F-Type automobile in 2012, for which "Burning Desire" served as a promotional single for the EP.

On September 19, the music video for "Blue Velvet" was released through H&M. On September 20, 2012; "Blue Velvet" was made available for purchase via digital download as the first promotional single from the EP. People who pre-ordered the EP received an immediate download of "Burning Desire". On February 14, 2013, the music video for "Burning Desire" was released. The song was made available for purchase via digital download on March 19, 2013 as the EP's second and final promo single.

Other songs

The third single from *Paradise* and the eighth single overall from *Born to Die* was unveiled to be "Cola" on 14 November 2012. To date, however, a release date for the single never materialized. Because the description of the trailer lists the song "Cola" as "Pussy", it has led to speculation about the song being titled "Pussy" or having a subtitle of that name. Despite this interpretation, it has been reported that the song is called "Cola" with no alternate titles. The official iTunes preorder does not acknowledge an alternate title. "Fresh" and "is-she-serious?" have been some of the reactions to the profane lyrics included on "Cola". *Hindustan Times* criticized the song snippet, saying it proved she was running out of ideas and that the songs all sounded strangely similar. When asked about the origin of the lyrics, Del Rey said: "I have a Scottish boyfriend, and that's just what he says!" Defending the track, she said that her record label had reservations about releasing the track.

The song, "Body Electric", alludes to Walt Whitman in the lyric, "Whitman is my daddy." The song's chorus of "I sing the body electric" is a direct reference to his poem "I Sing the Body Electric". Previously, Del Rey has cited Whitman as an inspiration, recalling his chapbook "Leaves of Grass" as instrumental to her songwriting. "Yayo" returns for a third release, after having appeared on Del Rey's first EP *Kill Kill* and her debut album, *Lana Del Ray a.k.a. Lizzy Grant*. A promotional video for the closing track, "Bel Air", was released on 8 November 2012. The video featured outtakes from the "Summertime Sadness" music video. In the video, Del Rey sings, "Roses, Bel Air, take me there/ I've been waiting to meet you/ Palm trees, in the light, I can see, late at night/ Darling I'm willing to greet you/ Come to me, baby." *Rolling Stone* praised the shift in persona Del Rey exhibited in the ballad's video, noting a significant difference from her usual Americana lounge singer, First Lady Onassis-Kennedy, and biker chick alter egos.

Film

Alongside *Paradise*, Del Rey plans to launch a short film titled *Tropico* that features the songs "Body Electric", "Gods and Monsters", and "Bel Air". "Tropico" was filmed in late June 2013; it was directed by Anthony Mandler, who also directed Del Rey's previous music videos for "National Anthem" and "Ride". Via social media platforms, Del Rey released several promotional images for the film, one depicting Del Rey in a wimple reminiscent of Mary, Mother of Jesus and another with Del Rey holding a snake and posing as Eve, the biblical wife of Adam from Genesis. In August 2013, Del announced on Twitter that the film would have two premieres: One at the Hollywood Forever Cemetery in Los Angeles and one in an unspecified location in New York; she referred to the short film as a "farewell". Critics noted that this contradicted other claims by Del Rey that she would release a third studio album, with a demo of the song "Black Beauty" leaking online. On November 22, 2013, an official trailer for "Tropico" was released; at the end of the trailer, it was announced that the film will be uploaded to Del Rey's official VEVO account on December 5, 2013. On December 3, 2013, Del Rey announced on Facebook and Twitter that "Tropico" will be screened at the Cinerama Dome in Hollywood, California on December 4, 2013 prior to its VEVO release.

Critical reception

Professional ratings	
Aggregate scores	
Source	Rating
Metacritic	(64/100)
Review scores	
Source	Rating
Allmusic	★ ★ ★ ★
American Songwriter	★ ★ ★ ★
Drowned in Sound	8/10
PopMatters	7/10
Rolling Stone	★ ★ ★ ★
Slant Magazine	★ ★ ★ ★
Sputnikmusic	3.5/5
Tiny Mix Tapes	★ ★ ★ ★

At Metacritic, which assigns a normalized rating out of 100 to reviews from mainstream critics, the EP has received an average score of 64, based on 9 reviews indicating "generally favorable reviews". Gil Kaufman of MTV wrote that "[the reissue] is as mellow and languorous... as she was on her debut." On the snippet video, he said, "...the new songs gives a peek at the gangster Nancy Sinatra's ongoing fascination with a sleepy, seductive sound and lyrics that mix old-fashion girl group obsession with sometimes profane, shocking new-school swagger." *Stuff* said the song titles were predictably pokerfaced. "Ride" received widely positive reviews, with the only qualms circling around the unrealistic cover art and coy song title. Of the cover art, Jessica Sager of PopCrush said it's unclear how the tire swing is suspended, with no visible trees nearby. Sager highlighted rumors circulating the internet about the music video for the single being recorded in Valley of Fire in Clark County, Nevada. Contactmusic.com noticed the track adheres to Del Rey's trademark sound, stating that the notion of her even having a trademark after one commercially successful album indicates that "we haven't seen the last of her just yet". Of the production itself, it was said that "Ride" is more accomplished than Del Rey's previous endeavors, with the strengths of the track outshining the flaws. The reviewer concluded by saying, "All that doe-eyed "you can be my full-time daddy / baby" shtick is going to start getting a little tired pretty soon, though, we reckon."

NME blogged that "Ride"'s most significant lyric read, "I'm tired of feeling like I'm fucking crazy", while stating that the accompanying music video may be produced solely by Del Rey, as the videos for "Carmen" and Video Games" were. Pitchfork Media agreed, saying the aforementioned lyric was a rare moment of raw emotion by Del Rey. *Billboard* wrote: "Ride' is a long, dreamy ballad that swells into full view during the chorus, when the singer declares, 'Been trying' hard not to get into trouble/But I, I've got a war in my mind… so I just ride." MTV called "Ride" a "slow burn" and "as mellow and languorous...as on her debut." Another MTV review said: "On 'Ride,' Rey sings what she knows best: loneliness, some daddy issues and day-drinking. All of this is probably a metaphor for something, but honestly, we're still trying to figure out what those 'Born To Die' tigers mean." Cameron Matthew of Spinner noted that Del Rey "amped up on the smokey vocals" with "Ride". Canada.com reviewer Leah Collins called "Bel Air" an Enya-channeled, eerie waltz.

Conversely, *The Huffington Post* called both "Bel Air" and "Yayo" filler-tracks. Disagreeing with this position, Carl Williot of Idolator wrote that "Yayo" should have been a single and was the best song on the EP. Calling the song Del Rey's most interesting song to date, Williot compared the narration on "Yayo" to the plight of Anna Nicole Smith and said it was "woozy" and "burlesque". As a whole, Williot noted the theme between *Born to Die* and *Paradise* shifted from infantilization to sexualization on the EP; songs such as "Burning Desire" and "Ride" were decisively more mature than tracks like "Video Games" from the singer's mainstream debut. Closing the review, Williot said the EP was best listened to: "While wearing formal cocktail attire that has become slightly rumpled following some sort of intense argument and/or sexual dalliance." Allmusic commented that the EP kept the glacial string arrangements and slow drums that inspired the cinematic atmosphere of *Born to Die*, while improving vocally. Her songwriting and lyricism, however, was criticized. John Bush, the Allmusic reviewer, canned the lyrical content of *Paradise*. For example, he

Del Rey is nominated for the Grammy Award for Best Pop Vocal Album in 2013.

highlighted the lyrics of "Body Electric", which state: "Elvis is my daddy/ Marilyn's my mother/ Jesus is my bestest friend/ We get crazy every Friday night/ drop it like it's hot in the pale moonlight.", as being "cliche" and "babyish", a trend pervading the entire album. On a positive note, Bush proposed that "Blue Velvet" proved Del Rey was more than capable of performing vocally when given tasteful content. Wrapping up the review, Bush concluded that, overall, Del Rey has lyrically remained in a stasis, with the album serving as fodder for her hype and image. According to Bush, Del Rey embodied the album with a simile from "Gods and Monsters": "Like a groupie incognito posing as a real singer, life imitates art." *Los Angeles Times* called the EP "surprisingly strong". *Digital Spy* said:

In "Body Electric", Del Rey lends tribute to both Elvis Presley (left) and Marilyn Monroe (right). Music reviewer Carl Williot considered the shout-out cliche, while other reviewers praised the songwriting.

> Current single "Ride" finds her wearing The Boss's influence on her sleeve most plainly with its galloping verses and sweeping melody, albeit delivered with Lana's '50s-styled Hollywood demeanour. Elsewhere, there's more talk of bad boys, cherry pie and other old fashioned glamourisms much like its parent album, but there's still progression to be found. The multiple hooks in "Cola" feel polished without compromising her rebellious nature (she opens it with the line: "My p***y tastes like Pepsi-Cola"), while the booming "Body Electric" sees her revisiting her Marilyn Monroe persona with more believable results than previous attempts. She treads close to being kooky for the sake of kooky on "Yayo", but when she gets it right in the case of "Bel Air" - a snowy, Tim Burton-inspired ballad - Lana proves there's plenty more to be excited for on album two.

Pointing to "Blue Velvet" and "Yayo" as the weaker songs, LGBT lifestyle magazine *So So Gay* thought this about *Paradise* as a whole: "The existing themes, stunning musicality, and lyrical strength of the original are complimented by a series of new tracks that give the listener 'more of the same'." Slant Magazine said the EP could not live up to *Born to Die*, with tracks "Gods and Monsters" and "Burning Desire" standing in its shadow. Slant Magazine challenged that *Paradise* was a "grubby cash grab". Drowned in Sound writer David Edwards mirrored Slant's position due to the release's proximity to the Christmas holiday. *Rolling Stone* called the album "conceptually stunning". *Billboard* praised the album's allusions to David Lynch, adding: "her vintage 60s charm just might kill you." Applauding Del Rey's rising stardom, *The Daily Record* celebrated the EP's commentary of the 2010s zeitgeist. *The Prophet Blog* wrote: "*Paradise*, sounds like the record she was always meant to make — not the one she had to. Whereas *Born to Die* was self-conscious and chart hungry, Paradise allows Lana the freedom to get a little more daring and fully indulge in her love of David Lynch."

Track listing

Paradise — Standard edition

No.	Title	Writer(s)	Producer(s)	Length
1.	"Ride"	• Lana Del Rey • Justin Parker	Rick Rubin	4:49
2.	"American"	• Del Rey • Rick Nowels • Emile Haynie	• Nowels • Haynie[a]	4:08
3.	"Cola"	• Del Rey • Nowels	• Nowels • DK[a]	4:20
4.	"Body Electric"	• Del Rey • Nowels	• Nowels • Dan Heath	3:53
5.	"Blue Velvet"	• Lee Morris • Bernie Wayne	Haynie	2:38
6.	"Gods & Monsters"	• Del Rey • Tim Larcombe	• Larcombe • Haynie[b]	3:57

7.	"Yayo"	Lana Del Rey	• Heath • Haynie	5:21
8.	"Bel Air"	• Del Rey • Heath	Heath	3:57
Total length:				**33:07**

Paradise — iTunes Store bonus track

No.	Title	Writer(s)	Producer(s)	Length
9.	"Burning Desire"	• Del Rey • Parker	Haynie	3:51
Total length:				**36:58**

Paradise — Special edition bonus tracks

No.	Title	Writer(s)	Producer(s)	Length
9.	"Blue Velvet" (Lindstrøm Remix)	• Morris • Wayne	• Haynie • Lindstrøm[c]	5:03
10.	"Blue Velvet" (Penguin Prison Remix)	• Morris • Wayne	• Haynie • Penguin Prison[c]	9:36
Total length:				**47:46**

Notes

- [a] signifies a co-producer
- [b] signifies an additional producer
- [c] signifies a remixer

Credits and personnel

Credits adapted from the liner notes of *Paradise*.

Performance credits

- Lana Del Rey - vocals (all tracks); backing vocals (track 7)

Instruments

- James Gadson - drums (track 1)
- Emile Haynie - drums (track 2, 7); additional keyboard (track 7)
- Dan Heath - percussion (track 4); horns (track 6); keyboard (track 7); strings (tracks 7, 8); piano (track 8)
- Devrim Karaoglu - drums (track 3)
- Jason Lader - bass guitar (track 1)
- Tim Larcombe - keyboards, guitar, drums (track 6)
- The Larry Gold Orchestra - strings (track 5)
- Songa Lee - violin (tracks 1, 8)
- Kieron Menzies - drum programming (track 3)
- Rick Nowels - synthesizer (track 2); keyboard (tracks 2, 3); bass guitar, acoustic guitar, drums (track 3); piano, mellotron, strings (track 4)
- Tim Pierce - electric guitar (track 2); slide guitar (tracks 3, 4)
- Zac Rae - piano, keyboard (track 1)
- Kathleen Sloan - violin (tracks 1, 8)

- Patrick Warren - electric guitar, synthesizer, piano (tracks 2, 3, 4); strings, glockenspiel, brass (track 3); organ (tracks 3, 4); dulcitone, bells, optigon, mellotron (track 4)

Technical and production

- Graham Archer - vocal engineering (track 7)
- Ben Baptie - mixing assistant (track 5)
- Spencer Burgess Jr. - recording assistant (track 5)
- Nikki Calvert - engineering (track 8)
- Jeremy Cochise Ball - mixing (track 7)
- John Davis - mastering (tracks 1, 2, 3, 4, 5, 6, 7, 8)
- DK - co-production (track 3)
- Tom Elmhirst - mixing (track 5)
- Chris Garcia - additional recording (tracks 2, 3); recording (track 4)
- Larry Gold - string arrangements (track 5)
- Emile Haynie - co-production (track 2); production (tracks 5, 7); additional production (track 6)
- Dan Heath - string arrangements (tracks 1, 6); orchestral arrangements (tracks 2, 4); production (tracks 4, 7, 8); engineering (track 8)
- Jason Lader - recording (track 1)
- Tim Larcombe - production (track 6)
- Eric Lynn - recording assistant (track 1)
- Kieron Menzies - recording, mixing (tracks 2, 3, 4)
- Rick Nowels - production (tracks 2, 3, 4)
- Sean Oakley - recording assistant (track 1)
- Robert Orton - mixing (track 6)
- Tucker Robinson - string recording (track 1); engineering (track 8)
- Jeff Rothschild - mixing (track 8)
- Rick Rubin - production (track 1)
- Andrew Scheps - mixing (track 1)
- Peter Stanislaus - mixing (track 8)
- Jordan Stilwell - additional recording (tracks 2, 3)

Commercial performance

Paradise debuted at number ten on the *Billboard* 200, selling 67,000 copies in its first week. It has since sold over 332,000 copies in the US.

Charts

Weekly charts

Chart (2012)	Peak position
Australian Albums (ARIA)[1]	19
Canadian Albums (*Billboard*)[2]	10
New Zealand Albums (Recorded Music NZ)[3]	19
US *Billboard* 200[4]	10
US Top Rock Albums (*Billboard*)[5]	4
US Top Alternative Albums (*Billboard*)[6]	4
US Top Tastemaker Albums (*Billboard*)[7]	5

Year-end charts

Chart (2013)	Position
US *Billboard* 200	115

Release history

Country	Date	Format
Australia	November 9, 2012	CD
Worldwide	November 12, 2012	12" Vinyl
Germany	November 13, 2012	CD
United States		CD, digital download

References

[1] " Lana Del Rey – Paradise" (http://www.australian-charts.com/showitem.asp?interpret=Lana+Del+Rey&titel=Paradise&cat=a). Australiancharts.com. Hung Medien.

[2] " Lana Del Rey Album & Song Chart History" (http://www.billboard.com/artist/306420/Lana+Del+Rey/chart?f=309) *Billboard* Canadian Albums Chart for Lana Del Rey. Prometheus Global Media.

[3] " Lana Del Rey – Born To Die - The Paradise Edition" (http://www.charts.org.nz/showitem.asp?interpret=Lana+Del+Rey&titel=Born+To+Die+-+The+Paradise+Edition&cat=a). Charts.org.nz. Hung Medien.

[4] "Lana Del Rey Album & Song Chart History" (http://www.billboard.com/artist/306420/Lana+Del+Rey/chart?f=305) *Billboard* 200 for Lana Del Rey. Prometheus Global Media.

[5] " Lana Del Rey Album & Song Chart History" (http://www.billboard.com/artist/306420/Lana+Del+Rey/chart?f=408) *Billboard* Top Rock Albums for Lana Del Rey. Prometheus Global Media.

[6] " Lana Del Rey Album & Song Chart History" (http://www.billboard.com/artist/306420/Lana+Del+Rey/chart?f=794) *Billboard* Top Alternative Albums for Lana Del Rey. Prometheus Global Media.

[7] " Lana Del Rey Album & Song Chart History" (http://www.billboard.com/artist/306420/Lana+Del+Rey/chart?f=407) *Billboard* Top Tastemaker Albums for Lana Del Rey. Prometheus Global Media.

The Observer

For other uses, see The Observer (disambiguation).

The Observer

Type	Weekly newspaper
Format	Berliner (ex-Broadsheet)
Owner(s)	Guardian Media Group
Editor	John Mulholland
Founded	1791
Political alignment	Centre-left
Language	English
Headquarters	Kings Place, 90 York Way, London
Circulation	214,644 (March 2014)
Sister newspapers	*The Guardian,* *The Guardian Weekly*
ISSN	0029-7712 [1]
OCLC number	50230244 [2]
Official website	observer.theguardian.com [3]

The Observer (International Edition)

ISSN	9976-1971 [4]
OCLC number	436604553 [5]

The Observer is a British newspaper, published on Sundays. In the same place on the political spectrum as its daily sister paper *The Guardian*, whose parent company Guardian Media Group acquired it in 1993, it takes a social liberal or social democratic line on most issues. First published in 1791, it is the world's oldest Sunday newspaper.

History

Origins

The first issue, published on 4 December 1791 by W.S. Bourne, was the world's first Sunday newspaper. Believing that the paper would be a means of wealth, Bourne instead soon found himself facing debts of nearly £1,600. Though early editions purported editorial independence, Bourne attempted to cut his losses and sell the title to the government. When this failed, Bourne's brother (a wealthy businessman) made an offer to the government, which also refused to buy the paper but agreed to subsidise it in return for influence over its editorial content. As a result, the paper soon took a strong line against radicals such as Thomas Paine, Francis Burdett and Joseph Priestley.

19th century

In 1807, the brothers decided to relinquish editorial control, naming Lewis Doxat as the new editor. Seven years later, the brothers sold *The Observer* to William Innell Clement, a newspaper proprietor who owned a number of publications. The paper continued to receive government subsidies during this period; in 1819, of the approximately 23,000 copies of the paper distributed weekly, approximately 10,000 were given away as "specimen copies", distributed by postmen who were paid to deliver them to "lawyers, doctors, and gentlemen of the town."[6] Yet the paper began to demonstrate a more independent editorial stance, criticising the authorities' handling of the events surrounding the Peterloo Massacre and defying an 1820 court order against publishing details of the trial of the Cato Street Conspirators, who were alleged to have plotted to murder members of the Cabinet. The woodcut pictures published of the stable and hayloft where the conspirators were arrested reflected a new stage of illustrated journalism that the newspaper pioneered during this time.

Clement maintained ownership of *The Observer* until his death in 1852. During that time, the paper supported parliamentary reform, but opposed a broader franchise and the Chartist leadership. After Doxat retired in 1857, Clement's heirs sold the paper to Joseph Snowe, who also took over the editor's chair. Under Snowe, the paper adopted a more liberal political stance, supporting the North during the American Civil War and endorsing universal manhood suffrage in 1866.[7] These positions contributed to a decline in circulation during this time.

In 1870, wealthy businessman Julius Beer bought the paper and appointed Edward Dicey as editor, whose efforts succeeded in reviving circulation. Though Beer's son Frederick became the owner upon Julius's death in 1880, he had little interest in the newspaper and was content to leave Dicey as editor until 1889. Henry Duff Traill took over the editorship after Dicey's departure, only to be replaced in 1891 by Frederick's wife, Rachel Beer, of the Sassoon family. Though circulation declined during her tenure, she remained as editor for thirteen years, combining it in 1893 with the editorship of *The Sunday Times*, a newspaper that she had also bought.[8]

20th century

Upon Frederick's death in 1905, the paper was purchased by the newspaper magnate Lord Northcliffe. After maintaining the existing editorial leadership for a couple of years, in 1908 Northcliffe named James Louis Garvin as editor. Garvin quickly turned the paper into an organ of political influence, boosting circulation from 5,000 to 40,000 within a year of his arrival as a result. Yet the revival in the paper's fortunes masked growing political disagreements between Garvin and Northcliffe. These disagreements ultimately led Northcliffe to sell the paper to William Waldorf Astor in 1911, who transferred ownership to his son Waldorf four years later.

During this period, the Astors were content to leave the control of the paper in Garvin's hands. Under his editorship circulation reached 200,000 during the interwar years, a figure which Garvin fought to maintain even during the depths of the Great Depression. Politically the paper pursued an independent Tory stance, which eventually brought Garvin into conflict with Waldorf's more liberal son, David. Their conflict contributed to Garvin's departure as editor in 1942, after which the paper took the unusual step of declaring itself non-partisan.

Ownership passed to Waldorf's sons in 1948, with David taking over as editor. He remained in the position for 27 years, during which time he turned it into a trust-owned newspaper employing, among others, George Orwell, Paul Jennings and C. A. Lejeune. Under Astor's editorship *The Observer* became the first national newspaper to oppose the government's 1956 invasion of Suez, a move which cost it many readers. In 1977, the Astors sold the ailing newspaper to US oil giant Atlantic Richfield (now called ARCO) who sold it to Lonrho plc in 1981. Since June 1993, it has been part of the Guardian Media Group.

In 1990, Farzad Bazoft, a journalist for *The Observer*, was executed in Iraq on charges of spying. In 2003, *The Observer* interviewed the Iraqi colonel who had arrested and interrogated Bazoft and who was convinced that Bazoft was not a spy.[9]

21st century

On 27 February 2005, *The Observer* Blog[10] was launched, making *The Observer* the first newspaper to purposely document its own internal decisions, as well as the first newspaper to release podcasts. The paper's regular columnists include Andrew Rawnsley and Nick Cohen.

In addition to the weekly *Observer Magazine* which is still present every Sunday, for several years each issue of *The Observer* came with a different free monthly magazine. These magazines had the titles *Observer Sport Monthly*, *Observer Music Monthly*, *Observer Woman* and *Observer Food Monthly*.

Content from *The Observer* is included in *The Guardian Weekly* for an international readership.

The Observer followed its daily partner *The Guardian* and converted to 'Berliner' format on Sunday 8 January 2006.[11][12]

The Observer was announced as *National Newspaper of the Year* at the British Press Awards 2007.Wikipedia:Citation needed

On 24 October 2007, it was announced that editor Roger Alton was stepping down at the end of the year to be replaced by his deputy, John Mulholland.

In early 2010, the paper was rejuvenated. An article on the paper's website previewing the new version stated that "The News section, which will incorporate Business and personal finance, will be home to a new section, Seven Days, offering a complete round-up of the previous week's main news from Britain and around the world, and will also focus on more analysis and comment."[13]

Supplements and features

After the paper was rejuvenated in early 2010, the main paper came with only a small number of supplements – *Sport*, *The Observer Magazine*, *The New Review* and *The New York Times International Weekly*, an 8-page supplement of articles selected from *The New York Times*, has been distributed with the paper since 2007. Every four weeks the paper includes *The Observer Food Monthly* magazine.

Previously, the main paper had come with a vast range of supplements including *Sport*, *Business & Media*, *Review*, *Escape* (a travel supplement), *The Observer Magazine* and various special interest monthlies, such as *Observer Food Monthly*, *Observer Women monthly* which was launched in 2006, *Observer Sport Monthly* and *The Observer Film Magazine*.

The Newsroom

The Observer and its sister newspaper *The Guardian* operate a visitor centre in London called The Newsroom. It contains their archives, including bound copies of old editions, a photographic library and other items such as diaries, letters and notebooks. This material may be consulted by members of the public. The Newsroom also mounts temporary exhibitions and runs an educational program for schools.

In November 2007, *The Observer* and *The Guardian* made their archives available over the internet.[14] The current extent of the archives available are 1791 to 2000 for *The Observer* and 1821 to 2000 for *The Guardian*. These archives will eventually go up to 2003.

Bans

The paper was banned in Egypt in February 2008 due to the publication of Prophet Mohammad's cartoons.

Editors

- W. S. Bourne & W. H. Bourne (1791–1807)
- Lewis Doxat (1807–1857)
- Joseph Snowe (1857–1870)
- Edward Dicey (1870–1889)
- Henry Duff Traill (1889–1891)
- Rachel Beer (1891–1904)
- Austin Harrison (1904–1908)
- James Louis Garvin (1908–1942)
- Ivor Brown (1942–1948)
- David Astor (1948–1975)
- Donald Trelford (1975–1993)
- Jonathan Fenby (1993–1995)
- Andrew Jaspan (1995–1996)
- Will Hutton (1996–1998)
- Roger Alton (1998–2007)
- John Mulholland (2008–)

Awards

The Observer was named the British Press Awards *National Newspaper of the Year* in 2007.[15] Its supplements have twice won "Regular Supplement of the Year" (*Sport Monthly*, 2001; *Food Monthly*, 2006).

Observer journalists have won a range of British Press Awards, including

- "Interviewer of the Year" (Lynn Barber, 2002; Sean O'Hagan, 2003; Rachel Cooke, 2006; Chrissy Iley (freelance for *Observer* and *Sunday Times* magazine), 2008)
- "Critic of the Year" (Jay Rayner, 2006; Philip French, 2009)

Bibliography

- Richard Cockett, *David Astor and The Observer*, André Deutsch, London, 1990, 294 pp. with index. ISBN 0-233-98735-5. Has endpapers which are facsimiles of *The Observer*, with other black-and-white photographic plates of personnel linked to the newspaper.

References

[1] http://www.worldcat.org/issn/0029-7712
[2] http://www.worldcat.org/oclc/50230244
[3] http://observer.theguardian.com/
[4] http://www.worldcat.org/issn/9976-1971
[5] http://www.worldcat.org/oclc/436604553
[6] Dennis Griffiths (ed.) *The Encyclopedia of the British Press, 1422–1992*, London and Basingstoke: Macmillan, 1992, p.159
[7] Observer text timeline (http://www.theguardian.com/gnm-archive/2002/jun/11/2)
[8] A brief history of The Observer (http://wayback.archive.org/web/20090917013231/http://www.adinfo-guardian.co.uk/the-observer/observer-history.shtml)
[9] Iraqi colonel admits Bazoft not a spy (http://www.theguardian.com/media/2003/may/18/Iraqandthemedia.iraq), accessed 4 April 2007
[10] Observer blog (http://www.theguardian.com/news/observerblog), accessed 27 February 2007

[11] Observer announces relaunch date (http://www.theguardian.com/media/2005/dec/19/theobserver.pressandpublishing), accessed 27
       February 2007
[12] The archive – summary of holdings (http://www.theguardian.com/gnm-archive), accessed 27 February 2007
[13] Guardian.co.uk (http://www.theguardian.com/help/insideguardian/2010/feb/21/new-observer)
[14] DigitalArchive (http://www.theguardian.com/info/2012/jul/25/digital-archive-notice)
[15] *Press Gazette*, Roll of Honour (http://www.pressgazette.co.uk/hybrid.asp?typeCode=99&navcode=92#), accessed 24 July 2011

External links

- *Observer* website (http://observer.theguardian.com/)
- Information about The Newsroom Archive and Visitor Centre (http://www.guardian.co.uk/newsroom)
- *DigitalArchive* paid-for service (http://www.theguardian.com/info/2012/jul/25/digital-archive-notice)
- History of Guardian Media Group 1990 – 1999, Guardian Media Group website; as of 2 March 2003; GMGplc.co.uk (http://www.gmgplc.co.uk/gmgplc/aboutus/abthistory/)Wikipedia:Link rot (link requires Flash to view timeline)
- History of the Observer (http://www.theguardian.com/gnm-archive/2002/jun/11/2)

Saturday Night Live

"SNL" redirects here. For other uses, see SNL (disambiguation).

For the current season, see Saturday Night Live (season 39).

Saturday Night Live	
Also known as	• NBC's Saturday Night (1975–77) • Saturday Night Live '80 (1980)
Genre	Variety show
Created by	Lorne Michaels
Written by	See List of Saturday Night Live writers
Directed by	• Dave Wilson (1975–86, 1989–95)
Starring	See List of Saturday Night Live cast members
Narrated by	• Don Pardo (1975–81, 1982–present)
Country of origin	United States
Original language(s)	English
No. of seasons	39
No. of episodes	766 (List of episodes)
Production	
Executive producer(s)	• Lorne Michaels (1975–80, 1985–present)
Location(s)	NBC Studios New York, New York
Running time	93 minutes (with commercials)
Production company(s)	• Broadway Video (1981–present)
Broadcast	
Original channel	NBC
Picture format	480i (4:3 SDTV) (1975–2005) 1080i (16:9 HDTV) (2005–present)
Original run	October 11, 1975 – present
Chronology	
Related shows	TV Funhouse Saturday Night Live Weekend Update Thursday
External links	
Website [1]	

Saturday Night Live (abbreviated as *SNL*) is an American late-night live television sketch comedy and variety show created by Lorne Michaels and developed by Dick Ebersol. The show premiered on NBC on October 11, 1975, under the original title *NBC's Saturday Night*. The show's comedy sketches, which parody contemporary culture and politics, are performed by a large and varying cast of repertory and newer cast members. Each episode is hosted by a celebrity guest (who usually delivers an opening monologue and performs in sketches with the cast) and features performances by a musical guest. An episode normally begins with a cold open sketch that ends with someone breaking character and proclaiming, "Live from New York, it's Saturday Night!," beginning the show proper.

In 1980, Michaels left the series to explore other opportunities. He was replaced by Jean Doumanian, who was replaced by Ebersol after a season of bad reviews. Ebersol ran the show until 1985, when Michaels returned; Michaels has remained since then. Many of *SNL*'s cast found national stardom while appearing on the show, and achieved success in film and television, both in front of and behind the camera. Others associated with the show, such as writers, have gone on to successful careers creating, writing, or starring in TV and film.

Broadcast from Studio 8H at NBC's headquarters in the GE Building, *SNL* has aired 766 episodes since its debut, and concluded its thirty-ninth season on May 17, 2014, making it one of the longest-running network television programs in the United States. The show format has been developed and recreated in several countries, including Spain, Italy, Brazil, Japan, and South Korea, each meeting with different levels of success. Successful sketches have seen life outside of the show as feature films, although only two met with critical and financial success: *The Blues Brothers* (1980) and *Wayne's World* (1992). The show has been marketed in other ways, including home media releases of "best of" and whole seasons, and books and documentaries about behind-the-scenes activities of running and developing the show.

Throughout more than three decades on air, *Saturday Night Live* has received a number of awards, including 36 Primetime Emmy Awards, a Peabody Award, and three Writers Guild of America Awards. In 2000, it was inducted into the National Association of Broadcasters Hall of Fame. It was ranked tenth in *TV Guide*'s "50 Greatest TV Shows of All Time" list, and in 2007 it was listed as one of *Time* magazine's "100 Best TV Shows of All-*TIME*". As of 2012, it has received 156 Emmy nominations, the most received by any one show in television history. The live aspect of the show has resulted in several controversies and acts of censorship, with mistakes and intentional acts of sabotage by performers and guests alike.

Development

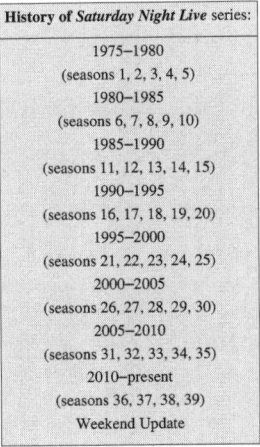

History of *Saturday Night Live* series:
1975–1980
(seasons 1, 2, 3, 4, 5)
1980–1985
(seasons 6, 7, 8, 9, 10)
1985–1990
(seasons 11, 12, 13, 14, 15)
1990–1995
(seasons 16, 17, 18, 19, 20)
1995–2000
(seasons 21, 22, 23, 24, 25)
2000–2005
(seasons 26, 27, 28, 29, 30)
2005–2010
(seasons 31, 32, 33, 34, 35)
2010–present
(seasons 36, 37, 38, 39)
Weekend Update

From 1965 until September 1975, NBC ran *The Best of Carson* reruns of *The Tonight Show*, airing them on either Saturday or Sunday night at local affiliates' discretion (originally known as *The Saturday/Sunday Tonight Show Starring Johnny Carson*). In 1974, Johnny Carson announced that he wanted the weekend shows pulled and saved so that they could be aired during weeknights, allowing him to take time off.[2]

In 1974, NBC president Herbert Schlosser approached his vice president of late night programming, Dick Ebersol, and asked him to create a show to fill the Saturday night time slot. At the suggestion of Paramount Pictures executive Barry Diller, Schlosser and Ebersol then approached Lorne Michaels. Over the next three weeks, Ebersol and Michaels developed the latter's idea for a variety show featuring high-concept comedy sketches, political satire, and music performances. By 1975, Michaels had assembled a talented cast, including Dan Aykroyd, John Belushi, Chevy Chase, Jane Curtin, Garrett Morris, Laraine Newman, Michael O'Donoghue, Gilda Radner, and George Coe. The show was originally called *NBC's Saturday Night*, because *Saturday Night Live* was in use by *Saturday Night Live with Howard Cosell* on the rival network ABC. NBC purchased the rights to the name in 1976 and officially adopted the new title on March 26, 1977.Wikipedia:Citation needed

Debuting on October 11, 1975, the show became an instant hit, and as a result the cast members became suddenly famous. Chase left the show during the second season and was replaced by the new and upcoming comic Bill Murray. Aykroyd and Belushi left the show after season four. In 1980 (after season five), Michaels—emotionally and physically exhausted—requested to put the show on hiatus for a year to give him time to pursue other ideas.[3] Concerned that the show would be cancelled without him, Michaels suggested writers Al Franken, Tom Davis, and Jim Downey as his replacements. However, NBC president Fred Silverman disliked Franken and—after Franken performed "Limo for a Lame-O", a scathing critique of Silverman's presidency—Silverman was furious at Franken and blamed Michaels for approving the sketch.[4] Unable to get the deal he wanted, Michaels chose to leave NBC for Paramount Pictures, intending to take his associate producer, Jean Doumanian, with him. Michaels later learned that Doumanian had been given his position at *SNL* after being recommended by her friend, NBC vice-president Barbara Gallagher.[5] Michaels' departure led to most of the cast and writing staff leaving the show.[6]

The reputation of the show as a springboard to fame meant that many aspiring stars were eager to join the new series. Doumanian was tasked with hiring a full cast and writing staff in less than three months, and NBC immediately cut the show's budget from the previous $1 million per episode down to just $350,000. Doumanian faced resentment and sabotage from the remaining Michaels staff, particularly males who did not appreciate a woman believing she could take Michaels' place.[7] The season was a disaster; ratings plummeted, and audiences failed to connect to the original cast's replacements, such as Charles Rocket and Ann Risley.[6] Doumanian's fate was sealed when, during a sketch, Rocket said "fuck" on live television.[8] After only ten months, Doumanian was dismissed.[9] Although executives suggested that *SNL* be left to die, network chief Brandon Tartikoff wanted to keep the show going, believing that the concept was more important to the network than money. Tartikoff turned to Ebersol, who previously had been fired by Silverman. Ebersol gained Michaels' approval in an attempt to avoid the same staff sabotage that had blighted Doumanian's tenure.[10]

> "He [Lorne Michaels] put me on TV, and no one else would have done that. Lorne created a show that's impacted culture for over 35 years. No one has ever really successfully been able to replicate it."
>
> -- Tina Fey on Michaels' influence on comedy.

Ebersol's tenure saw commercial success, but was considered lackluster compared to the Michaels era, except for the breakout of cast member Eddie Murphy.[11] Murphy, the main draw of the cast, left in 1984 to pursue his already successful film career, and Ebersol decided to again rebuild the cast. He broke from history by hiring established comedians such as Billy Crystal and Martin Short who could bring their already successful material to the show.[10] Ebersol's final year with this new cast is considered one of the series' funniest, but had strayed far from the precedent-shattering show that Michaels had created.[12] After that season, Ebersol wanted a more significant revamp, including departing from the show's established "live" format.Wikipedia:Citation needed Following unsuccessful forays into film and television, in need of money, and eager not to see Tartikoff cancel the show,[13] Michaels finally returned in 1985 after Ebersol opted not to. The show was again recast, with Michaels borrowing Ebersol's idea, and seeking out established acts such as Joan Cusack and Robert Downey, Jr.[14] The cast and writers struggled creatively, and in April 1986, Tartikoff made the decision to cancel the show, until he was convinced by producer Bernie Brillstein to give it one more year.[15] The show was renewed but for the first time in its history, for only thirteen episodes instead of the usual twenty-two.[16] Michaels again fired most of the cast and, learning his lesson from the previous seasons, sought out unknown talent such as Dana Carvey and Phil Hartman instead of known names.[16]

The show ran successfully again until it lost Carvey and Hartman, two of its biggest stars, between 1992 and 1994. Wanting to increase *SNL*'s ratings and profitability, then-NBC West Coast president Don Ohlmeyer and other executives began to actively interfere in the show, recommending that new stars such as Chris Farley and Adam Sandler be fired because Ohlmeyer did not "get" them, and critiquing the costly nature of performing the show live. The show faced increasing criticism from the press and cast, in part encouraged by the NBC executives hoping to weaken Michaels' position.[17] Michaels received a lucrative offer to develop a Saturday night project for CBS during this time, but remained loyal to *SNL*.[18] By 1995, Farley and Sandler were fired, and Mike Myers, another popular cast member, had left for a film career, but a new cast waited to replace them, featuring the likes of Will Ferrell, Jimmy Fallon, and Tina Fey.[19] The show focused on performers, and writers were forced to supply material for the casts' existing characters before they could write original sketches.[20] By 1997, Ohlmeyer renewed his focus on limiting Michaels' independence, forcing the removal of Downey and cast member Norm MacDonald.[21]

Cast and crew

Cast

Main article: Saturday Night Live cast members

The original 1975 cast of *SNL*, officially known on-air as "The Not Ready For Prime-Time Players", a term coined by writer Herb Sargent,[22] included Laraine Newman, John Belushi, Jane Curtin, Gilda Radner, Dan Aykroyd, Garrett Morris and Chevy Chase. Radner was the first person hired after Michaels himself. Although Chase became a performer, he was hired on a one-year writer contract, and refused to sign the performer contract that was repeatedly given to him, allowing him to leave the show after the first season in 1976.[23] Newman was brought aboard after having a prior working relationship with Michaels.[24] Morris was initially brought in as a writer, but attempts to have him fired by another writer led Michaels to have Morris audition for the cast, where he turned in a successful performance.[25] Curtin and Belushi were the last two cast members hired.[24] Belushi had a disdain for television and had repeatedly turned down offers to appear on other shows, but decided to work with the show because of the involvement of Radner, and writers Anne Beatts and Michael O'Donoghue.[26] Michaels was still reluctant to hire Belushi, believing he would be a source of trouble for the show, but Beatts, O'Donoghue and Ebersol successfully argued for his inclusion.[26] After Chase left the show he was replaced by Bill Murray, whom Michaels had intended to hire for the first-season cast, but was unable to due to budget restrictions.[27] When Chase returned to host in 1978, he found the remaining cast resentful at his departure and his success, particularly Belushi. Murray, goaded by the rest of the cast, and Chase came to blows shortly before the show.[28] Chase's departure for film made Michaels possessive of his talent; he threatened to fire Aykroyd if he took the role of D-Day in the 1978 comedy *Animal House*, and later refused to allow *SNL* musician Paul Shaffer to participate in *The Blues Brothers* (1980) with Aykroyd and Belushi after they left in 1979 to pursue film careers.[29] Michaels began to struggle to hold the remaining cast together in the wake of Chase, Aykroyd, and Belushi's independent successes. Radner had a one-woman Broadway show and Murray starred in the 1979 comedy *Meatballs*.[30] In 1980, when Michaels chose to leave the series to pursue other interests, he was followed by the remaining original cast, Curtin, Newman, and Morris, Murray, and additional cast members.

The Doumanian-era cast faced immediate comparison to the beloved former cast and were not received favorably.[9] Ebersol fired the majority of her hires, except for two unknown comedians: Eddie Murphy and Joe Piscopo.[31] Talent coordinator Neil Levy claimed Murphy contacted and pleaded with him for a role on the show, and after seeing him audition, Levy fought with Doumanian to cast him instead of Robert Townsend. Doumanian wanted only one black cast member and favored Townsend, but Levy convinced her to choose Murphy. Doumanian, however, also claimed credit for discovering Murphy and fighting with NBC executives to bring him onto the show.[32] Even so, Murphy would languish as a background character until Ebersol took charge,[33] after which Murphy was credited with much of that era's success.[34] Murphy's star exploded, and he quickly appeared in films such as *48*

Hrs. and *Trading Places*, before leaving for his film career in early 1984. Much of the Ebersol cast departed after the 1983–84 season and were replaced with established comedians who could supply their own material, but at an inflated cost; Billy Crystal and Martin Short were paid $25,000 and $20,000 per episode respectively, a far cry from earlier salaries.[10] Michaels' return in 1985 saw a cast reset that featured established talent such as Robert Downey Jr., Jon Lovitz and Dennis Miller.[35] The season was poorly received, and another reset followed in 1986. Learning his lesson from the previous season, Michaels avoided known talent in favor of actual ability. He kept Lovitz, Miller and Nora Dunn, and brought in new, untested talent such as Dana Carvey, Phil Hartman, and Jan Hooks, who together would define a new era on the show into the early 1990s.[36] The cast continued on for the next decade with the addition of new talent such as Mike Myers, Adam Sandler, and Chris Farley. Afraid of cast leaving for film, Michaels had overcrowded the cast, causing a divide between the veteran members and the new, younger talent, increasing competition for limited screen time.[37] By 1995, Carvey and Hartman had left, taking with them a virtual army of characters, Myers quit for his movie career, and increasing network pressure forced Michaels to fire Sandler and Farley. The show saw its next major overhaul, bringing in a new cast including Will Ferrell, Tina Fey, and Jimmy Fallon.[38] While cast members would leave over the following two decades, the show saw its next biggest transition in 2013, with the addition of 6 cast members to compensate for the departure of several longtime cast members like Bill Hader, Jason Sudeikis, and Fred Armisen.

SNL has featured over 130 cast members including Rachel Dratch, Amy Poehler, Chris Rock, David Spade, Will Forte, Julia Louis-Dreyfus, Tracy Morgan, Chris Parnell, Maya Rudolph, and Kristen Wiig. Darrell Hammond is the longest-serving cast member, having been a part of the cast for fourteen years between 1995 and 2009. Those selected to join the cast of *SNL* are normally already accomplished performers, recruited from improvisational comedy groups such as The Groundlings (Ferrell, Hartman,[39] Lovitz, Wiig) and The Second City (Aykroyd, Farley, Fey, Tim Meadows), or established stand-up comedians (Carvey, Sandler, Rock, Norm Macdonald), who already possess the training or experience necessary for *SNL*.

Of the many roles available in the show, one of the longest-running and most coveted is being the host of "Weekend Update", a segment which has alternated between having one or two hosts, and which allows the cast members involved to perform as themselves and be on camera for an extended period of time. Many of the "Weekend Update" hosts have gone on to find greater success outside of the show, including: Chase, Curtin, Murray, Miller, Macdonald,[40] Fey, Fallon,[41] and Poehler. From 2008, Seth Meyers was the solo host of "Weekend Update", before being partnered with Cecily Strong in 2013. After Meyers left for *Late Night with Seth Meyers* in February 2014, Strong was paired with head writer Colin Jost. The cast is divided into two tiers: the more established group of repertory players; and newer, unproven cast members known as featured players, who may eventually be promoted to the repertory stable.

2013–14 season cast[42]	
Repertory players	**Featured players**
• Vanessa Bayer (joined 2010) • Aidy Bryant (joined 2012) • Colin Jost (joined 2014) ⬚ • Taran Killam (joined 2010) • Kate McKinnon (joined 2012) • Bobby Moynihan (joined 2008) • Jay Pharoah (joined 2010) • Cecily Strong (joined 2012) ⬚ • Kenan Thompson (joined 2003)	• Beck Bennett (joined 2013) • Kyle Mooney (joined 2013) • Mike O'Brien (joined 2013) • Sasheer Zamata (joined 2014)
⬚ denotes Weekend Update anchor	

The cast were often contracted from anywhere between five and six years to the show, but starting with the 1999–2000 season, new hires were tied to a rewritten contract that allowed NBC to take a cast member in at least their second year and put them in an NBC sitcom. Cast are given the option of rejecting the first two sitcom offers but must accept the third offer, with the sitcom contract length dictated by NBC and potentially lasting up to six years. The move drew criticism from talent agents and managers who believed that a cast member could be locked into a contract with NBC for twelve years; six on *SNL* and then six on a sitcom. The contract also optioned the cast member for three feature films produced by SNL Films, a company owned by NBC, Paramount Pictures, and Michaels. The new contracts were reportedly developed after many previously unknown cast, such as Myers and Sandler, gained fame on *SNL* only to leave and make money for other studios. In a 2010 interview, Wiig was reported to be contracted to *SNL* for a total of seven years. The contracts also contain a network option which allows NBC to remove a cast member at any time.[43] In the first season of the show, cast were paid $750 per episode, rising to $2,000 by season two, and $4,000 by season four.[44] By the late 1990s, new cast members received a salary between $5,000 and $5,500 per episode, increasing to $6,000 in the second year and up to $12,500 for a cast member in their fifth year. Performers could earn an additional $1,500 per episode for writing a sketch which made it to air.[43] In 2001, Ferrell became the highest paid cast member, being paid $350,000 per season (approximately $17,500 per episode). In 2014, Sasheer Zamata was added as a cast member in mid-season after criticism about the show's lack of an African-American woman.

Writers

Main article: List of Saturday Night Live writers

As of the 2013–14 season, Colin Jost and Rob Klein are the show's co-head writers. Meyers had been co-head writer since 2005 and became the single head writer from 2008 to 2012. The "Weekend Update" segment has its own dedicated team of writers led by head writer and producer Alex Baze as of the 2011–12 season. Scenes on "Weekend Update" that involve members of the cast acting in-character alongside the host are often written by staff writers outside of the dedicated "Weekend Update" team, who know those characters better.

Lorne Michaels in 2010

SNL writers are often also performers or experienced in writing and improvisational comedy. Many are hired from similar backgrounds such as The Groundlings, Second City, Upright Citizens Brigade Theatre, and ImprovOlympic. Experienced writers with backgrounds in television shows are also sometimes brought into the *SNL* writing room. Like the *SNL* cast that step before the cameras, many of the writers have been able to find their own success outside the show such as O'Brien, who was brought into *SNL* from The Groundlings, went on to writing for *The Simpsons*, and eventually began hosting his own show, and former head writer Adam McKay who, along with performer Ferrell, founded the successful comedy website Funny or Die. In 2000, Fey became the first female *SNL* head writer and successfully transitioned into starring on the show, as well as writing and starring in feature films, and ultimately creating and starring in her own show *30 Rock*—partly based on her *SNL* experiences. In 2005, Fey was being paid $1.5 million per season for her dual role as head writer and performer.

Announcer

Don Pardo served as the announcer for the series when it first began, and has continued in the role for all but season seven between 1981 and 1982, when Michaels had left and Mel Brandt and Bill Hanrahan filled the announcing role. In 2004, Pardo announced that he would step down from his position, but then continued in the role until 2009 where he again announced his retirement, but then continued into the 2009–10 season. In 2010, then 92-year old Pardo was reported to be again considering his retirement, but as of the 2013–14 season, he continues to serve as the announcer. Apart from a brief period in 2006 in which Pardo pre-recorded his announcements at his home in Arizona, he has flown to New York City to perform his announcing duties live. Cast members Joe PiscopoWikipedia:Citation needed and Darrell Hammond also periodically impersonated Pardo and fulfilled his announcing duties when Pardo was unavailable.[45]

Hosts and musical guests

Main article: List of Saturday Night Live guests

A typical episode of *SNL* will feature a single host chosen for their popularity, novelty, or because they have a film, album or other work being released near the time of their appearance on the show.[46] The host delivers the opening monologue and performs in sketches with the cast. Traditionally the host of the show ends the opening monologue by introducing the musical guest for the night. Comedian George Carlin was the first to host *SNL* in the debut October 1975 episode; three episodes later, Candice Bergen became the first female host[47] and subsequently the first to host more than once.[48] Hosts have been drawn from a wide spectrum of backgrounds, from actors, such as Christopher Walken, Buck Henry, and John Goodman,[49] to musicians like George Harrison[50] and Dolly Parton,[51] to political activist Ralph Nader.[46] Guests who have hosted five or more times are sometimes referred to as belonging to the Five-Timers Club, a term that originated on a sketch performed on Tom Hanks' fifth episode. As of September 24, 2011, actor Alec Baldwin holds the record for most times hosting, having performed the duty on sixteen different occasions since 1990; Baldwin took the record from actor Steve Martin who had hosted fifteen times since 1976.

Each episode also features a musical guest, a solo act or a band, who perform two to three musical numbers. Occasionally, the musical guest has also simultaneously served as the host. As of May 19, 2012, Dave Grohl is the most frequent musical guest, performing on eleven shows since 1992. Michaels does not allow musical guests to perform using lip-synching tracks,[52] believing it diminishes the live aspect of the show. Exceptions are only made when the musical act is focused on intense dance routines instead of vocals, where it is difficult to be both heavily physically active and sing simultaneously. A 1975 performance by pop group ABBA was the first and only act to feature lip-synching,[52] until the controversial 2004 performance of Ashlee Simpson.

The *SNL* Band

Main article: Saturday Night Live Band

The Saturday Night Live Band (also known as "The Live Band") is the house band for *SNL*. Academy Award-winning composer Howard Shore served as the first musical director, from 1975 to 1980, appearing in many musical sketches, including Howard Shore and His All-Nurse Band and (backing a U.S. Coast Guard chorus) Howard Shore and the Shore Patrol. Over the years, the band has featured several New York studio musicians including Paul Shaffer (1975–1980), Lou Marini (1975–1983), David Sanborn (1975), Michael Brecker (early 1980s), Ray Chew (1980–1983), Alan Rubin (1975–1983), Georg Wadenius (1979–1985), Steve Ferrone (1985), David Johansen (performing as Buster Poindexter), Tom Malone (who took over as musical director from 1981 to 1985), and G.E. Smith (musical director from 1985 to 1995). The band is currently under the leadership of Tower of Power alumnus Lenny Pickett, keyboardist Leon Pendarvis and Eli Bruegemann who does not play in the band on the live show. The number of musicians has varied over the years, but the basic instrumentation has been three saxophones, one trombone, one trumpet, and a rhythm section featuring two keyboards, a guitar, bass, drums, and an extra percussionist, not a permanent part of the band until Valerie Naranjo's arrival in 1995. The 1983–1984 and 1984–1985 seasons featured the smallest band, a six-piece combo. The band plays instrumentals leading in and out of station breaks; affiliates who run no advertising during these interludes hear the band play complete songs behind a *Saturday Night Live* bumper graphic until the program resumes.[53]

Production

The studio

Since the show's inception, *SNL* has aired from Studio 8H, located on floors 8 and 9 of the GE Building (30 Rockefeller Plaza, or "30 Rock"). The studio had previously been used as a radio soundstage for Arturo Toscanini and his NBC Symphony Orchestra.[54] Michaels was dumbfounded when he originally inspected Studio 8H in 1975, and found it technically limited, outdated, in need of repair,[55] and lacking the capacity to host a live show.[54] Michaels demanded that NBC executives rebuild the studio and improve the acoustics to accommodate the intended musical acts,[54] at a cost of approximately $300,000.[54] Three of the first four shows of the 1976–77 season were shot at the former NBC Studios in Brooklyn, due to NBC News using Studio 8H for Presidential election coverage.[56]

During the summer 2005 shooting hiatus, crews began renovations on Studio 8H. With its thirty-first season premiere in October 2005, the show began broadcasting in high-definition television, appearing letterboxed on conventional television screens. The offices of SNL writers, producers, and other staff can be found on the 17th floor of "30 Rock".[57]

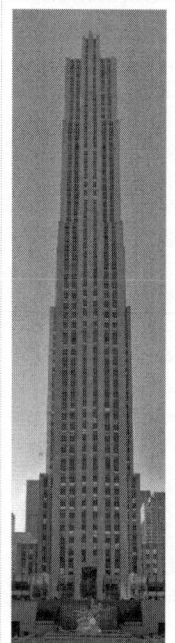

GE Building (30 Rockefeller Plaza, or "30 Rock") from where the show is broadcast.

Creating an episode

Production on an *SNL* episode will normally start on a Monday with a free-form pitch meeting[58][59] between the cast, writers, producers including Michaels, and the guest host, in Michaels' office, over two hours. The host is invited to pitch ideas during this meeting. Although some sketch writing may occur on the day, the bulk of the work revolves around pitching ideas. Tuesday is the only day dedicated purely to writing the scripts,[59] a process which can extend through the night into the following morning. Writing may not begin until 8pm on the Tuesday evening.[58] At 5pm on Wednesday, the sketches are read during a round-table meeting in the writers room, attended by the writers and producers present during the pitch meeting, technical experts such as make-up artists, who may be required to realize certain sketch ideas such as those using prosthetics, and other producers, resulting in an attendance of approximately fifty people.[60] At this point there may be at least 40 sketch ideas which are read-through in turn, lasting upwards of three hours.[60]

After completion of the read-through, Michaels, the head writer, the guest host, and some of the show producers will move to Michaels' office to decide the layout of the show and decide which of the sketches will be developed for air. Once complete, the writers and cast are allowed into Michaels' office to view the show breakdown and learn whether or not their sketch has survived.[61] Sketches may be rewritten starting the same day,[59] but will certainly commence on Thursday, work focuses on developing and rewriting the remaining sketches,[58] and possibly rehearsals. If a sketch is still scheduled beyond Thursday, it is rehearsed on Friday or Saturday[59] before moving to a rehearsal before a live audience at 8pm, again on Saturday before the live show.[58] After the rehearsal, Michaels will review the show lineup to ensure it meets a 90-minute length, and sketches that have made it as far as the live rehearsal may be removed.[62] This often results in less than two days of rehearsal for the eight to twelve sketches that have made it to the stage that then may appear on the live broadcast.[58] The opening monologue, spoken by the guest host, is given low priority and can be written as late as Saturday afternoon.[63]

According to an interview with Fey in 2004, the three- to four-member dedicated "Weekend Update" writing team will write jokes throughout the week. The host(s) of "Weekend Update" will normally not work with, or read the scripts from, the team until Thursday evening, after the main show sketches have been finalized. The host(s) will then work on contributing to the script where necessary.

Post-production

With onsite facilities housed on floors 8 and 17 of Rockefeller Plaza, post-production duties on live broadcasts of *Saturday Night Live* include the mixing of audio and video elements by the Senior Audio Mixer, coupled with additional audio feeds consisting of music, sound effects, music scoring and pre-recorded voiceovers. All sources are stored digitally, with shows captured and segregated into individual elements to reorganise for future repeats and syndication. The production tracking system was migrated from primarily analog to digital in 1998, with live shows typically requiring 1.5 terabytes of storage, consisting of audio elements and 5 cameras worth of visual elements. Elements of *Saturday Night Live* that are pre-recorded, such as certain commercial parodies, SNL Digital Shorts, and show graphics are processed off-site in the post-production facilities of Broadway Video.

Filming and photography

Studio 8H production facilities are maintained by NBC Production Services. Video camera equipment includes four Sony BVP-700 CCD cameras, and two Sony BVP-750 CCD handheld cameras, both using Vinten pedestals. A GVG 4000-3 digital component production switcher, and GVG 7000 digital component routing switcher are used to route visual feeds to the control room, with multiple digital and analogue video recorders used to store footage. Graphics are provided by a Chyron Infinit! character generator and a Quantel PictureBox. Audio facilities consist of a Calrec T Series digitally controlled analogue mixing console, and a Yamaha digital mixing console used for tape playback support and utility audio work.

As of 2009, the opening title sequence and opening montage is shot using the Canon EOS 5D Mark II and Canon EOS 7D digital SLR cameras. Typical elements are recorded at 30 fps, with slow-motion sequences shot at 60 fps, both in full 1080p high definition.

Edie Baskin was the original *SNL* photographer. She was hired after Michaels saw her photographs of Las Vegas and other work. Baskin helped create the opening title sequence for the show by taking photos of New York City at night.[64] The first episode used publicity photos of Carlin as transitional bumpers between the show and commercial breaks, the second episode used photos Baskin had already taken of host Paul Simon. It was then that Michaels suggested that Baskin photograph the hosts for the bumpers instead of using publicity photos, beginning a tradition which continues today.[65]

Since 1999, Mary Ellen Matthews has been the official photographer of *SNL*, responsible for devising distinctive photo layouts and aesthetics for still imagery used on the show. Matthews creates photo portraits of the hosts and musical guests of each episode which are used as commercial bumpers. The limited time frame between the host's involvement in the production process and the Live show requires Matthews to create makeshift photo studios on site at 30 Rock, with Matthews attempting to shoot the host on Tuesday and the musical guest on Thursday, although the availability of either can mean the photoshoot for both occurs as late as Thursday. Matthews employs flattering portrait lighting with hard lights to achieve a Hollywood style. On the lighting, Matthews commented: "I think it just helps the image pop off the screen...If you use soft or flat lighting, it becomes not as dimensional...The [classic Hollywood lighting] gives a little more contrast, and if I use edge lights and then light the background, it goes farther and farther back. I try to achieve that depth as much as I can." Matthews is also responsible for taking cast photos, behind the scenes images, documenting rehearsals, and promotional photos. As of 2010, she has also been involved in directing videos, including the show title sequence.

Broadcast

See also: List of Saturday Night Live episodes

The show usually begins at 11:30 p.m. (EST), unless a delay occurs. The show broadcasts for one and a half hours, ending at 1 a.m. For the Mountain[66] and Pacific time zones, NBC airs the prerecorded live show usually unedited, mistakes notwithstanding. Since the first opening in 1975 with Michael O'Donoghue, Chevy Chase, and John Belushi, the show has normally begun with a cold open sketch which ends with one or more cast members breaking character and proclaiming "Live from New York, it's Saturday Night!", launching the opening credits.

SNL's main stage, during rehearsal, 2008

Beginning February 2013, NBC has aired cut-down hour-long repeats at 10pm Saturday during the regular season, repeating the previous week's episode if it was original.

NBC and Broadway Video both hold the underlying rights to the show, while the copyright to every episode lies solely with NBC. From 1990 until 2004, Comedy Central and its predecessor Ha! re-aired reruns of the series, after which E! Entertainment Television signed a deal to reruns. Abbreviated thirty and sixty minute versions of the first five seasons aired as *The Best of Saturday Night Live* in syndication beginning in the 1980s and later on Nick at Nite in 1988. In September 2010, reruns of most episodes post-1998 began to air on VH1.

International

Because *SNL* has been a huge success in America, other countries have created their own versions of the show, including Spain, Italy, Japan and South Korea. SNL is aired in Israel on yes Comedy. SNL is also aired in the Middle East and North Africa on OSN Comedy every Saturday night, one week after it airs in the U.S.

Germany's version of the show, "RTL Samstag Nacht" was a hit in the 1990s on the RTL channel.

Spain's version of the show was short-lived, only lasting a few episodes which aired on Thursdays and not Saturdays as the title suggested. This version copied heavily from the American version, in that they did their own versions of sketches that were already done on the original series. Italy's *Saturday Night Live From Milan* uses original material.

The Japanese version *Saturday Night Live JPN*, which ran for six months in 2011, was created in part with Lorne Michaels' production company, Broadway Video and broadcast on Fuji TV networks. The show followed the same format with a few minor differences, being only 45 minutes long and hosted by a permanent host. The cast was made up of seasoned comedians who take center stage and newcomers who play the background roles. It was broadcast once a month, and ended after six episodes, as planned from the start.

On December 3, 2011, South Korea's *SNL Korea* premiered on cable channel tvN. As of July 20, 2013, it is in its fourth consecutive season, with 20 episodes.

In 2014, two 90-minute specials were broadcast in French on Télé-Québec in the Canadian province of Quebec under the title, *SNL Québec*; the specials were broadcast on February 8 and March 22, 2014. hosted by Louis-José Houde and Stéphane Rousseau, and is the same format and length as the original SNL series. Certain sketches from the original program, such as Debbie Downer and Schweddy Balls were adapted into French. On May 13, 2014, SNL Quebec was renewed for another 8 episodes to be broadcast monthly over the 2014-2015 season ending with a "Best Of" compilation. The entire cast is expected to return.

Delays

- The episode scheduled for October 25, 1986, hosted by Rosanna Arquette, was not aired until November 8 due to NBC broadcasting Game 6 of the 1986 World Series between the New York Mets and Boston Red Sox; the game entered extra innings, causing that night's broadcast of *SNL* to be cancelled. The show was recorded for the studio audience starting at 1:30 a.m. Eastern Time, and broadcast two weeks later with an "apology" by Mets pitcher Ron Darling. (He explained that the Mets players had all been happy and excited to win the World Series game, widely considered one of the most memorable in the event's 109-year history, but of course they all had become upset and glum when, in the locker room afterwards, they found out that they had caused the first-ever cancellation of *SNL*. Footage showed the depressed players sadly staring at the locker room floor in shame.)Wikipedia:Citation needed
- The episode scheduled for February 10, 2001, hosted by Jennifer Lopez, aired 45 minutes late due to an XFL game. Lopez and the cast were not told they were airing on a delay. Michaels was so upset by the delay that the episode was re-run a mere three weeks later, and the fledgling league actually changed the rules in order to speed up play so that no such incident would happen again.

Reception

In 2002, the show was ranked tenth on TV Guide's 50 Greatest TV Shows of All Time, while in 2007 it was honored with inclusion on *Time* magazine's list of "100 Best TV Shows of All-*TIME*." In June 2013, the show was placed at number 25 on the list of the 101 best written shows of all time by the Writers Guild of America, assessing series from the previous 70 years. In December 2013, *TV Guide* ranked it #18 on their list of the 60 Greatest Shows of All Time.

Accolades

Main article: List of awards and nominations received by Saturday Night Live

Saturday Night Live has won numerous awards since its debut, including 36 Primetime Emmy Awards, 2 Peabody Awards, and 4 Writers Guild of America Awards. In 2009, it received a total of 13 Emmy nominations for a lifetime total of 126, breaking the record for the most award nominated show in Emmy history, previously set with 124 by hospital drama *ER*. As of August 2012, it has received a record total of 156 Emmy nominations. Only 17 cast members have received individual Emmy nominations in the show's entire history. Of these only Chevy Chase and Gilda Radner have won, taking the award for Outstanding Individual Performance, in 1976 and 1978 respectively. In 1983, Eddie Murphy became the last male cast member to be nominated for a Best Supporting Actor Emmy until Bill Hader nearly thirty years later in 2012: Hader received a second nomination in 2013, making him the cast's only male multiple nominee.

Electoral impact

SNL has also had an effect on elections. Voters have reported that political sketches that were shown on the program influenced them in the voting booth. The media dubbed this the "The *SNL* Effect".Wikipedia:Citation needed The so-called *SNL* Effect was observed during the 2008 presidential campaign, according to Mike Dabadie. Two-thirds of voters who responded to a poll said they had seen a broadcast of politically charged content on *SNL*, with ten percent saying that it had made a difference in their decision. Barack Obama was the beneficiary of the political content, with 59 percent saying they did in fact cast a vote for the then-Democratic nominee.

Chevy Chase's bumbling impression of then-president Gerald Ford during the 1976 presidential election was cited as an influence on the election, and a quote commonly attributed to 2008 vice presidential candidate Sarah Palin stating "I can see Russia from my house" was actually spoken by SNL cast member Tina Fey while portraying Palin. Several politicians have appeared on *SNL*, including President Gerald Ford (in 1976), Senator (at the time) Barack

Obama (2007), Senator John McCain (2002 & 2008), Senator Hillary Clinton (2008), and Governor Sarah Palin (2008).

In other media

Home media

Main article: List of Saturday Night Live DVD releases

Currently, Universal Studios Home Entertainment and Lions Gate Entertainment hold video rights to the series. Universal has issued complete season DVD sets of the first few seasons, while Lionsgate's share of the rights are a result of prior contracts with NBC struck before the NBC Universal merger. A majority of Lionsgate's SNL DVDs are "Best Of..." compilations.

Books

Saturday Night Live (ISBN 0-380-01801-2), the first authorized book about the series, was published by Avon Books in 1977 and edited by Anne Beatts and John Head, with photography by Edie Baskin;[67] all three worked for *SNL* at the time the book was published. The oversized illustrated paperback included the scripts for several sketches by the 1975-1980 cast.[68] In 1986, Doug Hill and Jeff Weingrad authored *Saturday Night: A Backstage History of Saturday Night Live* (ISBN 0-688-05099-9), a behind-the-scenes look at the first ten seasons. *Saturday Night Live: The First Twenty Years* (ISBN 0-395-75284-1), by Michael Cader, was released in 1994, and presented information about the cast, characters, and other memorable moments seen on the show from 1975 to 1994.

Live From New York: An Uncensored History of Saturday Night Live, as Told By Its Stars, Writers and Guests (ISBN 0-316-73565-5) was released in 2002. The book, written by Tom Shales and James Andrew Miller, consists of interviews from people who have worked on the show. The interviews reveal personal experiences from what happened backstage and the difficulty of getting the show on air each week. In 2004, former cast member Jay Mohr released his memoir *Gasping for Airtime: Two Years in the Trenches of Saturday Night Live* (ISBN 1-401-30801-5), about his struggles during his two seasons on the show between 1993 and 1995, dealing with getting sketches on air and the intense work schedule. Cast member Bobby Moynihan described the book as "a handbook on what NOT to do at *SNL*."

Films

SNL has made several efforts to develop some of the more popular sketches into feature-length films, with varying degrees of commercial and critical success. The first foray into film came with the successful Aykroyd and Belushi vehicle, *The Blues Brothers* (1980), which earned over $115 million on a $27 million budget.

In 1990, Michaels oversaw the writing of a sketch anthology feature film titled *The Saturday Night Live Movie* with many of the show's current writing staff, including Al Franken, Tom Davis, Greg Daniels, Jim Downey, Conan O'Brien, Robert Smigel and George Meyer, contributing. The screenplay only got as far as a Revised First Draft dated July 26, 1990 before being abandoned.[69]

However, it was the success of *Wayne's World* (1992) that encouraged Michaels to produce more film spin-offs, based on several popular sketch characters. Michaels revived 1970s characters for *Coneheads* (1993), followed by *It's Pat* (1994); *Stuart Saves His Family* (1995); *A Night at the Roxbury* (1998); *Superstar* (1999) and *The Ladies Man* (2000). Some did moderately well, though others did not—notably, *It's Pat*, which did so badly at the box office that the studio that made the film, Touchstone Pictures (owned by The Walt Disney Company, which also owns NBC's rival ABC), pulled it only one week after releasing it,[70] and *Stuart Saves His Family*, which lost $15 million. Many of these films were produced by Paramount Pictures. The films based on *The Blues Brothers* were produced by Universal Studios, which merged with NBC in 2004 to form NBC Universal (Universal also has a joint venture with Paramount for international distribution of the two studios' films).

Film	Release date (United States)	Budget (estimated)	Box office revenue		
			United States	Elsewhere	Worldwide
The Blues Brothers	June 20, 1980	$27 million	$57,229,890	$58,000,000	$115,229,890
Wayne's World	February 14, 1992	$20 million	$121,697,323	$61,400,000	$183,097,323
Coneheads	July 23, 1993	$33 million	$21,274,717	N/A	$21,274,717
Wayne's World 2	December 10, 1993	$40 million	$48,197,805	N/A	$48,197,805
It's Pat	August 26, 1994	N/A	$60,822	N/A	$60,822
Stuart Saves His Family	April 14, 1995	$15 million	$912,082		$912,082
Blues Brothers 2000	February 6, 1998	$28 million	$14,051,384	N/A	$14,051,384
A Night at the Roxbury	October 2, 1998	$17 million	$30,331,165	N/A	$30,331,165
Superstar	October 8, 1999	$14 million	$30,636,478	N/A	$30,636,478
The Ladies Man	October 13, 2000	$24 million	$13,616,610	$126,602	$13,743,212
MacGruber	May 21, 2010	$10 million	$8,525,600	$797,295	$9,259,314

The character Bob Roberts from the Tim Robbins film of the same name (1992), first appeared on *SNL* in a short film about the conservative folk singer.

In addition, the 1999 comedy film *Office Space* originated from a series of animated short films by Mike Judge that aired on *SNL* in 1993.

The group The Folksmen first appeared on *SNL*, performing the song "Old Joe's Place" before later appearing in the film *A Mighty Wind* (2002). The three members of the Folksmen were the same three comedians: Harry Shearer, Michael McKean, and Christopher Guest, who also appeared on the same episode as the rock group Spinal Tap. At the time of the appearance (the 1984–85 season), Shearer and Guest were cast members.

Mr. Bill's Real Life Adventures is based off the Mr. Bill sketches from early seasons of *SNL*.

Music

In 2005, the comedy troupe The Lonely Island, consisting of *SNL* members Andy Samberg, Akiva Schaffer, and Jorma Taccone, gained national exposure after joining the show and debuting their skit music video "Lazy Sunday", written with fellow cast member Chris Parnell. The song became a surprise hit, and convinced Michaels to encourage the troupe to develop more comedy songs. Further successes with songs including "Like A Boss, "Jizz in My Pants," "I'm on a Boat," "We Like Sportz", "Boombox," and "Dick in a Box"—which won an Emmy for *Outstanding Original Music and Lyrics* in 2007—saw The Lonely Island go on to release two albums, *Incredibad* (2009) and *Turtleneck & Chain* (2011), containing *SNL*-developed songs and original works. The albums were released by Universal Republic Records who were provided with a license to the *SNL* songs by NBC and Broadway Video.

A cast album was released in 1976 on the Arista label including the song "Chevy's Girls" and comedy bits from the show ("Weekend Update", "Emily Litella", "Gun Control"); it was later re-issued on CD and MP3 download.

Other

Several programs have documented the behind-the-scenes events of the show. A *60 Minutes* report taped in October 2004 depicted the intense writing frenzy that goes on during the week leading up to a show, with crowded meetings and long hours. The report particularly noted the involvement of the guest host(s) in developing and selecting the sketches in which they will appear. Similarly, there has been an A&E episode of *Biography* which covered the production process, as well as an episode of *TV Tales* in 2002 on E!. In 2010, *Saturday Night*, a 94-minute documentary by actor James Franco in his directorial debut, was released; it follows the production process of the December 6, 2008, episode hosted by John Malkovich, from the concept stage to the episode actually airing live. Although it originated as a five-minute short film for Franco's New York University film class, Michaels granted Franco access to the process, allowing the project to be expanded.

In September 2011, ice cream company Ben & Jerry's released a limited-edition ice cream called "Schweddy Balls", inspired by a 1998 sketch of the same name starring Alec Baldwin, Ana Gasteyer and Molly Shannon. The ice cream became the fastest-selling Ben & Jerry's limited-edition flavor. The ice cream was also subject to criticism and boycotts by the One Million Moms organization over the "vulgar" name. Some retail chains chose not to sell the flavor, but declined to say if the decision was at their own discretion or based on the One Million Moms boycotts. In June 2014, two new flavours inspired by SNL sketches were introduced - *Lazy Sunday*, based on a sketch of the same name featuring Andy Samberg and Chris Parnell, and *Gilly's Catastropic Crunch* based on the recurring *Gilly* sketches featuring Kristen Wiig.[71] There are also plans for a further two flavours to be released later in the year commemorate the 40th anniversary of SNL.

Controversies

Andrew Dice Clay

Andrew Dice Clay was scheduled as host on the May 12, 1990, episode. Cast member Nora Dunn immediately announced to the press that she was boycotting the show in protest at Clay's perceived misogynistic, politically incorrect act, doing so without informing Michaels, the cast or most of the crew about her intent.[72] The backlash was immediate; casting Clay was compared to the Holocaust by an audience member during an interview with Michaels,[73] female members of the cast and crew were harassed by phone and mail for sticking with the show, and metal detectors were installed at the show to enhance security. NBC censors insisted that the episode be placed on a delay to compensate for anything Clay might say on air.[74] During the live show, some audience members heckled Clay and were immediately removed by the increased security detail.[75] Dunn's contract was already coming to an end, and with one episode left in the season, the staff voted against having her take part in the final episode or return.[76] Sinéad O'Connor was scheduled to be the musical guest for the episode, but she boycotted the show because of Clay's involvement, forcing the producers to find musical replacements.

Sinéad O'Connor

On October 3, 1992, Sinéad O'Connor was scheduled to appear, performing an a cappella performance of Bob Marley's "War". During the dress rehearsal, O'Connor held up a photo of a Balkan child as a protest of child abuse in war before bowing and leaving the stage, which the episode's director Dave Wilson described as a "very tender moment". However, during the live show, O'Connor altered the "War" lyric "fight racial injustice" to "fight child abuse" as a protest against the cases of sexual abuse in the Roman Catholic Church. She presented a photo of Pope John Paul II while singing the word "evil", before tearing the image into pieces and saying "Fight the real enemy". NBC had no foreknowledge of O'Connor's plan, and Wilson purposely failed to use the "applause" button, leaving the audience to sit in silence. Michaels made the decision to allow O'Connor to take the stage with the rest of the cast at the end of the show, for which he was later punished. NBC received thousands of irate calls in the aftermath of the incident, and protests against O'Connor occurred outside of the 30 Rock building, where a steamroller crushed dozens of her tapes, CDs and LPs. In the following weeks on *SNL*, guests Joe Pesci and Madonna both voiced their opposition to O'Connor.

As of 2012, NBC still declines to rebroadcast the sequence with the exception of an interview with O'Connor on MSNBC's *The Rachel Maddow Show*, which aired on April 24, 2010, when the clip was aired in full. In reruns the incident is replaced with the dress rehearsal performance. The original episode was made available on volume four of the *SNL* DVD special *Saturday Night Live - 25 Years of Music*, with an introduction by Michaels about the incident. On February 20, 2011, the clip was aired on the *SNL* special "Backstage" showing footage of the dress rehearsal and live performance side by side. The footage cuts to interviewees during the moment the photo was ripped.Wikipedia:Citation needed

The incident was mocked during a live episode of the television show *30 Rock*, in which an NBC page (Kristen Schaal) comes on stage and tears a picture of O'Connor in half.

Rage Against the Machine

On April 13, 1996, musical guests Rage Against the Machine (RATM) were scheduled to perform two songs. The show was hosted that night by billionaire Steve Forbes. According to RATM guitarist Tom Morello, "RATM wanted to stand in sharp juxtaposition to a billionaire telling jokes and promoting his flat tax by making our own statement."[77] To this end, the band hung two upside-down American flags from their amplifiers. Seconds before they took the stage to perform "Bulls on Parade", *SNL* and NBC sent stagehands in to pull the flags down. Following the removal of the flags during the first performance, the band was approached by *SNL* and NBC officials and ordered to immediately leave the building. Upon hearing this, bassist Tim Commerford reportedly stormed Forbes' dressing room, throwing shreds from one of the torn-down flags. Morello noted that members of the *SNL* cast and crew, whom he declined to name, "expressed solidarity with our actions, and a sense of shame that their show had censored the performance."

Ashlee Simpson

Ashlee Simpson appeared as a musical guest on October 23, 2004. Her first performance, "Pieces of Me," was performed without incident, but when she began her second song, "Autobiography," the vocals for "Pieces of Me" were heard again—before she had even raised the microphone to her mouth. Simpson began to do an impromptu jig, and then left the stage.[78] During the closing of the show Simpson appeared with the guest host Jude Law and said: "I'm so sorry. My band started playing the wrong song, and I didn't know what to do, so I thought I'd do a hoedown."

On October 25, Simpson explained that due to complications arising from severe acid reflux disease, she had completely lost her voice and her doctor had advised her not to sing. Her father wanted her to use a vocal guide track for the performance after she had suffered vocal issues during rehearsals. Simpson stated of the incident, "I made a complete fool of myself." According to Simpson, the drummer hit the wrong button, which caused the wrong track to be played. Lorne Michaels had been unaware of the plan to use lip synching, and said in an interview with *60 Minutes* that he would not have allowed it. Simpson is the only musical guest ever to walk off stage during a live performance.

Other incidents

- On December 13, 1975, the show was forced by the network to run on a five-second delay when controversial comedian Richard Pryor hosted.[79] Engineers at the show later said they did not run the delay because no one knew how to work it.[80]
- A stand-up routine by Sam Kinison in the October 18, 1986, episode was edited in West Coast and later airings to replace two parts of the routine with a silent image of the previous season's cast. The first cutaway occurred when Kinison began asking for the legalization of cannabis and said: "You can't get any more pot. If you give us back the pot, we'll forget about the crack". The joke violated NBC policy of the time that all references to drugs must be negative. The second, longer cutaway occurred when Kinison made a joke about the Crucifixion. During rehearsal, Kinison had not performed the drug joke; he had performed, and been asked to remove, the Crucifixion joke.
- In a "Wayne's World" sketch, the characters Wayne and Garth (portrayed by Myers and Carvey, respectively) made fun of Chelsea Clinton (the then 12-year-old daughter of the then President-elect Bill Clinton), implying that Chelsea was incapable of causing males to "Schwing!". This joke was subsequently edited out of all repeats

and syndication rebroadcasts of this sketch.

- A portion of Martin Lawrence's February 19, 1994, monologue concerning feminine hygiene has been removed from all repeats, replaced with a voice-over and intertitles stating that the excised portion "...was a frank and lively presentation, and nearly cost us all our jobs."
- In 1995, an Irish Bartender sketch, written by comedian Jay Mohr, was aired. By April 15, 1995, during the Saturday rehearsal, Mohr was brought to Michaels, and shown a video of the Irish Bartender act as performed by its creator, Rick Shapiro. Mohr denied any knowledge of Shapiro or his act at the time, but later admitted in his memoir that he had stolen the sketch word for word from Shapiro's work. Shapiro and his manager sued the show and gained an undisclosed settlement which included the sketch being removed from all reruns of the show.[81]
- In March 1998, a Robert Smigel animated short film, "Conspiracy Theory Rock", aired. The short is a scathing political sketch accusing corporations including Disney, FOX, and then-owners of NBC General Electric, of developing a media monopoly to manipulate public perception, and conceal questionable actions. The clip aired only once as part of the original *SNL* episode and was removed from syndicated repeats with Michaels explaining that it "wasn't funny". The clip was eventually released as part of the *Saturday TV Funhouse* compilation DVD in 2006.
- A sketch involving "butt pregnancy" during the first broadcast of the November 12, 2005, episode was replaced with a musical sketch about cafeteria food during the repeat.
- On September 26, 2009, Jenny Slate made her *SNL* debut in a biker babe sketch alongside Wiig and actress Megan Fox, where their characters repeatedly use the word "frickin'". During one instance Slate instead accidentally said "fuckin'", which was dubbed over with "freakin'" for subsequent airings.
- On December 15, 2012, actor Samuel L. Jackson, appearing on the recurring Kenan Thompson sketch "What Up With That?" as a talk show guest whose segment was cut for time, exclaimed what sounded like the words "fuck" and "bullshit." Thompson ad-libbed in response, "C'mon, Sam, that costs money!" Jackson later claimed he hadn't said the full word "fuck" and that Thompson was supposed to cut off his second expletive.

References

[1] http://www.nbc.com/Saturday_Night_Live/
[2] SNL's Beginnings (http://www.nbc.com/saturday-night-live/about/history.shtml) from NBC
[3] Shales & Miller 2002, pp. 121-122.
[4] Shales & Miller 2002, pp. 157-159,161.
[5] Shales & Miller 2002, p. 160-161.
[6] Shales & Miller 2002, p. 167.
[7] Shales & Miller 2002, pp. 166, 176.
[8] Shales & Miller 2002, p. 175.
[9] Shales & Miller 2002, p. 130.
[10] Shales & Miller 2002, p. 177-179.
[11] Shales & Miller 2002, p. 155.
[12] Shales & Miller 2002, p. 197.
[13] Shales & Miller 2002, p. 200.
[14] Shales & Miller 2002, p. 199.
[15] Shales & Miller 2002, p. 211.
[16] Shales & Miller 2002, p. 212.
[17] Shales & Miller 2002, pp. 352-353, 358.
[18] Shales & Miller 2002, pp. 350-351.
[19] Shales & Miller 2002, pp. 359.
[20] Shales & Miller 2002, pp. 361-362.
[21] Shales & Miller 2002, pp. 363.
[22] Shales & Miller 2002, p. 38.
[23] Shales & Miller 2002, p. 23.
[24] Shales & Miller 2002, p. 27.
[25] Shales & Miller 2002, p. 28.
[26] Shales & Miller 2002, p. 26.

[27] Shales & Miller 2002, p. 34.

[28] Shales & Miller 2002, pp. 82-83.

[29] Shales & Miller 2002, p. 81.

[30] Shales & Miller 2002, p. 118.

[31] Shales & Miller 2002, p. 140.

[32] Shales & Miller 2002, pp. 136-137.

[33] Shales & Miller 2002, p. 153.

[34] Shales & Miller 2002, pp. 161-163,165.

[35] Shales & Miller 2002, p. 198.

[36] Shales & Miller 2002, p. 209.

[37] Shales & Miller 2002, p. 308-309, 346-347.

[38] Shales & Miller 2002, p. 352-353,359.

[39] Shales & Miller 2002, p. 219.

[40] Shales & Miller 2002, p. 286.

[41] Shales & Miller 2002, p. 293.

[42] SNL Cast (http://www.nbc.com/saturday-night-live/bios/) from NBC

[43] Mohr 2004, p. 81.

[44] Shales & Miller 2002, p. 78.

[45] Shales & Miller 2002, p. 295.

[46] Shales & Miller 2002, p. 229.

[47] Shales & Miller 2002, p. 44.

[48] Shales & Miller 2002, p. 48.

[49] Shales & Miller 2002, p. 396.

[50] Shales & Miller 2002, p. 231.

[51] Shales & Miller 2002, p. 230.

[52] Shales & Miller 2002, p. 45.

[53] SNL Band (http://www.nbc.com/saturday-night-live/about/band.shtml) from NBC

[54] Shales & Miller 2002, p. 31.

[55] Shales & Miller 2002, p. 30.

[56] SNL's Studio (http://www.nbc.com/saturday-night-live/about/history.shtml) from NBC

[57] Shales & Miller 2002, p. 35.

[58] Mohr 2004, p. 27.

[59] Shales & Miller 2002, p. 79.

[60] Mohr 2004, p. 28.

[61] Mohr 2004, pp. 28-29.

[62] Mohr 2004, p. 30.

[63] Mohr 2004, p. 23.

[64] Shales & Miller 2002, p. 39.

[65] Shales & Miller 2002, p. 41.

[66] except for KSNG, KSNK, and KQCD, which air the live feed

[67] *Saturday Night Live* (1977) (http://lccn.loc.gov/78102562) from the Library of Congress Online Catalog

[68] Eric Idle Books (http://www.dailyllama.com/spam/books/idle.html) from dailyllama.com

[69] Script Review: THE SATURDAY NIGHT LIVE MOVIE (http://www.filmbuffonline.com/FBOLNewsreel/wordpress/2012/07/06/
script-review-the-saturday-night-live-movie/) from filmbuffonline.com

[70] Live, From New York, It's the Worst Movies From the Cast of SNL (http://www.filmcritic.com/features/2010/05/
snls-bad-boys----top-ten-worst-snlmovies/) from filmcritic.com

[71] http://eater.com/archives/2014/06/19/saturday-night-live-inspired-ben-jerrys-newest-flavors.php

[72] Shales & Miller 2002, pp. 224-225.

[73] Shales & Miller 2002, p. 225.

[74] Shales & Miller 2002, pp. 224,227.

[75] Shales & Miller 2002, p. 226.

[76] Shales & Miller 2002, pp. 225-226.

[77] Anon., Saturday Night Live Incident (http://www.musicfanclubs.org/rage/snl.htm), Public release and distribution. Retrieved November
12, 2007.

[78] http://www.today.com/id/6356035/ns/today-today_entertainment/t/ashlee-simpson-takes-snl-lip-sync-blame

[79] Shales & Miller 2002, p. 47.

[80] Furious Cool: Richard Pryor and the World that Made Him.

[81] Mohr 2004, p. 125.

Bibliography

- Mohr, Jay (2004). *Gasping for Airtime: Two Years in the Trenches of Saturday Night Live*. United States: Hyperion Books. ISBN 1-4013-0006-5.
- Shales, Tom; Miller, James Andrew (2002). *Live From New York: An Uncensored History of Saturday Night Live*. United States: Hachette Book Group USA. ISBN 0-316-73565-5.

Further reading

- Cader, Michael (1994). *Saturday Night Live: The First Twenty Years*. Boston: Houghton Mifflin. ISBN 0-395-70895-8.
- Hill, Doug, and Jeff Weingrad (1986). *Saturday Night: A Backstage History of Saturday Night Live*. New York: Beech Tree Books. ISBN 0-688-05099-9.
- Streeter, Michael (2005). *Nothing Lost Forever: The Films of Tom Schiller*. New York: BearManor Media. ISBN 1-59393-032-1.

External links

- Saturday Night Live (http://www.dmoz.org/Arts/Television/Programs/Comedy/Sketch_Comedy/Saturday_Night_Live/) at DMOZ
- Official NBC website (http://www.nbc.com/Saturday_Night_Live/)
- Official website (http://www.broadwayvideo.com/) for Broadway Video
- *Saturday Night Live* (http://www.imdb.com/title/tt0072562/) at the Internet Movie Database
- *Saturday Night Live* (http://www.tv.com/shows/saturday-night-live/) at TV.com
- Saturday Night Live video archive (http://screen.yahoo.com/snl/) at Yahoo Screen (http://screen.yahoo.com/)

Song of Myself

"**Song of Myself**" is a poem by Walt Whitman that is included in his work *Leaves of Grass*. It has been credited as "representing the core of Whitman's poetic vision."[1]

Publication history

The poem was first published without sections[2] as the first of twelve untitled poems in the first (1855) edition of *Leaves of Grass*. The first edition was published by Whitman at his own expense.

In the second (1856) edition, Whitman used the title "Poem of Walt Whitman, an American," which was shortened to "Walt Whitman" for the third (1860) edition.

The poem was divided into fifty-two numbered sections for the fourth (1867) edition and finally took on the title "Song of Myself" in the last edition (1881–2).

Steel engraving of Walt Whitman.

Reception

Following its 1855 publication, "Song of Myself" was immediately singled out by critics and readers for particular attention, and today, remains among the most acclaimed and influential poems written by an American.[3]

In 1855, the *Christian Spiritualist* gave a long, glowing review of "Song of Myself", praising Whitman for representing "a new poetic mediumship," which through active imagination sensed the "influx of spirit and the divine breath."[4] Ralph Waldo Emerson also wrote a letter to Whitman, praising his work for its "wit and wisdom".

Public acceptance was slow in coming, however. Social conservatives denounced the poem as flouting accepted norms of morality due to its blatant depictions of human sexuality. In 1882, Boston district attorney threatened action against *Leaves of Grass* for violating the state's obscenity laws and demanded that changes be made to several passages from "Song of Myself".

Literary style

The poem is written in Whitman's signature free verse style. Whitman, who praises words "as simple as grass" (section 39) forgoes standard verse and stanza patterns in favor of a simple, legible style that can appeal to a mass audience.[5]

Critics have noted a strong Transcendentalist influence on the poem. In section 32, for instance, Whitman expresses a desire to "live amongst the animals" and to find divinity in the insects.

In addition to this romanticism, the poem seems to anticipate a kind of realism that would only become important in United States literature after the American Civil War. In the following 1855 passage, for example, we can see Whitman's inclusion of the gritty details of everyday life:

"Song of Myself" includes passages about the unsavory realities of America before the Civil War, including one about a multi-racial slave

> The lunatic is carried at last to the asylum a confirm'd case,
> (He will never sleep any more as he did in the cot in his mother's bed-room;)
> The jour printer with gray head and gaunt jaws works at his case,
> He turns his quid of tobacco while his eyes blurr with the manuscript;
> The malform'd limbs are tied to the surgeon's table,
> What is removed drops horribly in a pail;
> The quadroon girl is sold at the auction-stand, the drunkard nods by the bar-room stove, ... (section 15)

"Self"

In the poem, Whitman emphasizes an all-powerful "I" which serves as narrator, who should not be limited to or confused with the person of the historical Walt Whitman. The persona described has transcended the conventional boundaries of self: "I pass death with the dying, and birth with the new-washed babe .... and am not contained between my hat and boots" (section 7).

There are several other quotes from the poem that makes it apparent that Whitman does not consider the narrator to represent a single individual. Rather, he seems to be narrating for all:

- "For every atom belonging to me as good belongs to you." (Section 1)
- "In all people I see myself, none more and not one a barleycorn less/and the good or bad I say of myself I say of them" (Section 20)
- "It is you talking just as much as myself... I act as the tongue of you" (Section 47)
- "I am large, I contain multitudes." (Section 51)

Literary critics Alice L. Cook and John B. Mason give interpretations as to the meaning of the "self" as well as its importance in the poem. Cook writes that the key to understanding the poem lies in the "concept of self" (typified by Whitman) as "both individual and universal,"[6] while Mason discusses "the reader's involvement in the poet's movement from the singular to the cosmic".[7] The "self" serves as an ideal, yet, in contrast to traditional epic poetry, this identity is one of the common people rather than a hero.[8]

Political context of "self"

Literary historian Betsy Erkkilä writes that "the drama of identity" in the poem is "rooted in the political drama of a nation in crisis," referring to tensions over slavery, women's rights, religious revival and free love that were sweeping across America when Whitman wrote "A Song of Myself".

References

[1] Greenspan, Ezra, ed. *Walt Whitman's "Song of Myself": A Sourcebook and Critical Edition*. New York: Routledge, 2005. Print.

[2] Loving, Jerome. *Walt Whitman: The Song of Himself*. California: University of California Press, 1999. Print.

[3] Gutman, Huck. "Walt Whitman's 'Song of Myself'". *The Oxford Encyclopedia of American Literature*. Ed. Jay Parini. Oxford University Press, 2004. *Oxford Reference Online*. Oxford University Press. Web. 20 October 2011

[4] Reynolds, David S. *Walt Whitman's America: A Cultural Biography*. New York: Alfred A. Knopf, 1995. Print.

[5] Redding, Patrick. "Whitman Unbound: Democracy and Poetic Form". *New Literary Theory* 41.3 (2010): 669-90. *Project Muse*. Web. 19 October 2011.

[6] Cook, Alice L. "A Note on Whitman's Symbolism in 'Song of Myself'". *Modern Language Notes* 65.4 (1950): 228-32. *JSTOR*. Web. 17 October 2011

[7] Mason, John B. "Walt Whitman's Catalogues: Rhetorical Means for Two Journeys in 'Song of Myself'". *American Literature* 45.1 (1973): 34-49. *JSTOR*. Web. 17 October 2011.

[8] Miller, James E. *Walt Whitman*. New York: Twayne Publishers, 1962. Print.

External links

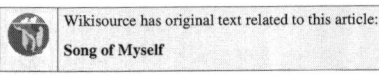

Wikisource has original text related to this article:
Song of Myself

- The University of Toronto's full text, with line numbers (http://rpo.library.utoronto.ca/poems/song-myself)
- Emerson's letter To Whitman (http://www.classroomelectric.org/volume1/belasco/whitman-emerson.htm)
- Alice L. Cook's "A Note on Whitman's Symbolism in 'Song of Myself'" (http://links.jstor.org/sici?sici=0149-6611(195004)65:4<228:ANOWSI>2.0.CO;2-5)
- John B. Mason's "Walt Whitman's Catalogues: Rhetorical Means for Two Journeys in "Song of Myself" (http://links.jstor.org/sici?sici=0002-9831(197303)45:1<34:WWCRMF>2.0.CO;2-V)

- WhitmanWeb's full text in 12 languages, plus audio recordings and commentaries (http://iwp.uiowa.edu/whitmanweb/)
- Audio: Robert Pinsky reads from "Song of Myself" (http://poemsoutloud.net/columns/archive/whitman_celebrates_himself/)

L'Officiel

L'Officiel

June - July 2013 cover

Director	Marie José Susskind Jalou
Editor-in-Chief (fashion)	Vanessa Bellugeon
Categories	Fashion
Frequency	monthly
Total circulation (2013)	135,000
First issue	1921
Company	Editions Jalou
Country	France
Language	French
Website	http://www.lofficielmode.com/

L'Officiel (French pronunciation: [lɔfisjɛl]) is a French fashion magazine published by *Les Editions Jalou*. It has been published in Paris since 1921 and targets upper-income, educated women aged 25 to 49.[1] *Les Editions Jalou* is a family media group based in Paris. It is 100% controlled by the Jalou family, and presided by Ms Marie-José Susskind-Jalou. As of 2013, it had a circulation of 135,000 A men's edition of *L'Officiel* called L'Officiel Hommes also published.

Both *L'Officiel* and L'Officiel Hommes are currently published in more than 20 countries, including Azerbaijan, Brazil, Central Asia, China, Germany, Greece, India, Italy, Korea, Latvia, Lebanon, Lithuania, Mexico, Morocco, the Netherlands, Russia, Singapore, Switzerland, Thailand, Turkey, Ukraine and the United Arab Emirates. Editions Jalou plan to launch L'Officiel magazine in Australia in 2015.

The complete name of the magazine is "*L'Officiel de la Couture et de la Mode de Paris*".

History

First issue of L'Officiel Paris, year 1921

L'Officiel was first published by Andrée Castaniée in 1921.[2] George Jalou joined the magazine as artistic director in 1932. Soon after, *L'Officiel* launched the careers of designers including Pierre Balmain, Cristóbal Balenciaga, Christian Dior, and Yves St. Laurent, and the magazine became "the Bible of fashion and of high society".[3] Jalou later became the magazine's general director, and ultimately purchased the publication. He transferred ownership of *L'Officiel* to his three children in 1986. Laurent became the president of Editions Jalou, Marie-José Susskind-Jalou directed its editorial content, and Maxime was responsible for publication. After Laurent died of a heart attack in January 2003, Marie-José Susskind-Jalou became the company's president. In recent years, the publication has taken a more youthful, energetic approach to fashion.

Editions Jalou, a family-owned company also comprises magazines including Jalouse, L'Optimum, L'Officiel Hommes, L'Officiel Art and L'Officiel Voyage. After launching L'Officiel in Indonesia and Azerbaijan this year, it is planning to launch editions in Switzerland and Australia for 2014 or 2015, which would bring the number of editions to more than 30. It is also eyeing the U.S. market, where it would launch with a partner. Meanwhile, Jalouse will have Chinese and Russian editions before the end of the year.

Editions Jalou generated a turnover of 31 millions euros, or $39.8 million at average exchange, in France in 2012, according to the company.

Collaboration

L'Officiel has tapped Vincent Darré, the fashion designer turned interiors maven, to design four issues, starting with October. Christmas, March, and June/July issues will follow. Known for his whimsical universe, Darré was named "curator" of the magazine. "We wanted to break with a classic conception of a magazine," said Benjamin Eymère, managing director of L'Officiel's publisher, Editions Jalou. "We want to do a luxury piece." There will be limited editions of Darré's issues, which will be numbered and could have a different format.

The gatefold cover of L'Officiel October 2013 issue, Photo By Karl Lagerfeld

Darré said his inspirations were publications like British quarterly Flair, surrealist-oriented publication Le Minotaure or art magazine L'Oeil. "It is a mix of fashion and art," he said. The magazine will have illustrations from the likes of Pierre Le-Tan. Contributors for the first issue include Karl Lagerfeld, Deborah Turbeville in tandem with Catherine Baba, Serge Leblon, Dominique Issermann and Olivier Zahm. "It will be a Parisian salon that resembles me. I invited my friends to participate," Darré said.

In October 2013, Karl Lagerfeld shot the gatefold cover of L'Officiel's October issue, which features cast members from the film "Opium," including Farida Khelfa, Audrey Marnay, Marisa Berenson and Arielle Dombasle. Vincent Darré, the fashion designer-turned-interiors-maven who was tapped earlier this year to be "curator" of L'Officiel, was the artistic director of the small-budget musical film about artist Jean Cocteau, set in Paris in the Twenties, while Dombasle directed it. The movie will be released on 2 Oct in France. The issue, which counts 377 pages including

100 advertising pages, priced at 4.50 euros, or $6 at current exchange.

In 2012, Les Editions Jalou has also launched a digital label, dubbed L'Officiel New Talents, geared to promoting blogger talents from the women's lifestyle and fashion domains. The selection committee for the bloggers includes André Saraiva, creative director of L'Officiel Hommes [4]. Men's bloggers will soon be added. The L'Officiel print magazine made by the bloggers will be released twice yearly, starting in May, with Marie-José Jalou, Jalou's president, as its editor in chief. "We need a magazine that defines the times," said Eymere, adding the bloggers get to maintain total independence for their blogs. Members include Kenza Sadoun-El Glaoui, Audrey Lombard, Marie Pottier and India Weber. The label will also represent the bloggers for special commissions with brands.

Related publications

L'Officiel Thailand

L'Officiel Thailand, November 2012. Model Rawiwan in DIOR

Editor-in-Chief	Kusuma Chaiyaporn
Fashion Director	Pop Kampol [5]
Categories	Fashion
Frequency	monthly
Total circulation (2012)	120,000
Company	Mass Connect ltd
Country	Thailand
Language	Thai
Website	http://lofficielthailand.com/

Beginning in 1996, *L'Officiel* began licensing its brand for use by publishers outside of France. Foreign editions of *L'Officiel* are now published in Russia, Japan, India, China, United Arab Emirates, Brazil, Greece, Latvia, Lithuania, Morocco, Netherlands, Ukraine, Serbia, Central Asia, Turkey, Italy, Thailand, Singapore. The men's edition of *L'Officiel*, called *L'Officiel Hommes*, is also published.

L'Officiel Italia [6] is the Italian edition of L'Officiel de la mode. Launched in September 2012, published by Martina Mondadori's Memoria Srl in collaboration with Paris-based Les Editions Jalou, the fashion magazine overseen by Memoria's chief executive officer Carlo Mazzoni. The men's Italian version, L'Officiel Hommes Italia, launched in 2009.

L'Officiel Thailand [7] (ลอฟฟิเซียล ประเทศไทย) is a luxury fashion magazine. It was launched in March 2012 with a circulation of 120,000. It's licensed by MASS Connect Ltd in Thailand. L'Officiel in Thailand includes L'Officiel de la mode, L'Officiel Hommes, L'Officiel Art, L'Officiel Watch&Jewelry and L'Officiel Wedding.[8] In July 2013

L'Officiel Thailand won the gold award on "Best Feature on Asian Fashion" and excellence award on "Best Feature on Interior Decoration" at The Asian Publishing Awards.[9]

L'Officiel India [10] is India's "premiere fashion and luxury magazine"; in 2007, its publishers announced that they would also publish *L'Officiel India* in the United Kingdom to target overseas Indians there.[11]

The Indian edition of French fashion and luxury magazine, L'Officiel, is now being brought out by MaXposure Media Group. The French magazine began operations in India in 2002 and was earlier published by Apricot Publications. Under the new company, Maxposure Media Group, the monthly magazine will be priced at Rs 100 and is aimed at well-heeled and well travelled Indian women who like to dress and are not short of spending for it. L'Officiel India now aims to be an ultimate fashion, style and luxury destination for the elite Indians and be an authoritative voice of the Indian fashion industry. The magazine is targeted at 35-year-old, educated women.

References

[1] "Lifestyle Mag L'Officiel to be Published in Latvia from Sept". Baltic News Service (10 March 2008). (Via LexisNexis.)

[2] Corine Moriou. "Le groupe édite L'Officiel, Jalouse, L'Optimum, etc.; Jalou, les magazines qui font des jaloux". *L'Entreprise* (1 September 2006), p. 54.

[3] "la bible de la mode et des élégantes"

[4] http://www.lofficielhommes.fr/

[5] http://kampoll.com/

[6] http://www.lofficielitalia.com/

[7] http://lofficielthailand.com/

[8] " Thai edition of French fashion mag launched. (http://www.nationmultimedia.com/business/ Thai-edition-of-French-fashion-mag-launched-30177707.html)" The Nation News. (12 March 2012)

[9] " Founder of Kompas Daily wins Lifetime Achievement Award at Gala APC dinner. (http://publishingconvention.com/pressrelease6/)" Asian Publishing convention (http://publishingconvention.com/). (12 July 2013)

[10] http://www.lofficielindia.com/

[11] "Fashion magazine launched in UK". Press Trust of India (14 June 2007).

External links

- Archive of the magazine (in French) (http://patrimoine.jalougallery.com/ lofficiel-de-la-mode-sommairepatrimoine-13.html)
- L'Officiel France (http://www.fashionmodeldirectory.com/magazines/lofficiel-france) – magazine profile at Fashion Model Directory

A Clockwork Orange

This article is about the novel. For the film, see A Clockwork Orange (film). For other uses, see A Clockwork Orange (disambiguation).

A Clockwork Orange

Dust jacket from the first edition	
Author	Anthony Burgess
Language	English/Nadsat
Genre	Science fiction, Novella, Satire, Dystopian fiction
Published	1962 (William Heinemann, UK)
ISBN	0-434-09800-0
OCLC	4205836 [1]

A Clockwork Orange is a dystopian novella by Anthony Burgess published in 1962. Set in a not-so-distant future English society that has a culture of extreme youth violence, the novel's teenage protagonist, Alex, narrates his violent exploits and his experiences with state authorities intent on reforming him. When the state undertakes to reform Alex—to "redeem" him—the novel asks, "At what cost?". The book is partially written in a Russian-influenced argot called "Nadsat". According to Burgess it was a *jeu d'esprit* written in just three weeks.

In 2005, *A Clockwork Orange* was included on *Time* magazine's list of the 100 best English-language novels written since 1923, and it was named by Modern Library and its readers as one of the 100 best English-language novels of the 20th century.[2] The original manuscript of the book is located at McMaster University in Hamilton, Ontario, Canada since that institution purchased the documents in 1971.

Plot summary

Part 1: Alex's world

Alex, a teenager living in near-future dystopian England, leads his gang on a night of opportunistic, random "ultra-violence". Alex's friends ("droogs" in the novel's Anglo-Russian slang, 'Nadsat') are: Dim, a slow-witted bruiser who is the gang's muscle; Georgie, an ambitious second-in-command; and Pete, who mostly plays along as the droogs indulge their taste for ultra-violence. Characterized as a sociopath and a hardened juvenile delinquent, Alex is also intelligent and quick-witted, with sophisticated taste in music, being particularly fond of Beethoven, referred to as "Lovely Ludwig Van".

The novel begins with the droogs sitting in their favorite hangout (the Korova Milk Bar), drinking "milk-plus", a drink consisting of milk, prodded with the customer's choice of certain drugs, including "vellocet", "synthemesc", or "drencrom" (which is what Alex and his droogs were drinking, according to Alex's own first-person narration). This drug, referred to as "knives", would "sharpen you up", as it did for Alex, in preparation of the night's mayhem. They assault a scholar walking home from the public library, rob a store, leaving the owner and his wife bloodied and unconscious, stomp a panhandling derelict, then scuffle with a rival gang. Joyriding through the countryside in a stolen car, they break into an isolated cottage and maul the young couple living there, beating the husband and raping his wife. In a metafictional touch, the husband is a writer working on a manuscript called "*A Clockwork Orange,*" and Alex contemptuously reads out a paragraph that states the novel's main theme before shredding the manuscript. Back at the milk bar, Alex punishes Dim for some crude behaviour, and strains within the gang become apparent. At home in his dreary flat, Alex plays classical music at top volume while fantasizing about more orgiastic violence.

Alex skips school the next day. Following an unexpected visit from P. R. Deltoid, his "post-corrective advisor," Alex meets a pair of ten-year-old girls and takes them back to his parents' flat, where he serves them scotch and soda, injects himself with hard drugs, and then rapes them. That evening, Alex finds his droogs in a mutinous mood. Georgie challenges Alex for leadership of the gang, demanding that they pull a "man-sized" job. Alex quells the rebellion by slashing Dim's hand and fighting with Georgie, then in a show of generosity takes them to a bar, where Alex insists on following through on Georgie's idea to burgle the home of a wealthy old woman. The break-in starts as farce and ends in tragic pathos, as Alex's attack kills the elderly woman. His escape is blocked by an attack by Dim, as payback for the earlier fight, leaving Alex incapacitated on the front step when the police arrive.

Part 2: The Ludovico Technique

Sentenced to prison for murder, Alex gets a job at the Wing chapel playing religious music on the stereo before and after services as well as during the singing of hymns. The prison chaplain mistakes Alex's Bible studies for stirrings of faith (Alex is actually reading Scripture for the violent passages). After Alex's fellow cellmates blame him for beating a troublesome cellmate to death, he agrees to undergo an experimental behaviour-modification treatment called the Ludovico Technique. The technique is a form of aversion therapy in which Alex receives an injection that makes him feel sick while watching graphically violent films, eventually conditioning him to suffer crippling bouts of nausea at the mere thought of violence. As an unintended consequence, the soundtrack to one of the films—Beethoven's Ninth Symphony—renders Alex unable to listen to his beloved classical music.

The effectiveness of the technique is demonstrated to a group of VIPs, who watch as Alex collapses before a walloping bully, and abases himself before a scantily-clad young woman whose presence has aroused his predatory sexual inclinations. Although the prison chaplain accuses the state of stripping Alex of free will, the government officials on the scene are pleased with the results and Alex is released into society early as a result.

Part 3: After prison

Since his parents are now renting his room to a lodger, Alex wanders the streets homeless. He enters a public library where he hopes to learn a painless way to commit suicide. There, he accidentally encounters the old scholar he assaulted earlier in the book, who, keen on revenge, beats Alex with the help of his friends. The policemen who come to Alex's rescue turn out to be none other than Dim and former gang rival Billyboy. The two policemen take Alex outside of town and beat him up. Dazed and bloodied, Alex collapses at the door of an isolated cottage, realizing too late that it is the house he and his droogs invaded in the first part of the story. Because the gang wore masks during the assault, the writer does not recognize Alex. The writer, whose name is revealed as F. Alexander, shelters Alex and questions him about the conditioning. During this sequence, it is revealed that Mrs. Alexander died of injuries inflicted during the gang-rape, while her husband has decided to continue living "where her fragrant memory persists" despite the horrid memories. Alex reveals in his description that he has been conditioned to feel intolerable deathly nausea on hearing certain classical music. Alexander, a critic of the government, intends to use Alex's therapy as a symbol of state brutality and thereby prevent the incumbent government from being re-elected, but a careless Alex soon inadvertently reveals that he was the ringleader during the night two years ago. Frightened for his own safety, Alex blurts out a confession to the writer's radical associates after they remove him from F. Alexander's home. Instead of protecting him, however, they imprison Alex in a dreary flat not far from his parents' residence. They pretend to leave, and then while he is sleeping in a locked bedroom subject him to a relentless barrage of classical music, prompting him to attempt suicide by leaping from a high window.

Alex wakes up in a hospital, where he is courted by government officials anxious to counter the bad publicity created by his suicide attempt. With Alexander placed in a mental institution, Alex is offered a well-paying job if he agrees to side with the government. As photographers snap pictures, Alex daydreams of orgiastic violence and reflects upon the news that his Ludovico conditioning has been reversed as part of his recovery: "I was cured, all right".

In the final chapter, Alex finds himself half-heartedly preparing for yet another night of crime with a new trio of droogs. After a chance encounter with Pete, who has reformed and married, Alex finds himself taking less and less pleasure in acts of senseless violence. He begins contemplating giving up crime himself to become a productive member of society and start a family of his own, while reflecting on the notion that his own children will be just as destructive—if not more so—than he himself.

Omission of the final chapter

The book has three parts, each with seven chapters. Burgess has stated that the total of 21 chapters was an intentional nod to the age of 21 being recognised as a milestone in human maturation. The 21st chapter was omitted from the editions published in the United States prior to 1986.[3] In the introduction to the updated American text (these newer editions include the missing 21st chapter), Burgess explains that when he first brought the book to an American publisher, he was told that U.S. audiences would never go for the final chapter, in which Alex sees the error of his ways, decides he has lost all energy for and thrill from violence and resolves to turn his life around (a slow-ripening but classic moment of metanoia—the moment at which one's protagonist realises that everything he thought he knew was wrong).

At the American publisher's insistence, Burgess allowed their editors to cut the redeeming final chapter from the U.S. version, so that the tale would end on a darker note, with Alex succumbing to his violent, reckless nature—an ending which the publisher insisted would be 'more realistic' and appealing to a U.S. audience. The film adaptation, directed by Stanley Kubrick, is based on the American edition of the book (which Burgess considered to be "badly flawed"). Kubrick called Chapter 21 "an extra chapter" and claimed that he had not read the original version until he had virtually finished the screenplay, and that he had never given serious consideration to using it. In Kubrick's opinion, the final chapter was unconvincing and inconsistent with the book.

Characters

- **Alex**: The novel's anti-hero and leader among his droogs. He often refers to himself as "Your Humble Narrator". (Having seduced two girls in his bedroom, Alex refers to himself as "Alexander the Large" while ravishing them; this was later the basis for Alex's claimed surname *DeLarge* in the 1971 film.)
- **George** or **Georgie**: Effectively Alex's greedy second-in-command. Georgie attempts to undermine Alex's status as leader of the gang. He is later killed during a botched robbery, while Alex is in prison.
- **Pete**: The most rational and least violent member of the gang. He is the only one who doesn't take particular sides when the droogs fight among themselves. He later meets and marries a girl, renouncing his old ways and even losing his former (Nadsat) speech patterns. A chance encounter with Pete in the final chapter influences Alex to realize that he grows bored with violence and recognises that human energy is better expended on creation than destruction.[4]
- **Dim**: An idiotic and thoroughly gormless member of the gang, persistently condescended to by Alex, but respected to some extent by his droogs for his formidable fighting abilities, his weapon of choice being a length of bike chain. He later becomes a police officer, exacting his revenge on Alex for the abuse he once suffered under his command.
- **P. R. Deltoid**: A criminal rehabilitation social worker assigned the task of keeping Alex on the straight and narrow. He seemingly has no clue about dealing with young people, and is devoid of empathy or understanding for his troublesome charge. Indeed, when Alex is arrested for murdering an old woman, and then ferociously beaten by several police officers, Deltoid simply spits on him.
- **The prison chaplain**: The character who first questions whether it's moral to turn a violent person into a behavioural automaton who can make no choice in such matters. This is the only character who is truly concerned about Alex's welfare; he is not taken seriously by Alex, though. (He is nicknamed by Alex "prison charlie" or "chaplin", possibly an allusion to Charlie Chaplin.)

- **Billyboy**: A rival of Alex's. Early on in the story, Alex and his droogs battle Billyboy and his droogs, which ends abruptly when the police arrive. Later, after Alex is released from prison, Billyboy (along with Dim, who like Billyboy has become a police officer) rescue Alex from a mob, then subsequently beat him, in a location out of town.
- **The prison governor**: The man who decides to let Alex "choose" to be the first reformed by the Ludovico technique.
- **The Minister of the Interior**, or *the Inferior*, as Alex refers to him. The government high-official who is determined that Ludovico's technique will be used to cut recidivism.
- **Dr. Branom**: Brodsky's colleague and co-developer of the Ludovico technique. He appears friendly and almost paternal towards Alex at first, before forcing him into the theatre and what Alex calls the "chair of torture".
- **Dr. Brodsky**: The scientist and co-developer of the "Ludovico technique". He seems much more passive than Branom, and says considerably less.
- **F. Alexander**: An author who was in the process of typing his *magnum opus A Clockwork Orange*, when Alex and his droogs broke into his house, beat him, tore up his work and then brutally gang-raped his wife, which caused her subsequent death. He is left deeply scarred by these events, and when he encounters Alex two years later he uses him as a guinea pig in a sadistic experiment intended to prove the Ludovico technique unsound.
- **Cat Woman**: An indirectly named woman who blocks Alex's gang's entrance scheme, and threatens to shoot Alex and set her cats on him if he doesn't leave. After Alex breaks into her house, she fights with him, ordering her cats to join the melee, but reprimands Alex for fighting them off. She sustains a fatal blow to the head during the scuffle.

Analysis

Background

A Clockwork Orange was written in Hove, then a senescent seaside town. Burgess had arrived back in Britain after his stint abroad to see that much had changed. A youth culture had grown, including coffee bars, pop music and teenage gangs.[5] England was gripped by fears over juvenile delinquency. Burgess claimed that the novel's inspiration was his first wife Lynne's beating by a gang of drunk American servicemen stationed in England during World War II. She subsequently miscarried.[6] In its investigation of free will, the book's target is ostensibly the concept of behaviourism, pioneered by such figures as B. F. Skinner.[7]

Burgess later stated that he wrote the book in three weeks.

Title

Burgess gave three possible origins for the title:

- He had overheard the phrase "as queer as a clockwork orange" in a London pub in 1945 and assumed it was a Cockney expression.Wikipedia:Citation needed In *Clockwork Marmalade*, an essay published in the *Listener* in 1972, he said that he had heard the phrase several times since that occasion. He also explained the title in response to a question from William Everson on the television programme, *Camera Three* in 1972, "Well, the title has a very different meaning but only to a particular generation of London Cockneys. It's a phrase which I heard many years ago and so fell in love with, I wanted to use it, the title of the book. But the phrase itself I did not make up. The phrase "as queer as a clockwork orange" is good old East London slang and it didn't seem to me necessary to explain it. Now, obviously, I have to give it an extra meaning. I've implied an extra dimension. I've implied the junction of the organic, the lively, the sweet − in other words, life, the orange − and the mechanical, the cold, the disciplined. I've brought them together in this kind of oxymoron, this sour-sweet word."[8][9] However, no other record of the expression being used before 1962 has ever appeared. Kingsley Amis notes in his *Memoirs* (1991) that no trace of it appears in Eric Partridge's *Dictionary of Historical Slang*.

- His second explanation was that it was a pun on the Malay word *orang*, meaning "man." The novel contains no other Malay words or links.
- In a prefatory note to *A Clockwork Orange: A Play with Music*, he wrote that the title was a metaphor for "...an organic entity, full of juice and sweetness and agreeable odour, being turned into a mechanism."

In his essay, "Clockwork Oranges,"Wikipedia:Citation needed Burgess asserts that "this title would be appropriate for a story about the application of Pavlovian or mechanical laws to an organism which, like a fruit, was capable of colour and sweetness." This title alludes to the protagonist's positively conditioned responses to feelings of evil which prevent the exercise of his free will. To induce this conditioning, the protagonist is subjected to a technique in which violent scenes displayed on screen, which he is forced to watch, are systematically paired with negative stimulation in the form of nausea and "feelings of terror" caused by an emetic medicine administered just before the presentation of the films.

Point of view

A Clockwork Orange is written using a narrative first-person singular perspective of a seemingly biased and unreliable narrator. The protagonist, Alex, never justifies his actions in the narration, giving a sense that he is somewhat sincere; a narrator who, as unlikeable as he may attempt to seem, evokes pity from the reader by telling of his unending suffering, and later through his realisation that the cycle will never end. Alex's perspective is effective in that the way that he describes events is easy to relate to, even if the situations themselves are not.

Use of slang

Main article: Nadsat

The book, narrated by Alex, contains many words in a slang argot which Burgess invented for the book, called Nadsat. It is a mix of modified Slavic words, rhyming slang, derived Russian (like *baboochka*), and words invented by Burgess himself. For instance, these terms have the following meanings in Nadsat: *droog* = friend; *korova* = cow; *gulliver* ('golova') = head; *malchick* or *malchickiwick* = boy; *soomka* = sack or bag; *Bog* = God; *khorosho* ('horrosho') = good; *prestoopnick* = criminal; *rooka* ('rooker') = hand; *cal* = crap; *veck* ('chelloveck') = man or guy; *litso* = face; *malenky* = little; and so on. Compare Polari.

One of Alex's doctors explains the language to a colleague as "odd bits of old rhyming slang; a bit of gypsy talk, too. But most of the roots are Slav propaganda. Subliminal penetration." Some words are not derived from anything, but merely easy to guess, e.g. 'in-out, in-out' or 'the old in-out' means sexual intercourse. *Cutter,* however, means 'money,' because 'cutter' rhymes with 'bread-and-butter'; this is rhyming slang, which is intended to be impenetrable to outsiders (especially eavesdropping policemen). Additionally, slang like Appypolly loggy (Apology) seems to derive from school boy slang. This reflects Alex's age of 15.

In the first edition of the book, no key was provided, and the reader was left to interpret the meaning from the context. In his appendix to the restored edition, Burgess explained that the slang would keep the book from seeming dated, and served to muffle "the raw response of pornography" from the acts of violence. Furthermore, in a novel where a form of brainwashing plays a role, the narrative itself brainwashes the reader into understanding Nadsat.Wikipedia:Citation needed

The term "ultraviolence," referring to excessive and/or unjustified violence, was coined by Burgess in the book, which includes the phrase "do the ultra-violent." The term's association with aesthetic violence has led to its use in the media.

Banning and censorship history in the US

In 1976, *A Clockwork Orange* was removed from an Aurora, Colorado high school because of "objectionable language". A year later in 1977 it was removed from high school classrooms in Westport, Massachusetts over similar concerns with "objectionable" language. In 1982, it was removed from two Anniston, Alabama libraries, later to be reinstated on a restricted basis. Also, in 1973 a bookseller was arrested for selling the novel. Charges were later dropped.[10] However, each of these instances came after the release of Stanley Kubrick's popular 1971 film adaptation of *A Clockwork Orange*, itself the subject of much controversy.

Writer's dismissal

In 1985, Burgess published *Flame into Being: The Life and Work of D. H. Lawrence*, and while discussing *Lady Chatterley's Lover* in his biography, Burgess compared that novel's notoriety with *A Clockwork Orange*: "We all suffer from the popular desire to make the known notorious. The book I am best known for, or only known for, is a novel I am prepared to repudiate: written a quarter of a century ago, a *jeu d'esprit* knocked off for money in three weeks, it became known as the raw material for a film which seemed to glorify sex and violence. The film made it easy for readers of the book to misunderstand what it was about, and the misunderstanding will pursue me until I die. I should not

Burgess in 1986

have written the book because of this danger of misinterpretation, and the same may be said of Lawrence and *Lady Chatterley's Lover*."[11] Burgess also dismissed *A Clockwork Orange* as "too didactic to be artistic".[12]

Awards and nominations and rankings

- 1983 – Prometheus Award (Preliminary Nominee)
- 1999 – Prometheus Award (Nomination)
- 2002 – Prometheus Award (Nomination)
- 2003 – Prometheus Award (Nomination)
- 2006 – Prometheus Award (Nomination)
- 2008 – Prometheus Award (Hall of Fame Award)

The novel was chosen by *Time* magazine as one of the 100 best English-language novels from 1923 to 2005.

Adaptations

The best known adaptation of the novel to other forms is the 1971 film *A Clockwork Orange* by Stanley Kubrick, starring Malcolm McDowell as Alex.

A 1965 film by Andy Warhol entitled *Vinyl* [13] was an adaptation of Burgess' novel.

After Kubrick's film was released, Burgess wrote a stage play titled *A Clockwork Orange*. In it, Dr. Branom defects from the psychiatric clinic when he grasps that the aversion therapy has destroyed Alex's ability to enjoy music. The play restores the novel's original ending.Wikipedia:Citation needed

In 1988, a German adaptation of *A Clockwork Orange* at the intimate theatre of Bad Godesberg featured a musical score by the German punk rock band Die Toten Hosen which, combined with orchestral clips of Beethoven's Ninth Symphony and "other dirty melodies" (so stated by the subtitle), was released on the album *Ein kleines bisschen Horrorschau*. The track *Hier kommt Alex* became one of the band's signature songs.

In February 1990, another musical version was produced at the Barbican Theatre in London by the Royal Shakespeare Company. Titled *A Clockwork Orange: 2004*, it received mostly negative reviews, with John Peter of *The Sunday Times* of London calling it "only an intellectual *Rocky Horror Show*," and John Gross of *The Sunday Telegraph* calling it "a clockwork lemon." Even Burgess himself, who wrote the script based on his novel, was disappointed. According to *The Evening Standard*, he called the score, written by Bono and The Edge of the rock group U2, "neo-wallpaper." Burgess had originally worked alongside the director of the production, Ron Daniels, and envisioned a musical score that was entirely classical. Unhappy with the decision to abandon that score, he heavily criticised the band's experimental mix of hip hop, liturgical and gothic music. Lise Hand of *The Irish Independent* reported The Edge as saying that Burgess' original conception was "a score written by a novelist rather than a songwriter." Calling it "meaningless glitz," Jane Edwardes of *20/20 Magazine* said that watching this production was "like being invited to an expensive French Restaurant - and being served with a Big Mac."

Vanessa Claire Smith, Sterling Wolfe, Michael Holmes, and Ricky Coates in Brad Mays' multi-media stage production of *A Clockwork Orange*, 2003, Los Angeles. (photo: Peter Zuehlke)

In 1994, Chicago's Steppenwolf Theater put on a production of *A Clockwork Orange* directed by Terry Kinney. The American premiere of novelist Anthony Burgess' own adaptation of his *A Clockwork Orange* starred K. Todd Freeman as Alex. In 2001, UNI Theatre (Mississauga, Ontario) presented the Canadian premiere of the play under the direction of Terry Costa.

In 2002, Godlight Theatre Company presented the New York Premiere adaptation of *A Clockwork Orange* at Manhattan Theatre Source. The production went on to play at the SoHo Playhouse (2002), Ensemble Studio Theatre (2004), 59E59 Theaters (2005) and the Edinburgh Festival Fringe (2005). While at Edinburgh, the production received rave reviews from the press while playing to sold-out audiences. The production was directed by Godlight's Artistic Director, Joe Tantalo.

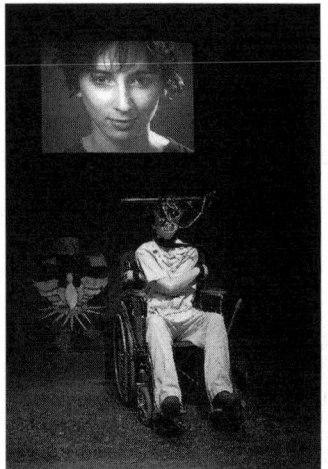

Vanessa Claire Smith in Brad Mays' multi-media stage production of *A Clockwork Orange*, 2003, Los Angeles. (photo: Peter Zuehlke)

In 2003, Los Angeles director Brad Mays and the ARK Theatre Company staged a multi-media adaptation of *A Clockwork Orange*, which was named "Pick Of The Week" by the *LA Weekly* and nominated for three of the 2004 LA Weekly Theater Awards: Direction, Revival Production (of a 20th-century work), and Leading Female Performance. Vanessa Claire Smith won Best Actress for her gender-bending portrayal of Alex, the music-loving teenage sociopath. This production utilised three separate video streams outputted to seven onstage video monitors - six 19-inch and one 40-inch. In order to preserve the first-person narrative of the book, a pre-recorded video stream of Alex, "your humble narrator," was projected onto the 40-inch monitor, thereby freeing the onstage character during passages which would have been awkward or impossible to sustain in the breaking of the fourth wall.

David Bowie referenced the book/film in various songs in his early 1970s oeuvre: "Suffragette City" mentions "droogie" in its lyrics, which is a reference to a term used in the book. Live appearances would include tracks from the soundtrack album, usually opening with Beethoven's Ninth Symphony segment "Ode To Joy" (as can be heard on live albums "Santa Monica '72" and the "Ziggy Stardust: The Motion Picture" soundtrack CD & DVD). The song "Sex and Violence" by American thrash metal band Carnivore (band) is about *A Clockwork Orange*. The Brazilian heavy metal group Sepultura used the plot of *A Clockwork Orange* for their concept album *A-Lex*. German punk rock band Die Toten Hosen wrote an album based on *A Clockwork Orange*, titled *Ein kleines bisschen Horrorschau* or "A Tiny Bit of Horrorshow." English punk rock band the Adicts became known for their "droog" image inspired by Kubrick's movie. Their third studio album was also entitled *smart alex*, referring to the book's protagonist.

- Rapper Cage previously rapped under the name of Alex, after the books protagonist, and he has since released the song Agent Orange which uses the title theme from the 1971 film as the beat

Release details

- 1962, UK, William Heinemann (ISBN ?), December 1962, Hardcover
- 1962, US, W. W. Norton & Co Ltd (ISBN ?), 1962, Hardcover
- 1963, US, W. W. Norton & Co Ltd (ISBN 0-345-28411-9), 1963, Paperback
- 1965, US, Ballantine Books (ISBN 0-345-01708-0), 1965, Paperback
- 1969, US, Ballantine Books (ISBN ?), 1969, Paperback
- 1971, US, Ballantine Books (ISBN 0-345-02624-1), 1971, Paperback,Movie released
- 1972, UK, Lorrimer, (ISBN 0-85647-019-8), 11 September 1972, Hardcover
- 1972, UK, Penguin Books Ltd (ISBN 0-14-003219-3), 25 January 1973, Paperback
- 1973, US, Caedmon Records, 1973, Vinyl LP (First 4 chapters read by Anthony Burgess)
- 1977, US, Ballantine Books (ISBN 0-345-27321-4), 12 September 1977, Paperback
- 1979, US, Ballantine Books (ISBN 0-345-31483-2), April 1979, Paperback
- 1983, US, Ballantine Books (ISBN 0-345-31483-2), 12 July 1983, Unbound
- 1986, US, W. W. Norton & Company (ISBN 0-393-31283-6), November 1986, Paperback (Adds final chapter not previously available in U.S. versions)
- 1987, UK, W. W. Norton & Co Ltd (ISBN 0-393-02439-3), July 1987, Hardcover
- 1988, US, Ballantine Books (ISBN 0-345-35443-5), March 1988, Paperback
- 1995, UK, W. W. Norton & Co Ltd (ISBN 0-393-31283-6), June 1995, Paperback
- 1996, UK, Penguin Books Ltd (ISBN 0-14-018882-7), 25 April 1996, Paperback
- 1996, UK, HarperAudio (ISBN 0-694-51752-6), September 1996, Audio Cassette
- 1997, UK, Heyne Verlag (ISBN 3-453-13079-0), 31 January 1997, Paperback
- 1998, UK, Penguin Books Ltd (ISBN 0-14-027409-X), 3 September 1998, Paperback
- 1999, UK, Rebound by Sagebrush (ISBN 0-8085-8194-5), October 1999, Library Binding
- 2000, UK, Penguin Books Ltd (ISBN 0-14-118260-1), 24 February 2000, Paperback
- 2000, UK, Penguin Books Ltd (ISBN 0-14-029105-9), 2 March 2000, Paperback
- 2000, UK, Turtleback Books (ISBN 0-606-19472-X), November 2000, Hardback
- 2001, UK, Penguin Books Ltd (ISBN 0-14-100855-5), 27 September 2001, Paperback
- 2002, UK, Thorndike Press (ISBN 0-7862-4644-8), October 2002, Hardback
- 2005, UK, Buccaneer Books (ISBN 1-56849-511-0), 29 January 2005, Library Binding
- 2010, Greece, Anubis Publications (ISBN 978-960-306-847-1), 2010, Paperback (Adds final chapter not previously available in Greek versions)
- 2012, US, W. W. Norton & Company (ISBN 978-0-393-08913-4) October 22, 2012, Hardback (50th Anniversary Edition, revised text version. Andrew Biswell, PhD, director of the International Burgess Foundation, has taken a close look at the three varying published editions alongside the original typescript to recreate the novel as Anthony Burgess envisioned it.

References

[1] http://www.worldcat.org/oclc/4205836

[2] "100 Best Novels" (http://www.modernlibrary.com/top-100/100-best-novels/). Modern Library. Retrieved 31 October 2012

[3] Burgess, Anthony (1986) *A Clockwork Orange Resucked* in A Clockwork Orange, W. W. Norton & Company, New York.

[4] A Clockwork Orange Resucked (http://thefloatinglibrary.com/2009/04/20/a-clockwork-orange-resucked/). The Floating Library.
     Retrieved on 2013-10-31.

[5] A Clockwork Orange (Penguin Modern Classics) (Paperback) by Anthony Burgess, Blake Morrison xv

[6] Burgess, A. *A Clockwork Orange*, Penguin UK, 2011, introduction by Blake Morrison, page 17 (http://books.google.fr/
     books?id=qUI8pbpCNJUC&pg=PT17&dq=Lynne) : « his first wife, Lynne, was beaten, kicked and robbed in London by a gang of four GI
     deserters ».

[7] *A Clockwork Orange* (Paperback) by Anthony Burgess, Will Self

[8] *An examination of Kubrick's A Clockwork Orange* (http://www.youtube.com/watch?v=ejM3odcn3Tk#t=7m23s) *Camera Three*: Creative
     Arts Television, 2010-08-04. **(Video)**

[9] *Clockwork Orange: A review with William Everson* (http://www.malcolmtribute.freeiz.com/aco/review.html). Retrieved: 2012-03-11.

[10] "Banned and/or Challenged Books from the Radcliffe Publishing Course Top 100 Novels of the 20th Century" (http://www.ala.org/
     advocacy/banned/frequentlychallenged/challengedclassics/reasonsbanned). American Library Association, 29 March 2007. (Accessed 24
     April 2012)Document ID: a6b9d0cb-cf04-dcc4-e1b3-acda735f48bd

[11] *Flame into Being: The Life and Work of D. H. Lawrence* (Heinemann, London 1985) Anthony Burgess, p 205

[12] *A Clockwork Orange* (Penguin Modern Classics) (Paperback) by Anthony Burgess, Blake Morrison xxii

[13] http://www.youtube.com/watch?v=IuENhAm5Tks

Further reading

- *A Clockwork Orange: A Play With Music*. Century Hutchinson Ltd. (1987). An extract is quoted on several web
  sites: Anthony Burgess from A Clockwork Orange: A play with music (Century Hutchinson Ltd, 1987) (http://
  pers-www.wlv.ac.uk/~fa1871/burgess.html), anthony burgess on 'a clockwork orange' - page 2 (https://web.
  archive.org/web/20051215190843/http://pages.eidosnet.co.uk/johnnymoped/aclockworktestament/
  aclockworktestament_anthonyburgessonaclockworkorange_page2.html) at the Wayback Machine (archived
  December 15, 2005), A Clockwork Orange - From A Clockwork Orange: A Play With Music (http://kubricks0.
  tripod.com/burgesam.htm)

- Burgess, Anthony (1978). Clockwork Oranges. In *1985*. London: Hutchinson. ISBN 0-09-136080-3 (extracts
  quoted here (http://web.archive.org/web/20060207052552/http://pages.eidosnet.co.uk/johnnymoped/
  aclockworktestament/aclockworktestament_beingtheadventures_page1.html))

- Vidal, Gore (1988). "Why I Am Eight Years Younger Than Anthony Burgess". *At Home: Essays, 1982–1988*.
  New York: Random House. p. 411. ISBN 0-394-57020-0.

- Tuck, Donald H. (1974). *The Encyclopedia of Science Fiction and Fantasy*. Chicago: Advent. p. 72.
  ISBN 0-911682-20-1.

External links

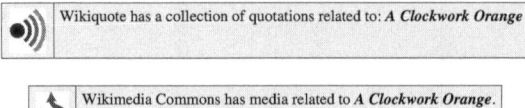

Wikiquote has a collection of quotations related to: *A Clockwork Orange*

Wikimedia Commons has media related to *A Clockwork Orange*.

- *A Clockwork Orange* (http://www.isfdb.org/cgi-bin/title.cgi?12305) title listing at the Internet Speculative
  Fiction Database
- *A Clockwork Orange* (http://www.sparknotes.com/lit/clockworkorange/) at SparkNotes
- *A Clockwork Orange* (http://literapedia.wikispaces.com/A+Clockwork+Orange) at Literapedia (http://
  literapedia.wikispaces.com/)

- *A Clockwork Orange* (1962) I Last chapter I Anthony Burgess (1917-1993) (http://chabrieres.pagesperso-orange. fr/texts/clockwork_orange.html)

Comparisons with the Kubrick film adaptation

- Dalrymple, Theodore. "A Prophetic and Violent Masterpiece" (http://www.city-journal.org/html/ 16_1_oh_to_be.html), *City Journal*
- Giola, Ted. "*A Clockwork Orange* by Anthony Burgess" (http://www.conceptualfiction.com/ a_clockwork_orange.html) at Conceptual Fiction (http://www.conceptualfiction.com/)
- Priestley, Brenton. "Of Clockwork Apples and Oranges: Burgess and Kubrick (2002)" (http://www. brentonpriestley.com/writing/clockwork_orange.htm)

American Cinematheque

The **American Cinematheque** is an independent, non-profit cultural organization in Los Angeles dedicated exclusively to the public presentation of the *Moving Image* in all its forms. It is considered among the premier organizations of its kind in America.

The Cinematheque was created in 1981 as an offshoot of the annual Filmex Los Angeles Film Festival which ran every year 1971–1983. After five years of fund-raising and planning, the Cinematheque launched its first series of screenings in 1987. It presents festivals and retrospectives that screen the best of worldwide cinema, video and television from the past and present - ranging from the classics to the outer frontiers of the art form. In addition to presenting and celebrating all aspects of the Moving Picture on the big screen - the Cinematheque also provides a forum where film-lovers and students can hear the world's leading filmmakers, actors, writers, editors, cinematographers and others discussing their work and craft.

The Cinematheque's two movie theatres

Between 1987 and 1998, the Cinematheque presented its programs at a variety of venues including the Directors Guild of America theater and the Raleigh Studios complex in Hollywood. In 1998 it opened its own permanent home in Hollywood - and in 2004 added a second theater in Santa Monica. It now presents festivals, retrospectives and assorted programs at these two theaters.

Grauman's Egyptian Theatre is the fabled Hollywood movie palace built in 1922 by legendary showman Sid Grauman (four years prior to opening his equally famous Chinese Theatre.) It was the location of Hollywood's first-ever movie premiere in 1922. In 1998 the American Cinematheque completed a major $12.8 million renovation that restored the theatre's exterior to its original glory - and added new film, video and audio technology. The Cinematheque has been presenting its programs there since December 1998.

Since its re-opening it has become a frequent choice for premieres and events in Hollywood. And it is the primary home for the Cinematheque's acclaimed year-round program of film, video & television festivals and retrospectives.

The Aero Theatre in Santa Monica is a 1940 landmark movie theatre that has also been renovated by the Cinametheque and it has been functioning as the organization's second theater, serving the Westside of Los Angeles, since 2004.

Programming

Among the Cinematheque's many recurrent annual festivals it has become well known for presenting the *Mods & Rockers Festival* [1] of rock-culture films first presented in 1999. The 2006 festival was a six-week retrospective that the *Los Angeles Times* noted was the largest-ever festival of rock-music films presented in the USA.

In addition to its year-round programs of film festivals and retrospectives, the organization presents the prestigious *American Cinematheque Award* annually to a filmmaker in recognition of contributions to the art form. In the 20 years since the award's inception many major filmmakers have been honored including directors such as Steven Spielberg, Martin Scorsese, Ron Howard, and Rob Reiner and actors including Sean Connery, John Travolta, Tom Cruise, Arnold Schwarzenegger, Mel Gibson, Bruce Willis, Nicolas Cage, Steve Martin, Al Pacino, George Clooney, Samuel L. Jackson, Denzel Washington, Jodie Foster, Nicole Kidman, and Julia Roberts. In recent years the gala evening presentations have been videotaped and aired as TV specials in the US by the TNT and AMC cable television networks and in 2010 (Matt Damon) by ABC.

Since 1994 the television special has been produced by Paul Flattery and the directors have included Spike Jonze Jr., Bruce Gowers, and Michael Dempsey.

American Cinematheque's distribution arm was set up in 1999, as Vitagraph Films.

Participation by industry leaders

The organization is governed by a Board Of Directors and a Board of Trustees. The two Boards include many prominent leaders in the entertainment industry including film directors and producers such as Sydney Pollack, Martin Scorsese, Mike Nichols, Francis Coppola, William Friedkin, Melvin Van Peebles, Brian Grazer, Joe Dante, Paula Wagner, and Steve Tisch. Other prominent Board members include: actors Candice Bergen and Goldie Hawn; studio chief Mike Medavoy; journalist Peter Bart (editor-in-chief of Variety); and talent agent Rick Nicita (Co-Chairman of Creative Artists Agency).

External links

- Official American Cinematheque website [2]

References

[1] http://www.modsandrockers.com/
[2] http://www.americancinematheque.com/

Summer Wine

For the sitcom, see Last of the Summer Wine.

"**Summer Wine**" is a song written by Lee Hazlewood. It was originally sung by Suzi Jane Hokom and Lee Hazlewood in 1966, but it was made famous by Nancy Sinatra and Lee Hazlewood in 1967. This version was originally released as the B-side of "Sugar Town" the previous year, before featuring on the Nancy & Lee LP in 1968. It was the first of Sinatra and Hazlewood's string of popular duets.

Lyrically, "Summer Wine" describes a man, voiced by Hazlewood, who meets a woman, Sinatra, who notices his silver spurs and invites him to have wine with her. After heavy drinking, the man awakens hungover to find his spurs and money have been stolen by the mysterious woman; the subtext of which being they experienced intercourse and as repayment she misappropriated his "silver spurs a dollar and a dime". He then declares a longing for more of her "wine". One interpretation, is that the man singing the song was seduced by the woman in order to steal his money and belongings. Another interpretation, sometimes cited, is that the song contains an allegorical description of drug use and that the lyric "she reassured me with an unfamiliar line" specifically refers to cocaine though that is anomalous for the apparent period setting. The song was used in the movie Stoker (film) and is also on the film soundtrack.

Covers

The song was later covered by Demis Roussos, Bono of U2 with The Corrs, Ultima Thule, Gry with FM Einheit and his Orchestra, Anna Hanski & Lee Hazlewood, Scooter (on the 2000 album *Sheffield*), Jack Grace, Moimir Papalescu and The Nihilists (with the male and female parts switched) and by Ville Valo & Natalia Avelon for the soundtrack of *Das Wilde Leben*. The version by Ville Valo & Natalia Avelon was the 4th best-selling single of 2007 in Germany[1] and was certified Platinum by the BVMI.

"Summer Wine" was also covered by Ed Kuepper and Clare Bowditch on the cult Australian music game show *Rockwiz*.[2]

A French cover called *Vin de l'été* was released by Marie Laforêt & Gérard Klein in 1969.Wikipedia:Citation needed

A Spanish cover called "Néctar de Verano" was released by Kela Gates -

A Dutch cover called *Toverdrank* (English: Potion) (on the album *Een man zoals ik* (English: A man like me)) was performed by Guido Belcanto and An Pierlé in 2011.

Two different German cover versions were released by Roland Kaiser (with Nancy Sinatra) in 1996 and by Claudia Jung & Nik P. in 2011.Wikipedia:Citation needed

Slovak cover called *Mladé víno* (Young wine) was released by Marcela Laiferová and Zdeno Sychra in 1967.Wikipedia:Citation needed

Also, Betty Chung covered it as 迷魂酒.

An Icelandic cover called *Sumarást* (Summer love) was released by Hljómsveit Ingimars Eydal in 1968 and by Helgi Björnsson og Ragnhildur Steinunn Jónsdóttir in 2007 for the movie Astrópía.Wikipedia:Citation needed

On April 18, 2013, Lana Del Rey released a music video for her and Barrie-James O'Neill's (from Kassidy) cover of "Summer Wine" by Lee Hazlewood.

References

[1] http://www.mtv.de/charts/Single_Jahrescharts_2007

[2] Rockwiz (http://www20.sbs.com.au/rockwiz)

Maleficent (film)

Maleficent	
Theatrical release poster	
Directed by	Robert Stromberg
Produced by	Joe Roth
Screenplay by	Linda Woolverton
Based on	• Disney's *Sleeping Beauty* • *La Belle au bois dormant* by Charles Perrault
Starring	• Angelina Jolie • Sharlto Copley • Elle Fanning • Sam Riley • Imelda Staunton • Juno Temple • Lesley Manville
Narrated by	Janet McTeer
Music by	James Newton Howard
Cinematography	Dean Semler
Edited by	• Chris Lebenzon • Richard Pearson
Production company	• Walt Disney Pictures • Roth Films
Distributed by	Walt Disney Studios Motion Pictures
Release date(s)	• May 28, 2014 (United Kingdom) • May 30, 2014 (United States)
Running time	97 minutes
Country	• United States
Language	English
Budget	$180 million
Box office	$716,719,000

Maleficent (/məˈlɛfɪsənt/ or /məˈlɪfɪsənt/) is a 2014 American fantasy film directed by Robert Stromberg from a screenplay by Linda Woolverton. Starring Angelina Jolie as the eponymous Disney villainess character, the film is a live-action re-imagining of Walt Disney's 1959 animated film *Sleeping Beauty*, and portrays the story from the perspective of the antagonist, Maleficent.

Principal photography took place between June and October 2012. The film premiered at the El Capitan Theatre in Hollywood on May 28, 2014, and was released in the United Kingdom that same day. It was released by Walt Disney Pictures in the U.S. on May 30, 2014 in the Disney Digital 3D, RealD 3D, and IMAX 3D formats, as well as in conventional theaters. The film was met with mixed reviews from critics, but was a commercial success, having grossed over $716 million worldwide.

Plot

An elderly narrator tells the story of Maleficent, a very strong and powerful faerie living in the Moors, a magical realm bordering a human kingdom. As a young girl, she falls in love with a human peasant boy named Stefan, but his mutual affection for Maleficent is overshadowed by his ambition to become king. As they grow older, Stefan stops seeing Maleficent. After Maleficent defeats the current king in battle when he attempts to invade the Moors, he offers to name whoever kills her as his successor. Stefan overhears this, goes to see Maleficent and deceives her into thinking that he has come to warn her of the king's plot. He drugs her and attempts to kill her but cannot bring himself to do so. Instead, he burns her wings off with iron, a lethal substance to faeries, and presents them to the king as proof of her death. Maleficent rescues a raven named Diaval to serve as her informant and he reports to her that Stefan has been crowned king. The realization that Stefan betrayed her to gain the throne devastates Maleficent and in retaliation, she declares herself queen of the Moors, forming a dark oppressive kingdom with Diaval as her one companion and confidant.

Some time later, Diaval informs Maleficent that King Stefan is hosting a christening for his newborn daughter, Aurora. Bent on revenge, Maleficent arrives uninvited and curses the newborn princess: on her sixteenth birthday, she will prick her finger on the spindle of a spinning wheel, which will cause her to fall into a death-like sleep. After Stefan is forced by Maleficent to beg for his daughter, she offers a caveat: the curse can be broken by true love's kiss. Terrified of Maleficent's vengeance, Stefan sends Aurora to live with three pixies until the day after her sixteenth birthday, while he destroys and burns all the spinning wheels in the kingdom and hides them in the deepest dungeon in the castle. He sends out his armies to find and kill Maleficent, but she surrounds her kingdom with an impenetrable shield of thorns.

Despite her initial dislike for Princess Aurora, Maleficent begins to care about the girl when the neglectful pixies fail to do so. After a brief meeting with the young Aurora, Maleficent watches over her from afar. When Aurora is 15, she meets Maleficent for the first time and calls her her "faerie godmother", as she recalled being watched over by her all her life. Realizing she has grown fond of the princess, Maleficent attempts to revoke the curse, but cannot as she herself had declared that "no power on Earth can change it". Aurora later meets Prince Phillip, and the two are intrigued by one another but have little opportunity to build a relationship. On the day before Aurora's 16th birthday, Maleficent, hoping to avoid the curse, allows the girl to move to the Moors, far away from any spindles. The pixies, however, inadvertently tell Aurora as she's moving out of her parentage and of Maleficent's true identity, and a furious Aurora runs away to her father.

Stefan brusquely locks Aurora away for safekeeping. She is drawn by the curse itself to the dungeon, where it assembles a spinning wheel. Aurora pricks her finger and falls asleep. Intent on saving her, Maleficent abducts Phillip and infiltrates Stefan's castle to have him kiss Aurora and break the curse. However, Phillip's romantic kiss has no effect, as the two are not truly in love. Maleficent apologizes to Aurora and swears no harm will come to her, kissing her forehead. This causes Aurora to awaken. Maleficent's curse has been broken as her motherly concern for Aurora constitutes "true love." Aurora forgives her and they attempt to flee the castle, but Maleficent is trapped in an iron net and attacked by Stefan and his guards. Maleficent transforms Diaval into a dragon and he lifts the net off her, but is driven back by the soldiers. Stefan beats Maleficent and taunts her, but before he can kill her, her wings, freed from his chamber by Aurora, fly back to her and reattach themselves. Maleficent overpowers Stefan, but cannot bring herself to kill him, instead declaring their feud over. Stefan attempts once more to kill her, but plummets to his death. Aurora is crowned queen of the human and faerie realms by Maleficent, unifying forever the two kingdoms with Phillip at her side. The narrator then reveals her own identity as "the one they called the Sleeping Beauty".

Cast

Angelina Jolie, Sharlto Copley and Sam Riley

- Angelina Jolie as Maleficent, the queen fairy of the Moors who casts a death-like sleep curse on Princess Aurora
  - Ella Purnell and Isobelle Molloy as young Maleficent
- Elle Fanning as Princess Aurora, daughter of King Stefan and princess of the human kingdom
  - Vivienne Jolie-Pitt and Eleanor Worthington Cox as young Princess Aurora
  - Janet McTeer as elderly Aurora (the film's narrator)
- Sharlto Copley as King Stefan, ruler of the human kingdom and Aurora's father
  - Michael Higgins as young Stefan
- Sam Riley as Diaval, a raven shapeshifter and Maleficent's confidant.
- Imelda Staunton as Knotgrass, a pink pixie charged with raising Aurora in secret until her 16th birthday.
- Juno Temple as Thistlewit, a green pixie charged with raising Aurora in secret until her 16th birthday.
- Lesley Manville as Flittle, a blue pixie charged with raising Aurora in secret until her 16th birthday.
- Brenton Thwaites as Phillip, a young prince who falls in love with Aurora while traveling through the forest.
- Kenneth Cranham as King Henry, a monarch determined to conquer the forest realm.
- Hannah New as Queen Leila, King Henry's daughter who marries Stefan and Aurora's mother.

Production

Angelina Jolie had long been attached to the project since May 2011, when Tim Burton, who had tentatively planned to direct, chose not to pursue it. Linda Woolverton was commissioned to write the script for the film. On January 6, 2012, Disney announced that Robert Stromberg, the production designer of *Alice in Wonderland*, and *Oz the Great and Powerful*, would direct the film. Joe Roth, Don Hahn, and Richard D. Zanuck were hired as producers, although Zanuck died later that year. Roth said the film would not have been made if Angelina Jolie had not agreed to take the title role: "She seemed like the only person who could play the part. There was no point in making the movie if it wasn't her."

In March 2012, Elle Fanning was reported to be in talks for the role of Princess Aurora. Her casting was officially announced in May 2012, along with Sharlto Copley as the male lead, Stefan, then described as the half-human, half-fairy son of a human king, along with Imelda Staunton; Miranda Richardson as Queen Ulla, then described as a fairy queen who is Maleficent's aunt with a dislike of her niece; Kenneth Cranham as a king; Sam Riley as Diaval, a raven who changes into human form and is Maleficent's right hand; and Lesley Manville.

Writing

"I was really moved by the script from first reading. It was like uncovering a great mystery. We all know the story of *Sleeping Beauty* and we all know Maleficent and what happened at the christening because we've all grown up with that. But what we've never known is, what happened before?"

—Angelina Jolie

Linda Woolverton's screenplay went through at least 15 versions as the film progressed in the production. Director Robert Stromberg said: "I met many times with Linda Woolverton, the writer. We did lots of roundtable discussions and sort of cut out the fat as much as we could and sort of purified the storyline as much as we could (...)" In some earlier versions of the story, Stefan was the half-human, half-fairy bastard son of King Henry. The version of the screenplay which went into shooting originally included two characters called Queen Ulla and King Kinloch, the fairy queen and the fairy king of the Moors, and the aunt and uncle of Maleficent. Miranda Richardson and Peter Capaldi were cast and shot the Queen Ulla and King Kinloch scenes, but they were cut in the editing process together with more than 15 minutes of the first act of the film. Stromberg said: "We spent a bit more time originally in the fairy world before we got into the human side of things (...) we wanted to get it [the film] under two hours. So we cut about fifteen minutes out of the first act, and then that had to be seamed together with some pretty basic reshoots."

Filming

With a budget estimated at $130–200 million, principal photography began on June 18, 2012 in London with the first pictures from set emerging and the first official look of Jolie as Maleficent. Rick Baker designed the special makeup effects for the film. Post-production began on October 5, 2012. Some filming took place in the Buckinghamshire countryside.

Re-shoots

John Lee Hancock assisted Stromberg with re-shoots for the film. Hancock, who had just finished overseeing the final post-production stages of *Saving Mr. Banks*, was approached by Roth, with whom both had worked on *Snow White and the Huntsman*. Roth said: "He's not directing. He wrote pages, and I hired a first-time director, and it's good to have him on set." Roth was asked why a "film of this magnitude was entrusted to a novice director", and he noted that Stromberg won Academy Awards for production design on *Avatar* and *Alice in Wonderland*. Roth said: "The movie is gorgeous to look at, and the last 75 minutes are really entertaining. The issue is the opening, which is being re-shot over eight days."

Music

James Newton Howard was hired to score the film in October 2012. On January 23, 2014, it was announced that recording artist Lana Del Rey would be covering the song "Once Upon a Dream", from the 1959 film *Sleeping Beauty* as the title song for *Maleficent*. Del Rey was handpicked by Angelina Jolie to perform the song. The single was released on January 26 and was made available for free for a limited time through Google Play.

Maleficent (Original Motion Picture Soundtrack)	
Film score by James Newton Howard	
Released	May 27, 2014
Recorded	Abbey Road Studios
Genre	Orchestral
Length	1:11:46
Label	Walt Disney

Professional ratings	
Review scores	
Source	Rating

All music composed by James Newton Howard (Tracks 1–22).

Maleficent (Original Motion Picture Soundtrack)

No.	Title	Writer(s)	Performer(s)	Length
1.	"*Maleficent* Suite"			6:38
2.	"Welcome to the Moors"			1:05
3.	"Maleficent Flies"			4:39
4.	"Battle of the Moors"			4:58
5.	"Three Peasant Women"			1:04
6.	"Go Away"			2:26
7.	"Aurora and the Fawn"			2:28
8.	"The Christening"			5:30
9.	"Prince Philip"			2:29
10.	"The Spindle's Power"			4:35
11.	"You Could Live Here Now"			2:26
12.	"Path of Destruction"			1:47
13.	"Aurora in Faerieland"			4:41
14.	"The Wall Defends Itself"			1:06
15.	"The Curse Won't Reverse"			1:21
16.	"Are You Maleficent?"			2:10
17.	"The Army Dances"			1:28
18.	"Phillip's Kiss"			2:20
19.	"The Iron Gauntlet"			1:35
20.	"True Love's Kiss"			2:33
21.	"Maleficent Is Captured"			7:42
22.	"The Queen of Faerieland"			3:25

| 23. | "Once Upon a Dream" | Jack Lawrence, Sammy Fain | Lana Del Rey | 3:20 |
| **Total length:** | | | | **1:11:46** |

Release

The film was originally slated for a March 2014 release, before it was changed to July 2, 2014. On September 18, 2013, the film's release date was bumped up from July 2, 2014 to May 30, due to Pixar's *The Good Dinosaur* having production problems and delays. In the UK, the film was released on May 28.

Marketing

On August 10, 2013, as part of the live action motion picture panel of the 2013 Disney D23 Expo in the Anaheim Convention Center at Anaheim, California, Disney unveiled its first look of *Maleficent* by revealing the new logo of the film's title and one-minute clip from the film. Angelina Jolie made a surprise visit to the expo and talked with the attendees about her fascination with Disney's *Sleeping Beauty* as a child, her working experience with the filmmakers on the film, and her love of Disney. She also remarked on how she scared little girls when she was in costume, makeup, and acting during shooting; this led to the decision of hiring her and Brad Pitt's daughter, Vivienne Jolie-Pitt, for the role of the young Princess Aurora, since she would not be scared of her own mother during principal photography.

Walt Disney Pictures released the teaser poster for *Maleficent* on November 12, 2013, featuring Jolie in costume and makeup, akin to the character's depiction in the original film. The first trailer was released the following day, on November 13. The first teaser trailer was attached to *Thor: The Dark World*, *The Hunger Games: Catching Fire*, *Frozen*, and *Vampire Academy: Blood Sisters*. Two more trailers were released in January 2014, revealing Maleficent's appearance. A third trailer featured Lana Del Rey singing "Once Upon a Dream". The final trailer was released on March 18, 2014. Starting April 18, 2014, Disney's Hollywood Studios and Disney California Adventure previewed the film inside the ABC Sound Studio and *It's Tough to Be a Bug!* theaters, respectively. *Disney Infinity 2.0* will feature Maleficent as a playable figure utilizing the look from the movie.

Home media

Maleficent is expected to be released by Walt Disney Studios Home Entertainment on DVD and Blu-ray November 4, 2014.

Reception

Box office

Maleficent has earned $233,468,131 in North America as of July 31, 2014, and an estimated $482,900,000 in other countries, for a worldwide total of $716,368,131. Worldwide, in its opening weekend, the film earned $175.5 million, $9 million of which was from IMAX locations. It is also the biggest debut among films starring Angelina Jolie, and the actress' highest grossing film of all-time worldwide, as well as the third highest-grossing 2014 film (behind *Transformers: Age of Extinction* and *X-Men: Days of Future Past*), and the 15th film distributed by Disney to surpass the $700 million mark at the worldwide box office.

North America

In North America, *Maleficent* earned $4.2 million in Thursday night showings, surpassing the midnight or late-night grosses of previous live-action fantasy films, *Alice in Wonderland*, *Oz the Great and Powerful* and *Snow White and the Huntsman*. By the end of its opening day (including late-night Thursday earnings), the film earned $24.3 million, similar to *Oz*, but ahead of *Snow White and the Huntsman* and behind *Alice*. *Maleficent* finished its debut weekend at first place with $69.4 million ($6.7 million of which was earned from IMAX locations and 35% of which was earned from 3D showings), which exceeded Disney's expectations of a $60 million opening and making it the largest opening weekend performance for Jolie (a record previously held by her 2008 film *Wanted*), as well as the third highest opening weekend for a solo female star (behind the first two films in *The Hunger Games* series). Disney reported that 46% of ticket buyers in Thursday previews were male, while weekend reports said family audiences accounted for 45% of the film's total audience, and couples and teens accounted for 38% and 18% respectively. Female audiences and moviegoers over 25 years old held respective proportions of 60% and 51%. Dave Hollis, head of Walt Disney Studios Motion Pictures, attributed this success to "some momentum and great word-of-mouth." During its first week, the film earned a total of $93.8 million, ahead of *Snow White* yet behind *Oz* and *Alice*. On its second weekend, *Maleficent* dropped by 50% to $34.3 million, finishing in second place. It experienced a smaller second-weekend drop than *Snow White*, yet still bigger than *Oz* and *Alice*. In North America, *Maleficent* is the fourth highest-grossing 2014 film.

Outside North America

Maleficent opened outside North America on the same weekend as North America, earning $20.1 million from 35 territories in its first two days (May 28–29, 2014). During its opening weekend, the film topped the box office with $106.1 million from 47 territories. Its largest opening weekends were in China ($22.2 million), Mexico ($14.0 million) and Russia and the CIS ($13.0 million). On the second weekend of release, *Maleficent* fell to $61.7 million, earning from 52 markets. It was in first place at the box office outside North America on three weekends, its first, third ($39.2 million) and fourth ($47.9 million).

Maleficent is the fifth highest-grossing 2014 film, and Angelina Jolie's highest-grossing live-action film. In total earnings, the film's top markets after North America are China ($46.5 million), Mexico ($45.3 million), Russia ($37.1 million), Brazil ($31.3 million), the United Kingdom ($30.3 million), Japan ($29.5 million) and Italy ($18.2 million).

Commercial analysis

Dave Lewis, writing for HitFix, predicted that although Disney fairy tales and Angelina Jolie's performance might attract audiences, *Maleficent* would not gross even as much as *Oz the Great and Powerful*, explaining that the film was released on the same time frame with competitive releases like *X-Men: Days of Future Past*, *Godzilla* and *A Million Ways to Die in the West*. Boxoffice wrote that *Maleficent* had a successful marketing campaign, featured Jolie in the title role, and its "female-driven" themes and plot aimed at women. However, the site also noted that the film would have to compete with other summer releases, and the character of *Maleficent* may not attract young children. Todd Cunningham of *The Wrap* shared the same opinion, writing that "[the film's] connecting with parents and that Jolie's considerable star power is having a big impact." Wells Fargo's Marci Ryvicker predicted that *Maleficent* might be "too dark and scary to be profitable" and was likely to force Disney "into a write-down", as reported by *The New York Times*; while RBC Capital Markets' David Bank commented that "It's definitely in the 'not a sure thing' bucket." *Wall St. Cheat Sheet* explained that the film approached to a more "grown-up" and "sinister" aspect of the classic, and targeted for an older audience like young adults. "It's just too scary for younger children," the site wrote. *ScreenRant* added that the PG rating of the film would "fill a void in the marketplace, which is currently without a traditional "family friendly" option." Box Office Mojo primarily compared the film with 2012's *Snow White and the Huntsman* (another film that also focused on a villain), predicting that *Maleficent* "has a good chance" of matching *Snow White*'s gross in North America box office.

Variety wrote that the film's opening weekend outperforming initial box-office projections was later attributed by analysts in part to Disney's successful marketing to the "potent demographic" (female audiences) much like the studio accomplished with *Frozen*, in which both films feature a strong female lead. Disney argued that a lack of family-friendly options in the marketplace would "bode well for *Maleficent*'s [box office] performance" in its two first weeks of release.

Critical response

The film received mixed reviews from critics, who praised Angelina Jolie's performance and the visual effects, but criticized its plot. It currently holds a 49% rating on the review aggregator website Rotten Tomatoes based on 184 reviews, with an average score of 5.6/10. The site's consensus reads, "Angelina Jolie's magnetic performance outshines *Maleficent*'s dazzling special effects; unfortunately, the movie around them fails to justify all that impressive effort." However, the audience rating is a "fresh" 75%, with an average score of 3.9/5 based on 128,117 responses. On Metacritic, the film has a rating of 56 out of 100, based on 44 critics, indicating "mixed or average reviews", while the user score is 7.2, indicating generally favorable reviews. CinemaScore gave the film an "A" rating on an A+ to F scale, based on polls conducted among audiences on its opening Friday.

Kate Taylor of *The Globe and Mail* was very positive about the film, writing that "[it] surprises not for its baroque visions of a colourful woodland enlivened by joyous fairies and a forbidding castle peopled by unhappy humans, but rather for the thematic richness of its story gloriously personified by Angelina Jolie in the title role." While criticizing the overuse of CGI and 3D effects, she particularly praised the positive message of the film and Jolie's performance. She concluded her review that "Long live the feminist revisionist backstory." On the contrary, Keith Staskiewicz, writing for the *Entertainment Weekly*, awarded the film a "B-" and wrote that "there's a lot of levitating cliffs and odd flora. But despite their bleeding-edge digital design, the backgrounds have all the depth of the old matte-painted backgrounds of the analog days," which made the film "[feel] classical in nature." She further commented that "The characters are boiled down to their essentials, the humor is timelessly broad." Michael Philips of *Chicago Tribune* gave the film two and a half stars, commenting that the recent "formula" that "a new angle on a well-known fairy tale appears in the light" "works" with *Maleficent*. He also said that the film "is all about second thoughts", as Maleficent "spends much of the film as Aurora's conflicted fairy godmother." Phillips particularly praised Jolie and Elle Fanning's acting, Rick Baker's makeup (for Jolie's "angular, serrated look"), but criticized James Newton Howard's "sloshy, pushy" musical score.

Angelina Jolie's performance in the film has been repeatedly singled out for praise by critics. Robbie Collin of *The Telegraph* wrote, "This Disney reimagining of *Sleeping Beauty* lacks true enchantment, but Angelina Jolie saves the day." Betsy Sharkey of the *Los Angeles Times* gave the film a positive review, writing "This is Jolie's film because of the Maleficent she makes. Everyone else, even Aurora, fades in her presence." Ann Hornaday of *The Washington Post* awarded the film three-and-a-half out of four stars, commenting that "Still, for all its limitations, "*Maleficent*" manages to be improbably entertaining to watch, due solely to its title character." Writing for Roger Ebert's website, Matt Zoller Seitz awarded *Maleficent* three out of four stars, praising the themes of the film and the acting of Jolie. Seitz also called the scene in which Maleficent discovers the loss of her wings "the most traumatizing image I've seen in a Hollywood fairy tale since the Christ-like sacrifice of Aslan in 2005's *The Chronicles of Narnia: The Lion, the Witch and the Wardrobe*." The review on *The Globe and Mail* further explained that "in the simple context of a fairy tale, Jolie does make both the terrifying horned creature and her gradual awakening heartfelt," extolling the "emotional richness" behind her physical acts. Richard Roeper of the *Chicago Sun-Times* felt more negatively, assigning it a D. Although Roeper praised the visuals, he criticized the acting and writing, stating that "the story itself might well put you into the same type of coma that befalls the heroine."

Themes

Multiple reviewers and commentators have noted that an early scene in the movie, where King Stefan drugs Maleficent and removes her wings from her unconscious body, is a metaphor for rape. Hayley Krischner of *The Huffington Post* interpreted the scene as an important reference to rape culture: "This is the horrific side of rape culture. We're so enmeshed in it that it's impossible to ignore a metaphoric rape that occurs in a Disney movie". She went on to praise the film for giving a positive and hopeful message to rape victims, ultimately allowing "the woman to recover. It gives her agency. It gives her power. It allows her to reclaim the story". Monika Bartyzel of *The Week* noted the scene's implications in her review: "In its first act, *Maleficent* offers a dark, surprisingly adult exploration of rape and female mutilation". However, Bartyzel went onto to opine that the film portrayed Maleficent's actions as "a rape revenge fantasy" and criticized the film for not following through on its early subtext, ultimately calling it less feminist and reductive compared to its 1959 counterpart: "In *Maleficent*, Aurora is the product of a cold and loveless marriage and a vengeful, unhinged rapist. Her safety relies on a trio of clueless and dangerously careless fairies, and her Godmother is the woman who cursed her — and who had, in turn, been violated by her own father". Angelina Jolie addressed the issue during an interview with BBC Radio on the *Women's Hour* programme and claimed that the subtext was intentional: "The question was asked: 'What could make a woman become so dark and lose all sense of her maternity, her womanhood, and her softness?' [...] We were very conscious, the writer and I, that [the scene] was a metaphor for rape". She further explained that the answer to the question "What could bring her back?" was still "an extreme *Disney*, fun version [of the story]", but "at the core it is abuse, and how the abused then have a choice of abusing others or overcoming and remaining loving, open people".

Jordan Shapiro of *Forbes* argued that the film's main subtext was the detrimental effects of ultimatums between capitalist and socialist societies. He pointed out that the Moors represented a socialist, nature-oriented, democratic society while the human kingdom was one of capitalism, industry and monarchy. Shapiro further commented that the character of Stefan, his theft of the Moors' riches (the jewel) and his mutilation of Maleficent's wings for the sake of his ambition were references of the American Dream. He conceived the wing-tearing scene as "a social commentary that any hierarchical rise to power inherently happens through the exploitation of others", explaining that it was the reason why "without her wings, Maleficent also becomes an oppressive ruler of the Moors. Everything she represents, believes and stands for has been grounded", and "like most victims of oppression", "she takes it out on those who are smaller and weaker". He concluded that through the merge of the two kingdoms at the end of the film, it sought to weave together capitalism and socialism and let go oppositions: "It is time to leave the kingdom of familiar partisan oppositions: let's replace *either/or* with *neither/nor* or *both/and*".

References

External links

- Official website (http://movies.disney.com/maleficent)
- *Maleficent* (http://www.imdb.com/title/tt1587310/) at the Internet Movie Database
- *Maleficent* (http://www.allmovie.com/movie/v559330) at AllMovie
- *Maleficent* (http://tcmdb.com/title/title.jsp?stid=892171) at the TCM Movie Database
- *Maleficent* (http://www.boxofficemojo.com/movies/?id=maleficient.htm) at Box Office Mojo
- *Maleficent* (http://www.metacritic.com/movie/maleficent) at Metacritic
- *Maleficent* (http://www.rottentomatoes.com/m/maleficent_2014/) at Rotten Tomatoes

West Coast (song)

"West Coast"	
Single by Lana Del Rey	
from the album *Ultraviolence*	
Released	April 14, 2014
Format	• CD single • digital download
Recorded	Nashville, TennesseeWikipedia:Citation neededWikipedia:Manual of Style/Dates and numbers#Chronological items
Genre	• Soft rock
Length	• 4:16 (album version) • 3:47 (radio edit)
Label	• Polydor • Interscope
Writer(s)	• Lana Del Rey • Rick Nowels
Producer(s)	• Dan Auerbach (album version) • Rick Nowels (radio edit)
Lana Del Rey singles chronology	
• "Once Upon a Dream" • "**West Coast**" • "Shades of Cool" • (2014) • (2014) • (2014)	

"**West Coast**" is a song by American singer-songwriter Lana Del Rey from her third studio album *Ultraviolence* (2014). It was released on April 14, 2014 by Interscope Records and Polydor Records as the lead single from the record. Del Rey collaborated with Rick Nowels during the songwriting process, while Dan Auerbach was enlisted to oversee its production.

Contemporary music critics commended "West Coast" in their reviews of the track; they expressed a particular appreciation for its unique production by comparison with songs from her major-label debut record *Born to Die* (2012), her follow-up extended play *Paradise* (2012), and mainstream radio stations in general. It debuted at number 17 on the U.S. *Billboard* Hot 100, and charted in the upper registers of several international record charts. Del Rey performed "West Coast" during the Coachella Valley Music and Arts Festival on April 13, while an accompanying music video directed by Vincent Haycock was premiered on May 7.

Background and composition

On April 3, 2014, Del Rey announced that the "West Coast" would be the lead single from *Ultraviolence*. Del Rey revealed the official single cover on April 10. Fearne Cotton played the song on her BBC Radio 1 show on April 14, 2014. On the same day the song was uploaded to her YouTube Vevo channel as an audio clip, featuring herself and Bradley Soileau on a beach, with the clip playing in a loop.

	"West Coast"
	"The tempo [of the song] shifts frequently, the instrumentation is jagged, and Lana's voice skips between breathy franticness and slurred, drugged-out ecstasy."

Problems playing this file? See media help.

"West Coast" is a ballad with an approximate length of four minutes and seventeen seconds. The song frequently shifts between a mid-tempo pop and soft rock verse and a surf rock slow-tempo chorus. Musically, its composition is built around reggae drum fills, blues-influenced guitar riffs, and draws influences from indie rock music. It was co-written by Del Rey with Rick Nowels, while production was handled by Dan Auerbach.

Vulture writer Lindsey Weber cited "West Coast" to be a mix of Stevie Nicks' 1982 song "Edge of Seventeen" with an outtake from a Quentin Tarantino film soundtrack. According to Harriet Gibsone of *The Guardian*, the song "oozes" with the "sultry sounds" and textures of "80s drive time".

Music video

On April 4, 2014, pictures surfaced of Del Rey shooting a music video in Los Angeles. She was on set with "Born to Die" and "Blue Jeans" star Bradley Soileau. On May 1, 2014, Del Rey posted a preview of the video on Instagram. On May 6, 2014, an unfinished version of the music video for "West Coast" was uploaded and taken down by Del Rey's label. The next day, the finished video was published. Jenn Pelly and Evan Minsker of Pitchfork Media remarked that at first, it "appears to function in small, romantic gestures—hanging near an ocean, smoking in the back of a car, much like a fashion ad in a magazine. And then, plot twist: It's Lana in flames."

The video opens with shots of the ocean and driving in LA intercut with scenes of Del Rey and Soileau walking down a beach with friends. Del Rey starts singing as more images of LA are shown. As the chorus comes in, scenes of Del Rey and Soileau playing in the ocean fade into Del Rey in a car with tattoo artist Mark Mahoney. The shot is more glamorous and withheld, he lights her cigarette and Del Rey leans her head on his shoulder. He whispers something in her ear before the second verse where the film returns to Del Rey and Soileau on the beach in a much more casual setting. For the second chorus the scenes of Del Rey in the car with Mahoney return until a shot of Del Rey in flames appears. While in flames she wears either a red dress and or a leather jacket.

Critical reception

The song has received universal acclaim from music critics, who commended its "atmospheric" and "hypnotic" production, as well as its maturity. Spin's Marc Hogan commented positively on the song, calling it "atmospheric". entertainmentwise lauded the track, calling it "stunning". *CultNoise* called the song a "vintage classic; soft around the edges, heartbreakingly beautiful and exquisitely composed" and awarded it a 9/10. MUUMUSE described the song as "revolutionary" and " entirely different from anything that's being offered in pop music at the moment", awarding it 5/5. A *Billboard* staff writer wrote that while it was less "moody" than her previous work, "West Coast" sounds "decidedly like Del Rey – airy vocals drenched in reverb and other effects plus a chorus/breakdown that shows off her vulnerability." Writing for VH1's website, Meghan O'Keefe wrote before asking readers their thoughts on the single, "Del Rey's newest single, "West Coast," boasts the singer's trademark combination of wistfully romantic lyrics and hypnotic beats, but it also signals a step forward."

MTV's Brenna Ehrlich wrote that "West Coast" is, "[a] dark, whisper-y jam, "West Coast" finds Del Rey as a more mature version of her "Lolita lost in the hood" persona", and that it "hints at a more subdued, rich side to Lana Del Rey's work". At *Rolling Stone*, Kory Grow writes, "Lana Del Rey shows off two different, moody sides of herself in "West Coast." Nolan Feeney at the *Time* wrote that the song has all the makings of her signature sound — plus a few new tricks. He added, "It's only right that during the most important music event on the West Coast — the Coachella music festival — pop music's endlessly polarizing flower child Lana Del Rey debuted a new song inspired by that very place." NME's Al Horner described the song as "a breathy, hip-moving blues grind", comparing it to the music of Stevie Nicks. He went on to say that "If 'West Coast' is anything to go on, 'Ultraviolence' should prove worth the wait". *The Guardian* said the song "oozes with the sultry sounds and textures of 80s drive time, based around a solitary guitar and anxiously breathy vocals". At the *Los Angeles Times*, Mikael Wood noted, "Lana Del Rey connects despite revealing little". He drew comparison stating, "it's a characteristically bleary number that sounds like Stevie Nicks' "Edge of Seventeen" slowed down to a narcotized crawl; there's a bit of "Wicked Game" by Chris Isaak in there too, as, indeed, there is in all of Del Rey's music."

Live performances

Del Rey premiered "West Coast" as part of her set at the Coachella music festival on April 13, 2014. According to Jason Lipshutz of *Billboard*, Del Rey's performance up until the point of premiering the song was "so strong" that she would have been forgiven if the song was a "dud". He concluded that thankfully the song "sounded like a winner when played live for the first time".

Track listing

- **UK Promo CD**[1]

1. "West Coast (Radio Edit)" – 3:44
2. "West Coast (Original)" – 4:15
3. "West Coast (Instrumental)" – 4:15

Credits and personnel

Credits adapted from the liner notes of *Ultraviolence*.

Performance credits

- Lana Del Rey - vocals, background vocals

Instruments

- Dan Auerbach - electric guitar, shaker, 12-string acoustic guitar, synthesizer
- Nick Movshon - bass guitar, drums
- Maximilian Weissenfeldt - drums

Technical and production

- Dan Auerbach - production
- John Davis - mastering
- Collin Dupuis - engineering

Charts

Chart (2014)	Peak position
Australia (ARIA)[2]	44
Belgium (Ultratip Flanders)[3]	4
Belgium (Ultratop 50 Wallonia)[4]	47
Canada (Canadian Hot 100)[5]	26
Denmark (Tracklisten)[6]	39
Finland (Suomen virallinen latauslista)[7]	21
France (SNEP)[8]	34
Germany (Media Control Charts)[9]	22
Greece Digital Songs (*Billboard*)	3
Hungary (Single Top 20)[10]	13
Ireland (IRMA)[11]	31
Israel (Media Forest)[12]	8
Italy (FIMI)	18
New Zealand (Recorded Music NZ)[13]	31
Portugal Digital Songs (*Billboard*)	39
Russian Digital Songs (*Lenta*)	1
Scotland (Official Charts Company)[14]	18
Spain (PROMUSICAE)[15]	12
Switzerland (Schweizer Hitparade)[16]	13
UK Singles (Official Charts Company)[17]	21
US *Billboard* Hot 100[18]	17
US Rock Airplay (*Billboard*)[19]	31
US Adult Alternative Songs (*Billboard*)[20]	8
US Alternative Songs (*Billboard*)[21]	29

Release history

West Coast (song) 104

Country	Date	Format	Label
Poland	April 14, 2014	Contemporary hit radio	Universal
Italy			
Canada	April 22, 2014	Digital download	
United States			Interscope
Belgium	April 23, 2014		Universal
France			
Finland			
Luxembourg			
New Zealand			
Netherlands			
Portugal			
Spain			
Sweden			
United Kingdom	May 25, 2014		Polydor
Germany	May 30, 2014		Vertigo / Capitol
United States	June 3, 2014	Modern rock radio	Interscope

References

[1] Lana Del Rey - West Coast (CDr) at Discogs (http://www.discogs.com/Lana-Del-Rey-West-Coast/release/5683968)
[2] " Australian-charts.com – Lana Del Rey – West Coast" (http://www.australian-charts.com/showitem.asp?interpret=Lana+Del+Rey& titel=West+Coast&cat=s). ARIA Top 50 Singles. Retrieved April 21, 2014.
[3] " Ultratop.be – Lana Del Rey – West Coast" (http://www.ultratop.be/nl/showitem.asp?interpret=Lana+Del+Rey&titel=West+Coast& cat=s) (in Dutch). Ultratip. Retrieved April 21, 2014.
[4] " Ultratop.be – Lana Del Rey – West Coast" (http://www.ultratop.be/fr/showitem.asp?interpret=Lana+Del+Rey&titel=West+Coast& cat=s) (in French). Ultratop 50. Retrieved April 21, 2014.
[5] " Lana Del Rey Album & Song Chart History" (http://www.billboard.com/artist/306420/Lana+Del+Rey/chart?f=793) Canadian Hot 100 for Lana Del Rey. Retrieved April 18, 2014.
[6] " Danishcharts.com – Lana Del Rey – West Coast" (http://www.danishcharts.com/showitem.asp?interpret=Lana+Del+Rey& titel=West+Coast&cat=s). Tracklisten. Retrieved April 25, 2014.
[7] " Lana Del Rey: West Coast" (http://www.ifpi.fi/tilastot/virallinen-lista/artistit/Lana+Del+Rey/West+Coast) (in Finnish). Musiikkituottajat – IFPI Finland. Retrieved April 22, 2014.
[8] " Lescharts.com – Lana Del Rey – West Coast" (http://www.lescharts.com/showitem.asp?interpret=Lana+Del+Rey&titel=West+ Coast&cat=s) (in French). Les classement single. Retrieved April 26, 2014.
[9] " Die ganze Musik im Internet: Charts, News, Neuerscheinungen, Tickets, Genres, Genresuche, Genrelexikon, Künstler-Suche, Musik-Suche, Track-Suche, Ticket-Suche – musicline.de" (http://musicline.de/de/chartverfolgung_summary/title/Lana+Del+Rey/West+Coast/single) (in German). Media Control Charts. PhonoNet GmbH. Retrieved June 4, 2014.
[10] " Archívum – Slágerlisták – MAHASZ – Magyar Hanglemezkiadók Szövetsége" (http://www.mahasz.hu/?menu=slagerlistak& menu2=archivum&lista=kislemez&ev=2014&het=23&submit_=Keresés) (in Hungarian). Single (track) Top 10 lista. Magyar Hanglemezkiadók Szövetsége. Retrieved June 12, 2014.
[11] " Chart Track" (http://www.chart-track.co.uk/index.jsp?c=p/musicvideo/music/archive/index_test.jsp&ct=240001&arch=t& lyr=2014&year=2014&week=16). Irish Singles Chart. Retrieved April 18, 2014.
[12] " {{{artist}}} – {{{song}}} Media Forest (http://www.mediaforest.biz/WeeklyCharts/HistoryWeeklyCharts.aspx?year=2014& week=25)". Israeli Airplay Chart. Media Forest. Retrieved July 11, 2014.
[13] " Charts.org.nz – Lana Del Rey – West Coast" (http://www.charts.org.nz/showitem.asp?interpret=Lana+Del+Rey&titel=West+ Coast&cat=s). Top 40 Singles. Retrieved April 25, 2014.
[14] " Archive Chart" (http://www.theofficialcharts.com/archive-chart/_/22/2014-06-07/). Scottish Singles Top 40. Retrieved July 3, 2014.

[15] " Spanishcharts.com – Lana Del Rey – West Coast" (http://www.spanishcharts.com/showitem.asp?interpret=Lana+Del+Rey& titel=West+Coast&cat=s) Canciones Top 50. Retrieved April 28, 2014.

[16] " Lana Del Rey – West Coast – swisscharts.com" (http://www.swisscharts.com/showitem.asp?interpret=Lana+Del+Rey&titel=West+ Coast&cat=s). Swiss Singles Chart. Retrieved June 8, 2014.

[17] " Archive Chart" (http://www.theofficialcharts.com/archive-chart/_/1/2014-06-07/) UK Singles Chart. Retrieved July 3, 2014.

[18] " Lana Del Rey Album & Song Chart History" (http://www.billboard.com/artist/306420/Lana+Del+Rey/chart?f=379) *Billboard* Hot 100 for Lana Del Rey. Retrieved April 18, 2014.

[19] " Lana Del Rey Album & Song Chart History" (http://www.billboard.com/artist/306420/Lana+Del+Rey/chart?f=1228) *Billboard* Rock Airplay for Lana Del Rey. Retrieved July 3, 2014.

[20] " Lana Del Rey Album & Song Chart History" (http://www.billboard.com/artist/306420/Lana+Del+Rey/chart?f=851) *Billboard* Adult Alternative Songs for Lana Del Rey. Retrieved July 3, 2014.

[21] " Lana Del Rey Album & Song Chart History" (http://www.billboard.com/artist/306420/Lana+Del+Rey/chart?f=377) *Billboard* Alternative Songs for Lana Del Rey. Retrieved July 10, 2014.

External links

- Official music video (https://www.youtube.com/watch?v=oKxuiw3iMBE) on YouTube

Shades of Cool

"Shades of Cool"	
Single by Lana Del Rey	
from the album *Ultraviolence*	
Released	May 26, 2014
Format	Digital download
Length	5:42
Label	• Polydor • Interscope
Writer(s)	• Lana Del Rey • Rick Nowels
Producer(s)	Dan Auerbach
Lana Del Rey singles chronology	
"West Coast" (2014) "**Shades of Cool**" "Ultraviolence" (2014)	

"**Shades of Cool**" is a song recorded by American singer-songwriter Lana Del Rey for her third studio album, *Ultraviolence* (2014). It was co-written by Del Rey, and Rick Nowels, and produced by Dan Auerbach. The song was released on May 26, 2014, by Polydor and Interscope Records, as the second single from *Ultraviolence*.

Composition

Consequence of Sound described the song as "a slow and slightly gloomy ballad marked by reverberated guitars, slight atmospherics, and Del Rey's vocals that alternate between a hushed whisper and ephemeral wailing." *Billboard* called it a "sweeping, atmospheric ballad that contrasts the more pop-savvy swaggering 'West Coast'". The song consists of "a chiming guitar, slow-burn bass line, and swelling orchestra" which surround Del Rey's vocals. Caryn Ganz of *Rolling Stone* described the song as "a waltz featuring a searing Auerbach guitar solo, swollen strings and Del Rey's operatic soprano."

Music video

Background

On June 12, 2014, Del Rey posted a preview of the video on Instagram. The video was uploaded to YouTube and Vevo on June 17, 2014. The video was filmed in Los Angeles in May and stars celebrity tattoo artist Mark Mahoney who previously appeared in the music video for "West Coast". It was directed by Jake Nava.

Synopsis

The video opens with Mahoney looking at the camera as a scene of an LA street at night fades in. Del Rey starts singing over shots of Mahoney driving a car before she appears superimposed over various dark blue plants and flowers, with the colors on her distorted and blurring. During the chorus, the scene with Del Rey shows red fireworks and birds while Mahoney is shown with blue shooting stars.

In the second verse, Del Rey walks down a street of LA in the daytime and sees Mahoney getting into his car. He notices her but gets in anyway.

In the next scene Del Rey swims by Mahoney by the glass side of a swimming pool as Mahoney crosses himself. Del Rey is then seen dancing in a living room while Mahoney drinks. Del Rey eats a strawberry then drinks and smokes in the pool while in another scene she playfully hugs and dances with Mahoney. She gets out of the pool as the shot references Marilyn Monroe in *Something's Got to Give*.

The video ends with a shot of Mahoney pulling a happy Del Rey off the floor into an embrace in reverse.

Critical response

"Shades of Cool" has received universal acclaim from music critics. Josh Wigler of MTV called it "fifty shades of great". Chris Coplan of Consequence of Sound complimented the song for its "grace and sophistication". Saran Shetty of *Slate* called "Shades of Cool" "a beautiful, brooding return to form [for Del Rey]" and compared it favorably to her previous single "West Coast". Critics have noted the similarity of her high-register vocals on the track to those of Cocteau Twins vocalist Elizabeth Fraser: "The haunting chorus of "Shades of Cool" and the reverb-drenched harmonies of atmospheric bonus track "Guns and Roses" unexpectedly recall the gorgeously ethereal vocals of Cocteau Twins singer Elizabeth Fraser. Del Rey has never sounded better."

Personnel

Credits adapted from the liner notes of *Ultraviolence*.

Performance credits

* Lana Del Rey - vocals

Instruments

* Dan Auerbach - electric guitar
* Collin Dupuis - drum programming
* Seth Kaufman - omnichord
* Leon Michels - mellotron
* Nick Movshon - bass guitar
* Russ Pahl - electric guitar
* Kenny Vaughan - electric guitar
* Maximilian Weissenfeldt - drums

Technical and production

* Dan Auerbach - production
* John Davis - mastering
* Collin Dupuis - engineering
* Robert Orton - mixing

Charts

Chart (2014)	Peak position
Australia (ARIA)[1]	50
Belgium (Ultratop 50 Wallonia)[2]	40
Canada (Canadian Hot 100)[3]	52
Czech Republic (Singles Digitál Top 100)[4]	79
Greece Digital Songs (*Billboard*)	3
France (SNEP)[5]	37
Hungary (Single Top 20)[6]	19
Russian Digital Songs (*Lenta*)	8
Spain (PROMUSICAE)[7]	31
Switzerland (Schweizer Hitparade)[8]	43
US *Billboard* Hot 100[9]	79

Release history

Country	Date	Format	Label
United States	May 26, 2014	Digital download	Interscope

References

[1] " Australian-charts.com – Lana Del Rey – Shades of Cool" (http://www.australian-charts.com/showitem.asp?interpret=Lana+Del+Rey&titel=Shades+of+Cool&cat=s). ARIA Top 50 Singles. Retrieved June 8, 2014.

[2] " Ultratop.be – Lana Del Rey – Shades of Cool" (http://www.ultratop.be/fr/showitem.asp?interpret=Lana+Del+Rey&titel=Shades+of+Cool&cat=s) (in French). Ultratop 50. Retrieved June 5, 2014.

[3] " Lana Del Rey Album & Song Chart History" (http://www.billboard.com/artist/306420/Lana+Del+Rey/chart?f=793) Canadian Hot 100 for Lana Del Rey. Retrieved June 5, 2014.

[4] " ČNS IFPI" (http://www.ifpicr.cz/hitparada/index.php?hitp=R) (in Czech). Hitparáda – Digital Top 100 Oficiální. IFPI Czech Republic. *Note: insert 201426 into search*. Retrieved July 3, 2014.

[5] " Lescharts.com – Lana Del Rey – Shades of Cool" (http://www.lescharts.com/showitem.asp?interpret=Lana+Del+Rey&titel=Shades+of+Cool&cat=s) (in French). Les classement single. Retrieved June 8, 2014.

[6] " Archívum – Slágerlisták – MAHASZ – Magyar Hanglemezkiadók Szövetsége" (http://www.mahasz.hu/?menu=slagerlistak&menu2=archivum&lista=kislemez&ev=2014&het=22&submit_=Keresés) (in Hungarian). Single (track) Top 10 lista. Magyar Hanglemezkiadók Szövetsége. Retrieved June 5, 2014.

[7] " Spanishcharts.com – Lana Del Rey – Shades of Cool" (http://www.spanishcharts.com/showitem.asp?interpret=Lana+Del+Rey&titel=Shades+of+Cool&cat=s) Canciones Top 50. Retrieved June 9, 2014.

[8] " Lana Del Rey – Shades of Cool – swisscharts.com" (http://www.swisscharts.com/showitem.asp?interpret=Lana+Del+Rey&titel=Shades+of+Cool&cat=s). Swiss Singles Chart. Retrieved June 15, 2014.

[9] " Lana Del Rey Album & Song Chart History" (http://www.billboard.com/artist/306420/Lana+Del+Rey/chart?f=379) *Billboard* Hot 100 for Lana Del Rey. Retrieved June 5, 2014.

External links

- Official music video (https://www.youtube.com/watch?v=rJABBmAMXnY) on YouTube

Brooklyn Baby

"Brooklyn Baby"	
Single by Lana Del Rey	
from the album *Ultraviolence*	
Released	June 8, 2014
Format	Digital download
Genre	Dream pop
Length	5:51
Label	• Polydor • Interscope
Writer(s)	• Lana Del Rey • Barrie O'Neill
Producer(s)	Dan Auerbach
Lana Del Rey singles chronology	
• "Ultraviolence" • (2014)	• "**Brooklyn Baby**" • (2014)

"**Brooklyn Baby**" is a song by American singer-songwriter Lana Del Rey for her third studio album *Ultraviolence* (2014). It was written by Del Rey, and Barrie O'Neill, while production was handled by Dan Auerbach. The song was released on June 8, 2014, by Polydor Records and Interscope Records, as the fourth single from *Ultraviolence*.

Composition

Miriam Coleman of Rolling Stone described Del Rey's vocals as "breathy" an called the melody of the song "reminiscent of 1960s girl-group hits". In the song, Del Rey pokes fun at the hipster subculture, referencing several cliches about them, Brooklyn, and Millennials. Del Rey said that she wrote the song with Lou Reed in mind. She was supposed to work with him and flew to New York City to meet him, but he died the day she arrived. He is referenced in the line "And my boyfriend's in a band/ He plays guitar while I sing Lou Reed".

Critical response

Miriam Coleman of Rolling Stone described it as a "dreamy song... with a breathy vocals and a melody before moving into Del Rey's typically languid, dreamy soundscape". Duncan Cooper of The Fader stated that "Brooklyn Baby" is the standout track of *Ultraviolence*, pointing out the "uncharacteristically self-assured gem", "Yeah, my boyfriend's really cool/ But he's not as cool as me.". Sharan Shetty of *Slate* complimented the melody of the song, however disliked the lack of "big, chewy vocal hooks".

Personnel

Credits adapted from the liner notes of *Ultraviolence*.

Performance credits

- Lana Del Rey - vocals, background vocals
- Seth Kaufman - background vocals

Instruments

- Dan Auerbach - electric guitar
- Seth Kaufman - electric guitar, percussion
- Leon Michels - mellotron, tambourine, percussion, tenor saxophone
- Nick Movshon - upright bass, drums
- Russ Pahl - pedal steel guitar, acoustic guitar
- Kenny Vaughan - acoustic guitar
- Maximilian Weissenfeldt - drums

Technical and production

- Dan Auerbach - production
- John Davis - mastering
- Collin Dupuis - engineering
- Robert Orton - mixing

Charts

Chart (2014)	Peak position
Australia (ARIA)[1]	35
Austria (Ö3 Austria Top 40)[2]	64
Belgium (Ultratop 50 Wallonia)[3]	32
Canada (Canadian Hot 100)[4]	60
Finland (Suomen virallinen latauslista)[5]	6
France (SNEP)[6]	33
Netherlands (Single Top 100)[7]	87
New Zealand (Recorded Music NZ)[8]	19
Russian Digital Songs (*Lenta*)	10
Spain (PROMUSICAE)[9]	36
Switzerland (Schweizer Hitparade)[10]	16
UK Singles (Official Charts Company)[11]	86
US Bubbling Under Hot 100 Singles (*Billboard*)	1

Release history

Country	Date	Format	Label
United States	June 8, 2014	Digital download	Interscope

References

[1] " Australian-charts.com – Lana Del Rey – Brooklyn Baby" (http://www.australian-charts.com/showitem.asp?interpret=Lana+Del+Rey& titel=Brooklyn+Baby&cat=s). ARIA Top 50 Singles. Retrieved June 16, 2014.

[2] " Lana Del Rey – Brooklyn Baby – Austriancharts.at" (http://www.austriancharts.at/showitem.asp?interpret=Lana+Del+Rey& titel=Brooklyn+Baby&cat=s) (in German). Ö3 Austria Top 40. Retrieved June 22, 2014.

[3] " Ultratop.be – Lana Del Rey – Brooklyn Baby" (http://www.ultratop.be/fr/showitem.asp?interpret=Lana+Del+Rey&titel=Brooklyn+ Baby&cat=s) (in French). Ultratop 50. Retrieved June 13, 2014.

[4] " Lana Del Rey Album & Song Chart History" (http://www.billboard.com/artist/306420/Lana+Del+Rey/chart?f=793) Canadian Hot 100 for Lana Del Rey. Retrieved April 18, 2014.

[5] " Lana Del Rey: Brooklyn Baby" (http://www.ifpi.fi/tilastot/virallinen-lista/artistit/Lana+Del+Rey/Brooklyn+Baby) (in Finnish). Musiikkituottajat – IFPI Finland. Retrieved June 12, 2014.

[6] " Lescharts.com – Lana Del Rey – Brooklyn Baby" (http://www.lescharts.com/showitem.asp?interpret=Lana+Del+Rey& titel=Brooklyn+Baby&cat=s) (in French). Les classement single. Retrieved June 16, 2014.

[7] " Dutchcharts.nl – Lana Del Rey – Brooklyn Baby" (http://www.dutchcharts.nl/showitem.asp?interpret=Lana+Del+Rey& titel=Brooklyn+Baby&cat=s) (in Dutch). Single Top 100. Retrieved June 14, 2014.

[8] " Charts.org.nz – Lana Del Rey – Brooklyn Baby" (http://www.charts.org.nz/showitem.asp?interpret=Lana+Del+Rey&titel=Brooklyn+ Baby&cat=s). Top 40 Singles. Retrieved April 18, 2014.

[9] " Spanishcharts.com – Lana Del Rey – Brooklyn Baby" (http://www.spanishcharts.com/showitem.asp?interpret=Lana+Del+Rey& titel=Brooklyn+Baby&cat=s) Canciones Top 50.

[10] " Lana Del Rey – Brooklyn Baby – swisscharts.com" (http://www.swisscharts.com/showitem.asp?interpret=Lana+Del+Rey& titel=Brooklyn+Baby&cat=s). Swiss Singles Chart. Retrieved June 15, 2014.

[11] " Archive Chart" (http://www.theofficialcharts.com/archive-chart/_/1/2014-06-28/) UK Singles Chart.

External links

- Official audio (https://www.youtube.com/watch?v=T5xcnjAG8pE) on YouTube

Article Sources and Contributors

Lana Del Rey *Source*: http://en.wikipedia.org/w/index.php?oldid=619429423 *Contributors*: 11JORN, 123dylan456, 1Sire, 1dee4mee, 3193th, 7, Aaa16, Acalamari, Acdx, Acroterion, Adriangl, Aeexo, Aerodynamica, Afavoritaweb, Ahmed R. Karam, Aidan hynes, Airmantx, Al.blackheart, AlbusPD, All Hallow's Wraith, Allens, AlligatorSky, Aloud212, Alyssaromano, Am86, Amaury, And we drown, Angel caboodle, Angelinthesnow, Another Believer, Antinate, Antiqueight, Antiuser, Apeloverage, Applelapacheeeer, Arbor to SJ, Arcandam, Arjayay, Armbrust, Arranrice, Articmonkeys, Artpop - volume 2, Aspieejmr, Atlantia, Auric, Avda-berlin, Ayylmaootori, BD2412, BDE1982, BaldBoris, Banshee01, Baseball Watcher, Basilisk4u, Batman194, Bearcat, Beatkickedin, Begoon, Bender235, Beyoncemil, Beyoncetan, Bgwhite, Bill shannon, Billyhill82, BizarreLoveTriangle, Bizzurp, Bkonrad, BluDaw, Bluefist, Bluemountain*14, Bluescarred, Bodhikun, Borntofreeze, Bradshawww, BrckoGOS, Bretonbanquet, Briegers, Brokenpassword, Brossow, BrotherDarksoul, BullRangifer, Burgermeister77, Burnberrytree, C.Fred, CPGirlAJ, Cameron Scott, CammieParkes, Candent shlimazel, Canuckian89, Captain Herbert, Carlosendra, Carolinek422, Cashie, Castncoot, Ceranthor, Cheezesatzu, Cheszy, ChrisBS, ChrisGualtieri, Chrishonduras, Chrism, Chrisseavey, Cinemantique, Closedmouth, CloudKade11, Cntras, Cobaltcigs, Cofapt, Collingwood, Connorzd, Cosmic Latte, Countercouper, Courcelles, Coyets, Crasshopper, Crazynas, Creationul, Crime-wmv, CrnoKrno, Crowdsurftn, Csa3dn, Cyrip, DVdm, DadaNeem, DanBLOO, Dana boomer, Danielhur21d13, Danno uk, Darcysmithxo, Dark Beauty Paradise, Darkparadises, Darylgolden, Dascill, DavidLeighEllis, Dawn Bard, Deadbeef, DedoGrin, DemirBajraktarevic, Deneuve15, Der Golem, Derek R Bullamore, Derpmir, DesignDeath, DieterMartinez, Discographer, Discospinster, Dizagaox, DjScrawl, Dkisnis, Dkspartan1, Dmgultekin, DocKino, Download, Dr.K., Drmies, Drpickem, Duphin, Dwpaul, DylanNZ, E.H.T.V., Eamontopleez, Easy4me, Edwardx, ElArLind, Electric Wombat, Electriccatfish2, Elineelene, Ellis.o22, Emerson7, Emiliehaugeballo, Emontie, Enervation, Epicurus B., Ericorbit, ErikHaugen, Ermidaphne, Erpert, Etc719, Eternal baby, EuroCarGT, EvergreenFir, Excirial, Extraordinary Machine, Eyesnore, Ezerty, Fadingaway121, Faizan, Fashwithin, Felix Folio Secundus, Ferdinand Pienaar, Feudonym, FieldMarine, Fiftyshades, Figgajon, Forevernoemi, Fraggle81, Francisco Bariffi, Frecklefoot, FromtheWordsofBR, Frostibrae, Frous, Fryn, FungasUK, Futuremama, Gabiarakelian, GagaARTPOP, Gamaliel, Gasjooz, Gbuvn, Genesis cz, Gilliam, Gio eleven, Giovanosky, GlitterDream, Gobonobo, GoingBatty, Gooey2504, Gossipbangbang, Greenock125, Greg Fasolino, Gregorik, Gruverja, Gungadin, Guy Harris, HC 5555, Hamiltonstone, Handsopened, Hardcorewhovian, Harland1, Hebrides, Helen Gretchen, Henry McClean, Hiddenid, Hidefromanna, Hihosilveraway89, Hohum, Hometown Kid, Hroðulf, Hy6e, I am One of Many, I just wanna edit stuff, IPadPerson, IXIA, Igordebraga, Ilovetati91, Imjustharrytho, Impavique, Inquiringmindz, InverseHypercube, IronGargoyle, Itistoday, Ivxiimmx, J36miles, Jabberwoch, Jackgill06, Jackmcbarn, Jagoperson, Jak Fisher, Jakec, Jalwikip, Jan256, Jatkins, Jay 1432, Jayjaykk13, Jean-Jacques Georges, Jediknightelectro1997, Jeffstev1127, JennKR, Jennica, Jim1138, Jjj1238, Jlujan69, John.james250, Johnevergreener, JohnnyMrNinja, Johnpacklambert, Johnvanbergen, Jordan Chuck, Jordanjharris, Jormesby, Josefhoracek, Joseistheway, Journalist, Jpvandijk, Jschnur, JuniorCaliBoii, Justasaddream, KTS821, Keagan888, Keanu banks, Keith D, Kieranmcdermott1, Kimiko20, Kingturtle, Koavf, KoshVorlon, Ktperry44, Kwesiidun91, Kww, LM2000, Lambiam, Lanadelrey12333, LeavemealoneNSA, Lectonar, LegacyOfValor, Lemonade51, Lentel soup, Liam987, Lindenhurst Liberty, Lionhead99, Littlecarmen, Littleharmonizer, LjubitelDr, Loginnigol, Lola212, Lopifalko, Lowellian, Lugia2453, Lxhizy, M.O.X, MER-C, Macarion, Macaronlover, Mad Hatter, Mad akhil 96, Magioladitis, Maine12329, Manfred(MANN)6, Marcelobing, Mark Arsten, Mason.Jones, Materialscientist, Matthew Proctor, MatthewTStone, Mauri96, Maxxie Le, Maxxyme, McCann27, Mcld, Mediran, Meganlenny, MelbourneStar, Melonkelon, MeltingObject, Meluvseveryone, Mercury McKinnon, Merveilles, Merxistan, Mfabzzz, MichaelSkinsFan, Michig, Michsonicfan, Mike Rosoft, MindNoGap, MindscapeDragon, Mongo460, Monsoongetback, Mpwilliams, Mselmani, Mtirrell38, Muhali, Muhandes, Mungo Kitsch, Murmuration, Musicprovider2, MusikAnimal, My love is love, My name is not dave, Mystarnia, Myxomatosis57, Napeterson18, Natmessina, NawlinWiki, Need some hypnotherapy, Neil Clancy, Nick2501, NickCT, Nicotineandgravy, Noozgroop, Noremac2001, NorwegianMarcus, Novusuna, Ntonto55, OccasionallyCrazy12345678910, Octopus12, OfTheGreen, Officially Mr X, Ohnoitsjamie, Okay nick, Oliviazerweck, Omnisci88, Onedirectionandselenagomez, Onlythetruthisappropriate, Ontario101, Orginalinfo, Over Hill and Under Hill, Oyoxxxoyo, Ozkithar Salas, PKimage, Parrotshake, Part of me 2, Patrickwilken, Paul Erik, PauloLochs, Pburka, Pemilligan, Perelka, Philippemorin123, Poopoobear25252, Postdlf, PrivateMasterHD, Protenpinner, Puongdauline11, Puramyun31, Putoro, Q1445, Q43, QuasyBoy, Quebec99, REKupp, RGCorris, Racklever, RafikiSykes, Rameses MMX, Random Ranaun, Rcsprinter123, ReblFleur, Redd Foxx 1991, Redrose64, Reece Leonard, Rfkzsaok7, Ribberboy, RichardMills65, Rjwilmsi, Ro7586, Robert Moore, RobertCWebb, Robsinden, Robynloud, RomualdoJavi, RoyTek, Rui78901, Rustypup49, Rwalker, Ryansuzuki, Ryulong, SNAAAAKE!!, SNUGGUMS, Salvadorcases, SamanthaPuckettIndo, Samjohnzon, Sammylovesyouxx, Sanogo700, Sauloviegas, Sayonaramynameis..., Scottdoesntknow, Scratchy7929, Seaphoto, Seduisant, Shadowjams, ShelfSkewed, Shuipzv3, SidCurtis10, Slideshot, Slon02, Smarty9108, Smilingsuzy, SnapSnap, Sofffie7, Sola2012, Solino, Someko1999, Somervillain, SpecialK, Splarks, Ss112, Sserdde, StAnselm, Stallions2010, Status, Steel, Stemonitis, Stevenciara, Steveo2, StoneProphet11, Strawberry Slugs, Strike Eagle, Supernature91, Supervehicle, Suriel1981, Suzranish, Svernon19, Swalkeroo, Swatjester, Sxphruggi, TLSuda, TV, Tabletop, Tassedethe, Tav2244, Tbhotch, Tdslk, TeaDrinker, Teammathi, Teammm, Teatreez, TenPoundHammer, Terhorst, Thaliagrace15, Thatdudecray, The Determinator, The Interior, The JPS, TheOnlyOne12, Theonlycab, Thevampireashlee, Thicknick 5, Thumperward, Thunderbolt93, Tim1357, Toccata quarta, Tomlawrence95, Toripante, Trollabate, U-Mos, Uffeadz, Ulrikke1994, UltraRainbows, Unfriend12, Unreal7, Usfbull2121, Utcursch, Vanished user 352535, Vanished user alaij23jrkef8hj4fiu34t34, Vanished user v8hjw98h4iufv8j23iortualifjhoi3, Vegaswikian, WJBscribe, WQUlrich, Werldwayd, Whatcha know bout us, Whatever318, Whitestorm17, Widr, Wiki13, WikiRedactor, Wikiepdiax818, With my body, Woohookitty, Worldwideswifty, Writerchic99, Wtwilson3, Xmetov, Y2kcrazyjoker4, Yeanolia, Yegeo, Yintan, Yworo, Zagibbs, Zak Hammat, Zarcadia, Zero over zero, Zolfianyarvelling, Zymurgy, İsaocel, Ὁ οἶστρος, 913 anonymous edits

Ultraviolence (album) *Source*: http://en.wikipedia.org/w/index.php?oldid=619259920 *Contributors*: (CA)Giacobbe, 2Flows, Aaa16, Acalamari, AddWittyNameHere, Afavoritaweb, Ahmedfarhat, Airmantx, Aj91892, Americancupcakeclub, Andise1, AndrewAllen15, Angelordemon, Another Believer, Antique Ruby, Arjann, Armen Balabanyan, Articmonkeys, Axeldarkdreamer, Babykitsune, Badpiggy, Ben.nes13, Billinghurst, Bleff, Blueriver94, Brambleclawx, BrothaTimothy, Brysonj, Caseymary, ChrisCarss Former24.108.99.31, Cnwilliams, ConnorGissing, Creationul, Crikko, Criss Smith Lewis, Cxleb, Dan1025, DanWiki2011, DantODB, Deneuve15, Digital0000, Dkisnis, Dusomething, Eduardow10, Elassint, ElectraViolence, Esquelet, Fadingaway101, FotoPhest, Francisco Bariffi, FranklinG, Funnysox24, Gabiarakelian, Gaknowitall, GoingBatty, Goncalor, Hangshimkim, Hardcorewhovian, Helder Monter, Holiday56, Homeostasis07, I just wanna edit stuff, IPadPerson, Indietime4991, Isa3211, JennKR, John.james250, Jonesey95, JovanMonster, K9Monsta, Katelynne420, Kieranmcdermott1, KirrVlad, Kirtap92, Kissmycody, Ladyseashell, Leo Mercury, LillyJacobs, Limbsaw, Little gansta17, LittleWink, Littlecarmen, Livelikemusic, Lsrdiy, Lucas Thoms, Lugia2453, Magioladitis, MariAna Mimi, Maridiem, Mayast, Michsonicfan, Mistressmaryam, Moderngguilt, Monstermathiaz, Mr. LuxeTH, My love is love, Myxomatosis57, NightmareWorks, Nxtgenration, Older and ... well older, Puisque, QuasyBoy, R3troguy420, Rainbows&beef, RazorEyeEdits, RealDealBillMcNeal, ReblFleur, RileyBoudreau, Roisin kj, RoyThomasMusic, Rsicxs, SNTMcentral, STATicVapor, Salvio giuliano, Samjohnzon, Scottdoesntknow, Sean gallen24, Smarty9108, Soulparadox, Splarks, Starcheerspeaksnewslostwars, Status, Stealstrash, Thatguy0823, TheDarkKnight180, TheOnlyOne12, Thisiskyle.n, Thomasamuse, Tom Morris, Tommes14, Tpmunkee, U990467, UltraviolenceDeluxe, Werldwayd, Whatcha know bout us, Whatscrackin555, Whoknew?123, WikiRedactor, Ymblanter, Z33k, Zamaira13, 352 anonymous edits

Tropico (film) *Source*: http://en.wikipedia.org/w/index.php?oldid=617708271 *Contributors*: Alexfilipe, Another Believer, Artpop - volume 2, Bender235, Bleff, ChrisGualtieri, Cnilep, Cnwilliams, Creationul, David Condrey, HĐ, Littlecarmen, Lsrdiy, MagicatthemovieS, Mogism, Myonlywishthisyear, Pratyya Ghosh, Prettygirlglam0, QuasyBoy, Ryulong, Samjohnzon, Sunny Nights, The Orience, Thevampireashlee, Thomasamuse, U990467, Verne Equinox, Xxvid, 25 anonymous edits

Lana Del Ray (album) *Source*: http://en.wikipedia.org/w/index.php?oldid=618593749 *Contributors*: Another Believer, Azkamalik, Discospinster, Esquelet, Josh3580, Kieranmcdermott1, Koavf, Littlecarmen, Materialscientist, Status, WikiRedactor, 23 anonymous edits

Born to Die (Lana Del Rey album) *Source*: http://en.wikipedia.org/w/index.php?oldid=619625108 *Contributors*: (CA)Giacobbe, 12345abcxyz20082009, 1Sire, 6060852zoo, 97198, Aaa16, Acalamari, Afutinadoa, Agbnsd, Akulun37, Alezk90, Alf.laylah.wa.laylah, Allens, AlligatorSky, Ambersimms, Amkilpatrick, And we drown, Andrzejbanas, Anniev33, Another Believer, Artpop - volume 2, Ary29, Awais66, Awu1996, Axeldarkdreamer, BD2412, BTVS34, Beatflow, Ben Ben, Bender235, BenjaniBoy139, Bgwhite, BionicLotus, BluDaw, Bluesatellite, Bnewall1, Bretonbanquet, Broden, Bumazhka, CJBR, Caladonia, Caldape95, CaroleHenson, Cheszy, Chris the speller, ChrisGualtieri, Chronisgr, Cianu, Ciphers, Clay KH, Clem69420, Complete confection, ConcernedVancouverite, Countercouper, Creationul, Crowdsurftn, Cyrip, DAP388, Dan3231, Dan56, Dark Beauty Paradise, Dbmelo123, Deathlasersonline, DeeONEjay, Deneuve15, Derek R Bullamore, Didigodot, DieterMartinez, Digital0000, Discospinster, Dissolve, Dkisnis, Doc Strange, Drmies, Drpickem, Duphin, EagerToddler39, Easy4me, Emilyjem, Emyro, Envyofthetown, EricEnfermero, Ericorbit, Esquelet, Eternal baby, Evannotkelley, Fadingaway121, Faigl.ladislav, Fashwithin, Feudonym, Fire of your loins babe, FisherQueen, Francisco Bariffi, Frostibrae, Frous, FungasUK, Gabiarakelian, Gaknowitall, Ged UK, Get it started and put it down, GlitterDream, GoingBatty, Greenock125, HC 5555, Happenssofast, Harout72, Heartsingsvibes, Henry McClean, IPadPerson, Ichigonyan, Imperatore, InterIOV111.111, Jack1755, Jackattaaaack, Jackgill06, Jak Fisher, Jamesx12345, Jarble, Jean louis van doe, Jevansen, Jexral, Jim1138, JimVC3, Jj227, Jjj1238, John.james250, Johnvanbergen, Jonesey95, Jonkerz, Joseistheway, Joseph jupiter, Josve05a, Journalist, JovanMonster, Joyrider2, Juanc1317, Kieranmcdermott1, Kiko4564, Killbill22, Kinu, KirrVlad, Kirtap92, Kiss me on my open mouth, Koavf, Kww, LanaDelReyGrammyCommitee, LeviLucienFoster, LilHelpa, LindseyHugs, LittleWink, Littlecarmen, Loginnigol, Lopifalko, Lovebritneynet, Lowrijones1988, Lsrdiy, Lugia2453, Luke08091995, Madvillain2010, Magioladitis, MariAna Mimi, Mathiiuz, Mauri96, Maxxie Le, Mayast, Mburrell, Mcdonalds, Meadow Gate, Melonkelon, Meluvseveryone, Melvalevis, Merynancy, MetroPlayer, Michig, Mihelpl, Mlpearc, Mmrsofgreen, Mogism, MoiRobin, Monsoongetback, MontyPhyton, Mr JKX, Mr. Sedge, Mrramyon74$$, Muhandes, Murmuration, My love is love, Myxomatosis57, NXL1997, Need some hypnotherapy, Nobbyson123, Noboyo, Ntonto55, Nycpirate2, Oiv8, Omnisci88, Onedaylemurswillruletheworld, OngakuKougou, Onlythetruthisappropriate, Ozkithar Salas, PASTALOVERMATEWANK83, PKimage, Pafcool2, PancakeMistake, Part of me 2, Patdog, Paul Erik, Peeta-june, PorlBond1, Prism, Puisque, Puongdauline11, QuasyBoy, Querido0328, RGCorris, RafaelPPascual, ReblFleur, Redrose64, Reece Leonard, Reza 1389, Richard3120, Roie3600, Rwalker, Ryulong, STATicVapor, Samlikeswiki, Samuka Rodrigues, Sanjeetpearnest, Sauloviegas, Sayonaramynameis..., Scottdoesntknow, Scratchy7929, Selfan, SilentShout666, Silvergoat, Silvrous, Smurfandbuffalo, SnapSnap, Sofffie7, Sola2012, Sonyatvintern, SpecialK, Ss112, StAnselm, Starcheerspeaksnewslostwars, Status, Steakbuns, Stee888, Sun Creator, Supernature91, Swalkeroo, TLSuda, TV, Tabletop, Taras98, Tbhotch, Teammathi, Teatreez, TenPoundHammer, Tgeairn, The Certificater, The Interior, The wub, TheOnlyOne12, Therealdavo2, Thevampireashlee, Thismightbezach, Thomson200, TomPynch, Tombo671, Tomica, Uion, Uncleangelo, Unreal7, Vanished user alaij23jrkef8hj4fiu34t34, Vanished user v8hjw98h4iufv8j23iortualifjhoi3, Vegaswikian, Vinokurov Demis, WWETrishMickiefan, WeAllSquidward, Werieth, WesleyDodds, Whatever318, Widr, WikHead, WikiRedactor, Xiku1, Y2kcrazyjoker4, Yuvalbleich, Z33k, Zagibbs, 956 anonymous edits

Paradise (Lana Del Rey EP) *Source*: http://en.wikipedia.org/w/index.php?oldid=619312878 *Contributors*: (CA)Giacobbe, Aaa16, Acalamari, Andrzejbanas, Another Believer, Artpop - volume 2, Awu1996, Bbbnbbb, BenjaniBoy139, Biotroll, Caladonia, CaliforniaDreamsFan, Callanecc, Charliemilne, ChrisGualtieri, Creationul, Crikko, Cyrip, Dan56, Dark Beauty Paradise, Derpmir,

Dkisnis, Dresx, Easy4me, Eduardow10, Eyeball4000, Fadingaway121, Flyer22, Gabriel bier, GagaARTPOP, GenQuest, Gio eleven, GoingBatty, Greg Fasolino, Hadji87, Hahc21, Harout72, IPadPerson, Ivanaaj, Jackattaaaack, JoCalderone99, John.james250, JustAGal, Kafka1251, Kieranmcdermott1, Kworbi, LK8995, Lil-unique1, LilHelpa, Little Professor, Littlecarmen, Lsrdiy, MadSkilz252, Magioladitis, MariAna Mimi, Meadow Gate, Melonkelon, MrX, MusikAnimal, Myrnostrum, Myxomatosis57, Niceguyedc, Noboyo, Not your damn cat, PancakeMistake, PokerFace3, Puongdauline11, QuasyBoy, ReblFleur, Reece Leonard, Rsrikanth05, Rwalker, STATicVapor, Samlikeswiki, Scottdoesntknow, Shannon Tucker, Slather, Someguy1221, SoushokukeiDino, StAnselm, Status, TV, Tassedethe, Tbhotch, Teammathi, Thevampireashlee, Thomasamuse, Tombo671, U990467, Unreal7, Uppppp, Vanished user v8hjw98h4iufv8j23iortualifjhoi3, Vasilevs12, Vegaswikian, VoluntarySlave, Whatever318, Widr, WikiRedactor, Wikkitywack, With my body, Zagibbs, 201 anonymous edits

The Observer *Source*: http://en.wikipedia.org/w/index.php?oldid=617356708 *Contributors*: (, 119, 711joel, Abberley2, Academe, Acegikmo1, Adlestrop, Aidsoo, Alexius08, Amencorner1, Andreasegde, AndrewWTaylor, Arash red, Ark25, ArtVandelay13, Auric, Autolycus, Autospark, Barnabypage, Bbb2007, Beao, Bearcat, Blurpeace, Bobblewik, Bobo192, Breno, Brycehughes, C.Fred, CalJW, Capitalismojo, Charles Matthews, Chris the speller, Chrism, Colonies Chris, CommonsDelinker, Crashandspin, Crosbiesmith, D6, Darkieboy236, Deansfa, Den fjättrade ankan, DennyColt, Devourer09, Digifiend, Docu, Echuck215, Egeymi, Esperant, Exok, Fences and windows, Finlux, Formica rufa, Gareth E Kegg, Gigi men, Gimmetrow, Gobonobo, Good Olfactory, GrahamHardy, Grahams7, Greeeeeen, Green Tentacle, GregLoutsenko, Hammer Raccoon, Headhitter, Hephaestos, Hoary, Hqb, IJA, Icecold7, IrishIurnman4Lyfe, JD554, JK the unwise, Jamesmorrison, Jaraalbe, JillandJack, Jimbo Wales, Joebloggsy, Joechuck, John, Jös, KSTP31, Kaihsu, Katieh5584, Kesac, Kind Tennis Fan, Lakewindemere, Ldonna, Lightmouse, Lotje, Luckystars, Maarten1963, Magnusllewellin, Mais oui!, Markbrough, Mav, Maxí, Me677, Mick gold, Mistere, Mklobas, Mpntod, Mr Taz, N-HH, NaidNdeso, NathanLee, Neutral Milk Hotel, NeutralPoint, Nikai, Nytsyn, Ohconfucius, Onorem, OpenToppedBus, Oscarblend, Otbon, Parkerlovescider, Patstuart, Pedro, Petri Krohn, Philip Cross, Picapica, Pigsonthewing, Pinar, Pneumaman, Possum, RadicalBender, Rangoon11, Razorflame, Rbrwr, Rd232, Riddley, Rje, Rjwilmsi, Robertvan1, RobinCarmody, Rodhullandemu, Roferbia, Roo72, Rwendland, SMcCandlish, Saga City, Sam Francis, Save-Me-Oprah, SchwarzeMelancholie, ScottyBoy900Q, Shakehandsman, Slazenger, SlimVirgin, Snigbrook, Snooo, SoLando, Solidice190, Squalla, Supertask, Svick, Tarquin, TerriersFan, The Geography Elite, The Vintage Feminist, TheParanoidOne, Theresa knott, Thomas Peardew, Till, Tim!, Toddst1, Tony Sidaway, TonyDodson, Tonzo, Towel401, Trident13, Velella, WLU, Wackywace, Walden, WhisperToMe, Wikipediatastic, WillowW, Xn4, Zeibeks, Zeibex, Zimbabweed, 87 anonymous edits

Saturday Night Live *Source*: http://en.wikipedia.org/w/index.php?oldid=619372450 *Contributors*: 17Drew, 198.144.10.xxx, 1wolfblake, 209.75.42.xxx, 23skidoo, 4wajzkd02, 75pickup, 803290, A More Perfect Onion, A Train, A bit iffy, A.lanzetta, AMK1211, Aaron Bowen, Aaronh7, Aaronjhill, Ab85, Abbey09, AbigailAbernathy, Ableadded, AbsoluteGleek92, Ace Class Shadow, Ace Mendiola, Acegikmo1, Acourt323, Acps110, Adamahill, Adavidw, Addihockey10, Aerisence, Aerotheque, Ahpook, Aia94, Aido2002, Aladdin Zane, Alai, Alan smithee, Alansohn, Albert109, AlbertSM, Alden1998, Ale jrb, Alexander Vince, Alexwcovington, Algetrig91, Algocu, Alix195, Allamericanbear, Allenstone, Aloha princess, Alsandro, Altenmann, Amaury, Amchow78, AmericanCentury21, Amphytrite, Amstaton, Anabanana1021, Anand999, Anarchy10110021, Andrew Levine, Andruil, Andux, AndyBQ, Angel caboodle, Anonymous 57, Antandrus, Antonrojo, Apparition11, Applehead77, ApprenticeFan, Arbor to SJ, Argyle2006, ArkansasTraveler, Arms & Hearts, Arniep, Arsene, Arteitle, Artiyom, As5n, Asbl, Ashadeofgrey, AstroZombieDC, Astronautics, Atario, AtashiAtsuka, Atomsmith, Auntof6, Authalic, Autoin123456, Avamos, Avillia, Avoided, Axle2009, Azumanga1, BBCNYC, BD2412, Bachrach44, Bakedlays5447, Banaticus, Barbatus, Baronvon, Baseballfan, Basement12, Bcarlson33, Bdesham, Bdragon, Bearcat, Beginning, Beinsane, Bellatrix Kerrigan, Belpit, Bender235, Bento00, Berean Hunter, Bevo, Bezbozhnik, Bfahome, Bgold4, Bhugh, BigJolly9, Bigbluefish, Biglovinb, Bird-Phobia, Birdienest81, Bjones, Bjs50, Bkkbrad, Blackjack48, Blahblahblahblahblahperson, Bleh999, Bloobear, Blubberboy92, BlueChair, Bmb8609, Bmitchelf, Bobblewik, Bobbydiggy08, Boisemedia, Boneyard90, Bongwarrior, Boobies987654321, Bookemdano63, Borgx, Bornhj, BornonJune8, BostonRed, Bovineboy2008, Bozhawk, Bped1985, Brainscar, Branddobbe, Bratsche, BreakfastJr, Bret "The Beast" Michaels, Briaboru, BrianGriffin-FG, Brianis19, Brianstr4, Bricaniwi, Broadway video, Broco03, Broha7, Brooker, Bruxism, Bry456, Bryan Derksen, Btboy500, Bucklerbuckets, BudMann9, Bull Market, Bull-Doser, Bullzeye, Bunchofgrapes, Buntz. Butros, Butterfly0fdoom, CIS, CJS102793, COMPFUNK2, CR85747, Cable1tvdealerz, Caf3623, CalebNoble, Camboy8, Can't sleep, clown will eat me, CanOfWorms, CapitalQ, Capmango, CardinalDan, Caringtype1, Carlj7, Carlover08, Carolynmathis, Carruthers, Cartoon Boy, Cbrown1023, Cburnett, Ccacsmss, Ccradio, Chadig, Chall rule baby, Chandler, Chavando, Cheesesteaks3, Chickenmonkey, Chilla, Chowbok, Chrisbolt, Christian75, Chrysaor, Chukpeev, CiaraBeth, Cjosefy, Ckatz, Ckelsh, Clarkcj12, Classicfilms, Claymort, Claytonian, Cleared as filed, Cleo20, Clerks, Cliffb, Cloogle12, Closedmouth, Cman517, Cmdrjameson, Cnota, Cnwilliams, CobraWiki, Colfer2, ColinBlair, Colonies Chris, Comatmebro, Cometstyles, Commander Keane, CommonsDelinker, Connerb312, ConorMaguire1995, Conti, Conversion script, Coolbeans39, Coolcars76, CowboySpartan, Crazysane, Crestville, CrestwoodRocks, Croat Canuck, Cruel Irony, Cubs Fan, Curvebill, Cytkory, Czolgolz, D bovair1988, DFS, DJBullfish, DPH1110, DVdm, Dabears12345, Dabigtrain, Dacxjo, Dale Arnett, Dalejenkins, Dalillama, Dan653, Danny Rathjens, Dante Alighieri, Dapilars, DarkNITE, Darkwarriorblake, Darthbob100, Darz Mol, Davbenson, DaveJB, Davemackey, Davemcarlson, Davenbelle, David J Walker, David Levy, David Reject, David Rush, David Shankbone, Davidpatrick, Dbrasco23, Dc2016, Dcalloway, Dcljr, Ddk1138, De728631, Deandean1998, Deansfa, Decumanus, Deej30, DefLeppardVanHalen, Delirium, Deltabeignet, Demomoke, Dercyachaporra, Derek R Bullamore, Derek Ross, Devanjedi, Dfmock, Dgabbard, Dhartung, Dhodges, Dhp1080, Diddlyman2004, Diderot's dreams, Digamma, Dina, Dinnerbone, Dirknoel, Discolash, Discospinster, Djyourazn, Dk1965, Dmarquard, Dnyhagen, Dobie80, DocGratis, DocWatson42, Doctorindy, Doczilla, Dodgeballrocks, Dominus, Donaldd23, DonsTib, Doppy88, Dori, DougHill, Dpm12, DragonflySixtyseven, Dragons flight, Drew4991, Drive Time, Drmies, Drn211, DropDeadGorgias, Drunkenpeter99, Dryridge, Dsemaya, DtownG, Duf Davis, Duke33, Dukemeiser, Dunks58, DuoDeathscyther 02, Dwanyewest, Dwlkr51, Dwo, Dwpaul, Dwslassls, Dynamite XI, E2e3v6, EVula, Ead88, Eagles247, Easterbradford, Easton12, Eayankeefan73, Ebp112002, Ed, Ed g2s, Eddie.willers, Edgar181, EditorKid, Edsanville, Edward, EfrenIII, Egern, Ehccheehcche, Ejfetters, Elcapitane, Elkinfencer7, Ellsworth, Eloquence, Emerson7, EmiOfBrie, Emily8164478683, Epbr123, Erebus555, ErikNY, Eshlare, Esprit15d, Evanh2008, Evanreyes, Evercat, Everyking, Evil Monkey, Evildevil, Evilosity, EwingMan, Excirial, Exitthewayyoucame, Exp HP, FMAFan1990, Falcon8765, Fallgelb, Fantailfan, Favonian, Favre1fan93, Fenderman250, Fernandobouregard, Fhb3, FieldMarine, Firsfron, Fishal, Fisherjs, Flibbert, Floaterfluss, Flockmeal, Flyguy33, Forgetaboutit4000, Formeruser-81, Fourthords, Fpmfpm, Fraggle81, Freakofnurture, Freshacconci, Freshmutt, Friday13, Frigax, Frizzcat, Frze, Fuddle, Funguy06, Fuzzy510, GCW50, GH200, GPHemsley, GVOLTT, Gaff, GageSkidmore, Gaius Cornelius, Gareth, Gargaj, Gary, Gecafe, Gershwinrb, Get It, Gh24ever, Ghirlandajo, Ghosts&empties, Gidtanner, Gigi head, Gildir, Gilliam, Giraffedata, Glickmam, Gmosaki, Gnfnrf, GoPurpleNGold24, Gobonobo, Gogo Dodo, GoingBatty, Golbez, GoldenGoose100, Gonzonoir, Good Olfactory, Goodnightmush, Gordon Ecker, Gothbag, Graham87, Grandma Got Divorced, Granpuff, Grant.Alpaugh, Grapesoda22, Graphiteblimp72, Greba, Gregorof, Ground Zero, Grouse, Grutness, Guat6, Guinness2702, Gus Polly, Gyrferret, HJensen, Hailey C. Shannon, Hajor, Hans Dunkelberg, Happysailor, Harej, Harley Hudson, Harris7, Hawkinsbiz, Headbomb, Helloeveryone!22, Hephaestos, HexaChord, Hfs, HiMom, Hillock65, Hipgnostic, Hiphats, Hippieanger, Hit bull, win steak, Hlodynn, Honette, Hullaballoo Wolfowitz, Hut 8.5, Huw Powell, Hvn0413, I c u trippin, ILikeThings, Iamjrm, IanManka, Ianblair23, Ianjones50, Ianthegecko, Ike9898, Ilikepielol, Illbeyourtennant, Iluvliz, Imbeutiful, ImmortalAl, Imnotminkus, In Defense of the Artist, Informationfountain, InsaneZeroG, Interlingua, InterruptorJones, Into The Fray, Invincible Ninja, Iohannes Animosus, Iowaiowa12, Irishguy, Irk, IronGargoyle, IsleofPlan, Ivanvector, Ixfd64, Iyannaholmes, J Di, J Hofmann Kemp, J.delanoy, JBFrenchhorn, JDspeeder1, JForget, JGKlein, JHK, JHP, JHunterJ, JKPrivett, JMacGill, JMyrleFuller, JYi, Jabooty212, Jack Cox, Jackel, Jackohare, Jacob.Flax, Jacobsons129, Jagarin, Jaknouse, Jaldridge86, James Luftan, JamesB3, JamesBWatson, Jamie jca, Jammedic, Jar789, Jas9946, Jasonglchu, Jay Gatsby, JayJay, Jayann, JazzCarnival, Jbhammon, Jcrct, Jeff G., Jeff schiller, JeffyJeffyMan2004, Jendeyoung, Jengod, Jennica, Jennifer Brooks, Jeremy Butler, JerryLewisOverdrive, Jerzy, Jester29, JetLover, Jfiling, Jgera5, Jgm, Jgroub, Jhiner, Jim Apple, Jim1138, Jimregan, Jippiisfriends, Jjj055, Jjjjjcccccczzzzz, Jkazoo, Jlahorn, Jlesage, Jm91698, Jmcook120, Jnestorius, Joanberenguer, JodyB, Joe o. is beast, Joe21983813, John Cline, John Price, John Quincy Adding Machine, John R Murray, John of Reading, JohnI, Johnny Cade, Johnskeller, Jolomo, Joltman, Jon513, JonMoore, Joseph A. Spadaro, Josh3580, Jsonitsac, Jtant2, Juliancolton, Julianortega, Jusdafax, JustAGal, JustPhil, Jvcdude, Jwy, KConWiki, KUsam, Kacoco, Kafziel, Kaiserm, Kalathalan, Kanamekun, Kane5187, Kapow, Karenjc, Karl 334, Kaseydear, Katebrown83, Katydidit, Kbh3rd, Kchishol1970, Keaton, Kesla, Kevinbrogers, Kevinmac81, Keyser Söze, Kharker, Khatru2, Kicking222, Kidwiki91, Kinabrew, KineticEnergy, KirbyMaster14, Kitch, Kjammer, Koala15, Koavf, Kocio, Kostmo, Kraftlos, Krich, Ktr101, Kurt Shaped Box, Kvangend, Kwanesum, L1759, LOL, Lakeshark, Lambertman, Lamrock, Lanford, LarryG888, Larrymcp, Laszlo Panaflex, Lauren.klika, Laurenboukas, Laurinavicius, Lawikitejana, Lazareth, Ldubs48, Leadpipevigilante, Lear's Fool, LeaveSleaves, Legolas173, Legomyeggo252, Lemnaminor, Leszek Jańczuk, LetItBe, Levineps, Lexein, Life of Riley, Lighthead, LilUnderwood12, Lilpinoy 82, LindsayH, Lionelt, Loansince, Loft, Loginnigol, Lokicarbis, Longhair, Lord of the Vulcans, LordBleen, Lordhart, Loserjay10, LouScheffer, Lovemephone, Lovepollution, Lrg8607, LuK3, Lucnitrj, Luspari, Lvillealumni, MARKLA123, MBtheI, MER-C, MKCordova, MKoltnow, MONGO, MZMcBride, MaJic, Macarion, Mackensen, Mackeriv, Madchester, Madhu Mathew Wiki, Magioladitis, Magister Mathematicae, Magkaz, Mainly.generic, MakeRocketGoNow, Maksdo, Malikbek, Malinaccier, Malkus, Manufracture, Manway, ManymerrymenmakingmuchmoneyinthemonthofMay, Marchije, Marcus Brute, Marek69, Mariacer Cervantes, Markt3, Martarius, Martin19, Martpol, Martyn Lovell, Masonprof, MasqueIV, Matches10, Mathteach4u, Mato, Matt Deres, MattRotFace, Mattbrundage, Mattderojas, Matthewrbowker, Mattworld, Mav, Maxim, Mbstone, McGeddon, McSly, Mdf, Mdomino2011, Mechanic93, MegX, MegaJD, Megan1967, Megapixie, MegastarLV, MelbourneStar, Melonkelon, Melsaran, Mendoza215, Mercurywoodrose, Mfk91, Mgcsinc, Michael 2247778, Michael L. Kaufman, Michael Rawdon, Michaela den, Michaelbeckham, Mike Selinker, MikeAllen, MikeWazowski, Mikereynolds4444, Mikeyhurricane43, MikkoM, Mimzy1990, Minaker, Minesweeper, Mintguy, Miquonranger03, Misterrick, Mitsukai, Mjesuele, Mkeranat, Mlaffs, Mmholla33, Mo0, Modulatum, Mogism, Moncrief, Mooveeguy, Moshe Constantine Hassan Al-Silverburg, Mpgmatthew, Mr Snrub, Mr. Chicago, Mraandthebigbrother, Mrblondnyc, Mrmiscellanious, Mrschimpf, Mtjaws, Mtroy, Mtstroud, Mttcmbs, Mukyboy, Mulad, Musdan77, Mushroom, Mwparenteau, Myscrnnm, Mysdaao, N5iln, NJA, NTox, Nais, Nakon, Nathan Ladd, NathanielTheBold, Nazarian1, Nehrams2020, NeilN, Neilc, Neilka, NekoDaemon, Nenog, Neolandes, NewTestLeper79, Newsflash930, Nick Dillinger, NickCatal, Nico Tarango, NightSnoop, Nightscream, Nippy13, Nishiwarrior, Nj-educator, Nlu, Nman91, Nobody of Consequence, Noommos, Norman21, NormanEinstein, Not a dog, Not a slave, NuclearWarfare, Nuggetboy, ONEder Boy, OUNorton, Off-the-air, Onebravemonkey, Onemoretillhome, Only, Onlyonforonedit, Onorem, OrangeDog, Ost316, Out-of-focus, OutRider2003, OverlordQ, Oxguy3, Oxymoron83, P4k, PScooter63, Paat, Pacific Coast Highway, PacificBoy, Padme na, Panastasia, Papacha, Patiferoolz, Patrolmanno9, Paul Benjamin Austin, Paul Erik, Paul Richter, Pdb, PeaceNT, Pedro thy master, Pegship, Percederberg, Pete.k, Peter G Werner, Peter Karlsen, Peterhansen2032, Petero9, Pfalstad, Phi beta, PhilTLL, Philg88, PinkCake, Pinkadelica, Pipedreambomb, Pixelface, Pizzafrisbee, Pjoef, Plasma Twa 2, Pnevares, Podzemnik, Pokey5945, Polarbear97, Pop19711, Postdlf, PowerWindows, Prodego, ProhibitOnions, Prometheus235, Pseudomonas, PsychoJason, Pumapayam, Punjabihater, Purplebackpack89, Qaqaq, Qrc2006, Quase, QuasyBoy, Qutezuce, Quuxplusone, RHodnett, Raafia, Raaj1290, Racconish, RachC, Racingstripes, Radagast83, Radiant chains, Radicalsubversiv, RadioActive, Radiofreewill, Radiohawk, Radius, Rainbowsunshine86, Rajah, Ral315, RattleandHum, Rayna Jaymes, Rayquazados, Rbraunwa, Rebelguy93, Recollected, Redrocket, Redthoreau, Registered user 92, Reign of Toads, Renesis, Renosecond, RevAladdinSane, RexNL, Rfc1394, Rice33, Rich Farmbrough, Richard Arthur Norton (1958-), RichardMills65, Richardman363, RichieGB, RickK, Rillian, Ring2011, Rivemont, Rje, Rjwilmsi, Rkpuffate, Rlquall, RobJ1981, Robert K S, Robert Moore, Robertb-dc, Rockhopper10r, Rockin56, Rodrigogomespaixao, Rodriguez ochoa 31, Rogue Gremlin, Ronhjones, Ronny8, Rontrigger, Rorschach, Rory096, Rosekelleher, RoyBatty42, Rtkat3, Rustyshacklford, Rutld001, RyanLV, Ryanatthedisco7, S0uj1r0, SD6-Agent, SFC9394, SINFJ, SS451, ST47, Saginaw-hitchhiker, Sajt, Salamurai, Saltine, SaltyBoatr, Samdod2427, Samwisebruce, Sandcherry, SandraBullock2007, Saopaulo1, Satan666123666, Saturdaynightlive, Savethemooses, Scarce, Scarian, Schappy, Schlabobble, Schmendrick, Schmidt26, Schroeder74, SchuminWeb, Scooby7292, Scope creep, Scott MacGillivray, Scottf929, Sd-100, Seabear3ty, SeanO, Seanmathis26, Seanzimmer, Seattlefan68, Secret Saturdays, Semper discens, Seokhun, Seresin, Seth Ilys, Sewing, SeymoreAwesome, Seyon, Shadowjams, Shadowlynk, ShakingSpirit, Shamrox, Shatner, Sheepnacidadegrande, Shoeofdeath, Showdown, Shsilver, SidP, Siege72, SigKauffman, Sik0fewl, SilentGuy, Silentph03nix, Simbry, Simpsons2010, Sinistrum, Sirex98, Sisko199, Sjones23,

Sjorford, Sjschultz, Sky Attacker, SkyWalker, Slightsmile, Slimer42, SmartGuy Old, Smdo, Smoke Rulz, SmokeDetector47, Smurdah, Snicket01, Snowfreak91287, Snowy150, SoM, Socalspongebob, Sohollywood, Soliloquial, Someguy1221, Someoneinmyheadbutit'snotme, Son of Somebody, Soonercary, Sorry about your dog, Souldier77, Soulpatch, Soundslikealotofhooplah, South Philly, Soxwon, SpacemanSpiff, Spalding, Sparkdogvbdapdnw, Spatronic, Speed010, Spellmaster, Spencer, Spinningspark, Spitfire, Splash, Splashmo, Spongefan, Spoonkymonkey, Squandermania, Srleffler, Srushe, Srxt81, Stacecom, Stacyv.v, Steam5, Steelers45, Steve2011, Stevietheman, StewartNetAddict, StewieBaby05, Stickee, Stlsportsfan2316, Stonesoup99, Stormie, Stormwatch, Str1977, Strings42, Strom, Struway, Stusutcliffe, SubwayEater, Sugar Bear, Sunray, SuperFlash101, Survivorfan101, Susan118, Sven Manguard, Swingkid570, Sxzas, Szyslak, TA3M YM TA3, TAnthony, THollan, TJ Spyke, TMC1982, TPIRFanSteve, TPREX, TUF-KAT, TVFAN24, Tadishere2, Tarc, Tassedethe, Tbhotch, Tdi7457, Techman224, TehBrandon, Telefan, Tempshill, Ten-pint, Terrocomtor, Tgeairn, Tha*Lunat!k, The Cunctator, The Filmaker, The Lake Effect, The Man in Question, The Mystery Man, The Obento Musubi, The Rogue Penguin, The Smartest and Coolest, The man stephen, The monkeyhate, TheCustomOfLife, TheEvilBlueberryCouncil, TheHYPO, TheRedPenOfDoom, Theaterfreak64, Thefourdotelipsis, Themalpal, Themindset, TheoFleury89, Theoldsparkle, Therealdede, Therequiembellishere, Theshibboleth, Thingg, Thinking-ape, Thomprod, Thonil, Thunderbunny, Tide rolls, Tidus the BlitzStar, TigerShark, Tim Ivorson, Tim Messer, Tim010987, Timc, TimothyHorrigan, Timrollpickering, Tinton5, Tiptoety, Tk hylian, Tkgd2007, Tktru, Tkynerd, Tntdj, Tobias Hoevekamp, TonicBH, Tonster, Tony Fox, Tony1, TonyTheTiger, Tpbradbury, Tree Biting Conspiracy, Trivialist, Trusilver, Truthiness Jones, Tsuchiya Hikaru, Tubby23, Tutelary, TutterMouse, Tverbeek, Twang, Twintone, Twistedkombat, Tyler306, Tylerdmace, Tylerl82, Ultraexactzz, Umrguy42, Uncle Dick, Uncle Milty, UncleDouggie, Unclemikejb, Unicycledude42, User2004, UserNameless, UtherSRG, Vaniac, Vaoverland, Varlaam, VeiledAbyss, Veinor, Veldin963, Velella, Verloren, Versus22, Vidor, Viewdrix, Vincelord, Violetriga, Vkil, Voidxor, Vonspringer, Vranak, Vrray people1000, Vsm87, Vsmith, Vzbs34, WOSlinker, Wackywace, Waffleslice, Wafulz, Wahkeenah, Walter Humala, Walterbrunswick, Walterego, Wapcaplet, Ward3001, Wasted Time R, Water78, Wavy G, Wayward, Wcquidditch, Wctaiwan, Wdflake, Webgrunt, Wencer, Weregerbil, Werideatdusk33, WesleyDodds, Wetman, Wfaulk, Wik4, WikiPlayer, WikiTome, Wikialexdx, Wikipedical, Wikiwiki1237, WildWildBil, WillC, William Graham, Williamborg, Williamnilly, Williamsburgland, Willking1979, Willsmith47, Wingdude88, Wolfnix, Woohookitty, Wtmitchell, X201, X292FirefighterX, XLerate, XadXgamerX, Xanzzibar, Xavierhollandaise, Xezbeth, Xgottagetoutx, Xihix, Xinoph, Xm2631, Xunflash, XuxiRawe22, Y2kcrazyjoker4, YOMHER, YUL89YYZ, Yagmonster, Yamaguchi先生, Yamla, Yarnover, Yavoh, Yellid23, Yelling Bird, Yomher, Yoni90, YoungImpressionist129, Youngamerican, Your mother1234567890, ZRetro, Zacharysyoung, Zanimum, Zaphod-Swe, Zenohockey, Zephyrnthesky, ZhaoHong, Zoe, Zoicon5, Zsero, Zzyzx11, Δ, زرشک, 3656 anonymous edits

Song of Myself *Source*: http://en.wikipedia.org/w/index.php?oldid=613155682 *Contributors*: Aksi great, Alansohn, Allens, Atorpen, Benjwgarner, Brtom1, Bryan Derksen, Btstevens89, DoubleBlue, Drmies, Eliz81, Engineer Bob, Ewulp, Fanra, Fieldday-sunday, Firks19, Fluffernutter, Freakofnurture, Gipperfish, Golfandme, Goodsmonth, Hu12, IWP, Igoldste, Ipoellet, Johnuniq, Junius49, KConWiki, Kirrages, Koavf, Kyle824, Leon..., Leonard^Bloom, Lkjhgfdsa, Lucretius3659, MakeRocketGoNow, Mav, Merlinsorca, Midnightdreary, Mrmrbeaniepiece, Mtfr, Muhandes, Noq, Ohnoitsjamie, Oscarfan, Otto4711, PaladinWhite, Palayla, Parkwells, Pcpcpc, Pharos, PhnomPencil, R.Ahmd, Rainier Schmidt, Rivertorch, Rostz, Sandycx, Squash, Srleffler, T e r o, Tony Sidaway, TonyTheTiger, Whichiswhich, Wimt, Wmahan, Wolfman, Wwnorton, X!, Xndr, 143 anonymous edits

L'Officiel *Source*: http://en.wikipedia.org/w/index.php?oldid=603388265 *Contributors*: Calliopejen1, Colonies Chris, Danno uk, Dawnseeker2000, Dawynn, Delirium, Grutness, Lofficielthailand, Mean as custard, Neoeros, Od Mishehu AWB, Ohconfucius, Poppilundo, Racconish, Robomod, Zvonko, 47 anonymous edits

A Clockwork Orange *Source*: http://en.wikipedia.org/w/index.php?oldid=618769577 *Contributors*: 05kinjac, 06whitec, 10metreh, 1297, 5 albert square, 54mp0 X 70rg0, 6afraidof7, 7&6=thirteen, 8mmfilm!, A1r, ABCD, AEMoreira042281, AOC25, AV3000, Aaron.a.high, Abductive, Abercromby3, Aberwulf, Aeusoes1, Ahoerstemeier, Ahpook, Aim Here, Akseli9, Alansohn, Albany NY, Alekzia, Alexforcefive, Alfcab, Alison, AlistairMcMillan, Allens, Allseeingi, Altenmann, Alvonruff, Amccarter, Ameotoko, Amorim Parga, Anamnisia, Andishepartovi, Andonic, Andrew777, Andrewc1453, Andy G, Andycjp, Andyo, Angelic Wraith, Angr, Animum, Anjouli, AnnaFrance, Anomo, Anonymous from the 21st century, Anonymous from the 21th century, Anrod, Antandrus, Ante Aikio, Anthony, Anthony Ivanoff, Antiuser, Anville, Aranel, Archer888, Arjayay, Arthena, Artist Formerly Known As Whocares, Ascepanovic, Ashmoo, Atenea26, Athletes Foot, AuJH, Auréola, Austinmohr, Aveeck, BD2412, Baba Alex, BadSeed, Bender235, Beno1000, Bfarrell5, Bgwhite, BiT, Bill shannon, Blades95, Blue63duck, Bmunden, Bobo192, Bobzchemist, Bodnotbod, Bogdangiusca, Boing! said Zebedee, Breez, Brendanmiddleton, Brian G. Crawford, Brianhe, Brianski, Bridesmill, BrokenSegue, Brossow, Browned, BruceDLimber, Bt8257, C0n724l10n, CLW, Cajunstrike, Calabane, Calliopejen, Calmer Waters, Camembert, Cammoore, Can't sleep, clown will eat me, Canterbury Tail, CaptainFugu, Carlos Rojas77, Cburnett, Cerejota, CesarFelipe, Chafe66, Chatfecter, Chcknwnm, Chicagofan69, Chiton magnificus, Choor monster, Chris Capoccia, Chris the speller, Chris77xyz, ChrisGualtieri, Christine Saliba, Christophernandez, ChuckyDarko, Chudster92, Chuq, Cid935, Citymovement, Clarkcj12, Clintjf, CoNFuseDEnD, Coemgenus, Commander Keane, Commander Peace13, Compfreak7, Comradesandalio, Conti, Contrivance, Conversion script, CorrectorofErrors, Courcelles, CowboySpartan, Crazy Fox, Csmiller, Csmth, Cult of the Sacred Or nge, Cumulus Clouds, CutOffTies, Cybercobra, Czolgolz, D420182, DARTH SIDIOUS 2, DadaNeem, Dan100, Dancey2, Daniel Case, Darguz Parsilvan, Darrenhusted, Dave souza, Davetron5000, David Edgar, David Gerard, David depaoli, Davidbspalding, Dawkeye, Db102291, Dbenbenn, Dead Horsey, DeadEyeArrow, Deathphoenix, Deb, Debracica, Den fjättrade ankan, Denisarona, DennisDaniels, Dethomas, Devilmaycare, Dewrad, Digipak, Dikke poes, Dismas, Dissidia Fan, Djallal, Djdaedalus, Dl2000, Dlloydp, Doc glasgow, Dolph, Donfbreed, Donreed, Dougweller, DrBat, Draconiszeta, Dreamscapist, Druff, DubbleM, Dumpendebat, Dylan Lake, Dysprosia, E0steven, EEMIV, Eastlaw, Eclecticology, EconoPhysicist, Ed g2s, Eddie.willers, Eddiewiilover1555, Edgar181, EditorInTheRye, Edward, El Comandante, ElTyrant, Electric.tapir, Elizabell, Ellmist, Ellsworth, Epiphany11, Epolk, Erviale, Esperant, Esrever, Evalpor, Everyking, Evil Monkey, Explainer, Eyrian, FT2, Fan-freaken-tasic, Farrtj, Feliceallegra, FestivalOfSouls, Fetchcomms, Fieldday-sunday, Filippof, Firelightcorvett, FirstPrinciples, Fitch, Fixer23, Flammifer, Flat Out, Flowanda, Flyer22, Footsoldier, Fparnon, Frecklefoot, Frecklegirl, Fredcondo, Fullmetalkubrick, Funeral, Furkhaocean, GSlicer, Gabriel Yuji, Gaius Cornelius, Gamaliel, Garrick92, Gary Jones, Gauss, Gavindow, Gavins., GeZe, Geevee, Gekritzl, Ghettoeskimo, Giggleguy, Gilliam, Gizzakk, Glane23, Glassbreaker5791, Gmcole, Gobbleswoggler, Gogo Dodo, GooTuM, GorgeCustersSabre, GrahamHardy, Greatgavini, Greatrobo76, Gregalodon, Gregbard, Grrowl, Gurumeditation64, Gustave the Steel, GuyverArt, Gyrofrog, H2g2bob, Haham hanuka, Hajor, Hakluyt bean, HalJor, HarryHenryGebel, Hashar, Hbdragon88, Heliogabalus227, Henderson@aol.com, Heron, Herve Reex, Heslopian, Hmains, Hushpuckena, I am One of Many, Idontwantausernameman, Ike, Ike9898, Ikiroid, Ilikepie2221, ImperatorExercitus, Inter, Interwiki gl, Iron Ghost, JB82, Jaberwocky6669, Jackelfive, JamesAM, Jareha, JasticE, Java13690, Jay, Jayjg, Jbsuperfly, JesseRafe, Jiang, Jihg, Jim1138, Jim62sch, Jkta97, JoanneB, Jodon1971, Joeyrahimi, John, John Lake, John Vandenberg, JohnElder, JohnOwens, Johnny 42, JonHarder, Jonadin93, Jonathan Gr, Jonathan.s.kt, Joseph Wajsberg, Jpardey01, Jpisdandy, Juansidious, Just plain Bill, JustAGal, KDLarsen, Kaijucole, Kaizokuo, Kappa, Karynannestuckey, Katieh5584, Kbhoyt, Kdau, Keilana, Kelly Martin, Kelvingreen, Kesac, Kevinalewis, Kghose, Kingturtle, Kirkwb, Kitabparast, KnowBuddy, KnowledgeOfSelf, Koavf, Koccur3, Korath, Kouban, Koyaanis Qatsi, Krazeycarl, Kubrickchick, Kukini, Kuralyov, Kusma, Kyleslat, Kzollman, L Kensington, L.Crono, L33th4x0rguy, LGagnon, LM2000, La marts boys, Lacrimosus, Larry V, Laura S, Lefty, Lesser Shadow, Lightmouse, Ling.Nut, Linkster123, Llywrch, Lokifan at LJ, Lolmaster, Loren.wilton, LostLeviathan, Lot49a, Lotje, LucasVB, LudwigK, Luigibob, Lukevader, Luna Santin, Lunakeet, Lung salad, MASQUERAID, MC10, MER-C, MFlet1, MK8, Ma'ame Michu, Mackinaw, Madcoverboy, Madskile, Magioladitis, Mahlon, MakeRocketGoNow, Malcolm Farmer, Mancune2001, Manic2, Manny Clockwork Orange, Marc Kupper, MarcoTolo, Marcready, Marcus Bowen, Mark Forest, Mark Zelinka, MarnetteD, Martarius, Martinor, Martpol, Martyring, Masked Mutant, Matthew voros, MatthewUND, Mattnad, Max Terry, Mcrfan44, Mdebets, Melanippa, Mentifisto, Merkwurdigliebe, Merovingian, Metahacker, Michaelkvance, Michel.SLM, Mick V, Midgrid, Mike E Fresh, Mike Searson, Mike6271, MikeBriggs, Milliped, Mimi-t-m-c-26, Mirateca, Missmarple, Mkckim, Mkweise, Mogism, Mohamed mashaly, Molly-in-md, Moondust9358, Mordemur, Morningstar2651, MrDarcy, Mrdude, MuZemike, Mushroom, MusicMaker5376, N5iln, N8chz, Nakon, Nalvage, Nandesuka, NargleFishHat, Nasenatmer, Natcase, NawlinWiki, Neilbeach, Neilc, Neko-chan, NeoBatfreak, Neokamek, Neptune's Trident, Niceguyedc, Nick Cooper, NickPenguin, Nikai, Nikkimaria, Ninmacer20, Noctibus, NotSuper, Notinasnaid, Noumero888, O'Dea, OccultZone, Oceancetaceen, Octane, Olaf Davis, Omnipaedista, One Salient Oversight, Opponent, Originalname37, Orrc, Oscabat, Ouro, P2bpc, Pablo X, Paffka, PamukSoundystem, Patrick, Paul A, Paul Magnussen, Pazuzu413, Pegship, Percy Snoodle, Peter Winnberg, Phantommont, Pharaoh of the Wizards, Phil Bridger, PicBook, Pip2andahalf, PisspunkDK, Pit, Pjimenez, Plasticup, Poccil, Polisher of Cobwebs, Poopyloopsy, Porlob, Portillo, Ppntori, Profoss, Prosit, Ptryxxx, Quadell, Quasimondo, Queenmomcat, Quuxplusone, R Lowry, R. fiend, RA0808, RJHall, RL0919, RaCha'ar, RadioEverleigh, Ranger Duke, Raven4x4x, Ray Dassen, Razorflame, Repku, Reveree, RexNL, Rfc1394, Rhobite, Rhododendrites, Rich Farmbrough, Rillian, Ringbang, Ripe, RjCan, Rjanag, Rjwilmsi, RobertG, RobertIl, Ronhjones, Rorro, Rosenknospe, RoyBoy, Royboycrashfan, Rsrikanth05, Rtrace, Ruakh, Rubicon, Rudybowwow, RunOrDie, Runefrost, RxS, Ryan Norton, Ryan124, S3000, SCEhardt, SJP, ST47, Sadads, Saksham, Sallyberta, Salmanazar, Samulili, Sandstein, Sanfazer, SarekOfVulcan, Sburcher, Sc147, Schatman, SeanLegassick, Seatdistrict, Sepulwiki, Sethmahoney, Sgt Pinback, ShadowyCaballero, Shakurazz, Shirt58, Shoejar, Shuffdog, Sierra 1, Simon Peter Hughes, Simon Wardell, SimonP, SingingZombie, Sintermerte, Sjc, Skapur, Skarebo, Skyraider, Sleddog116, Slightsmile, Snotduck, Snow0r, Snowolf, Snoyes, SofterWorld, Softlavender, Some jerk on the Internet, Someguy1221, Sophitus, Sosthenes12, SpNeo, Spacelib, Spencer444, Springerak, Spylab, Sroc, Starwiz, Stefan Kruithof, Stefanomione, Stephenb, Stevenmitchell, StewieBaby05, Sturman, Subsume, SubtleWreck, SuperMarioMan, Swattie, Synthetic, TK Floyd, TZe, Tagtheatre, Tangerines, Tarquin, Tartan, Tassedethe, Tc triangle, Tdowling, Techman224, Technomad, Ted 3000, TedKendall, Tedernst, Teh Squonkz, TehRealJesus, Template namespace initialisation script, TenPoundHammer, TerriersFan, Thatguyflint, The Anome, The Blade of the Northern Lights, The Cunctator, The Rock And Roll Pirate, The Singing Badger, The Uncyclopedian, The undertow, The wub, TheCoffee, TheMidnighters, ThePersonOverTheRainbow, TheSeez, Theaterfreak64, Thelos1, Theodolite, Theshibboleth, Thestanwyks, Thomas Blomberg, ThomasK, Thorsten1, Thoughtcat, Thrawn03, ThreeAnswers, Thumperward, Tientao, Tim!, Tim1357, Timo Honkasalo, Tkessler, Tkrokli, Tkynerd, Tom harrison, Tomlillis, Tomwhite56, Tony Sidaway, Tony360X, TonyW, Tonyfuchs1019, Topbanana, Trevor Andersen, Treybien, Trianam, Trilobite, Triona, Trusilver, Tufflaw, Turnstep, Tweaker214, Typhoon, Ulric1313, Uman88, Unicorn19, Unint, Uucp, Vague Rant, Valenciano, Vanished User 1004, Vanished user g454XxNpUVWvxzlr, Varangian, Ventifact, VeryVerily, Victor Lopes, Victory93, VioLetJade, Violentbob, Violncello, VivianCastiera, Vlemaic, VolatileChemical, Vrenator, WIERDGREENMAN, Wakuran, Wanhamies, WashUrslfInTears, Wenli, Wereon, Western John, Westknife, Whittsnake1, Whyismynamebeth, WickerGuy, WikHead, Wiki Raja, Wiki alf, WikiHannibal, Wikiborg, William (The Bill) Blackstone, Woohookitty, Xanchester, Xenocidic, Xephedrinex, Xezbeth, Xhojux, Year 2144, Yorick8080, Yvwv, ZENmud, ZacBowling, Zap Rowsdower, ZapThunderstrike, Zappaz, Zaruyache, Zeisseng, Zepheus, Zephyrad, Zer0faults, Zombie433, ZombieRamen, Zosodada, Zotdragon, Zpb52, Zteller, Zyqqh, דוד, דוד ש', 1546 anonymous edits

American Cinematheque *Source*: http://en.wikipedia.org/w/index.php?oldid=601719776 *Contributors*: 2moms4life, Chris the speller, ChrisGualtieri, CineSight, Davidpatrick, Grayfell, John of Reading, Levineps, Lquilter, Melonkelon, Merseymasala, PacificBoy, Quentin X, Simon12, Steve, 5 anonymous edits

Summer Wine *Source*: http://en.wikipedia.org/w/index.php?oldid=616313781 *Contributors*: ACSE, ASaltzman, Ahoerstemeier, Beardo, Bolgar12, Caleson, ChrisGualtieri, Clausthal, DocWatson42, DougDean, Druzhnik, Earbox, Floquenbeam, Frous, GoingBatty, InnocuousPseudonym, JD554, Jax 0677, KaragouniS, Keilana, Lankeymarlon, LeoFrank, Liberatus, Lightlowemon, MagicatthemovieS, Materialscientist, MisterVista, Mogism, Muhandes, Nikita.Kostylev, Poco a poco, Quadibloc, Raps1970, Richhoncho, Sinnyo, Stemonitis, Stevewilkins, Syxx,

Teammathi, The Amazing Pudding, VicVega123, Waacstats, 91 anonymous edits

Maleficent (film) *Source*: http://en.wikipedia.org/w/index.php?oldid=619731098 *Contributors*: 16danielv, 1ST7, Acalamari, Action Parker, Alan19951, Aldy, Alexbrombal, Alien Putsch resistant, All Hallow's Wraith, AlphaKate, Amanda7207, Amandajohnson3000000465, Amducker, Amy50632, And1987, Andrestreamz, Angus Wright, Anonymous from the 21st century, Another Believer, Aquila89, Arcadina, Articmonkeys, Asciiavatar, Ashdenej, AussieLegend, Backendgaming, Bender235, BiH, Blalthazar, Bloggersingh, Bluerules, Bollyjeff, Bovineboy2008, Brandmeister, Brazzy, Brendin24, BrettofMoore, Bry4n esp, Caecae99, ChipmunkRaccoon, ChrisAnorthosis, Cmcalpine, Connymenzel, CoolDude13, Crboyer, Creationul, Daniel J. Leivick, De Disney, Deflective, Deltasim, DemirBajraktarevic, Deor, Derek R Bullamore, Diego Moya, Discospinster, Dogmad87, Dougweller, DrNegative, Draco9904, Dragonzbb11, DrummerSteve69, EVula, EamonnPKeane, Easy4me, ElHef, Elizium23, Faizhaider, Farshad.h, Favre1fan93, FilmandTVFan28, FlawlessViper, Flax5, Flyer22, FraDany, Freshh, Garyoak99, Geraldo Perez, Giggett, Goustien, Hammersoft, ILoveOlaf, Igormachado21, IronGargoyle, IsmailAwang, Italian1980, J.Dontrell, Jakeleereed, Jec178, Jedi94, Jim1138, Joeyc97, John Ozyer-Key, Jonathansuh, Junewinters, Kailash29792, Karisaamelia, Katana geldar, Kazu-kun, Koala15, Lady Lotus, LadyofShalott, Leonardo Lazov, Lg16spears, LiluMultipass, Little Jimmy, Lord Opeth, Lquilter, Lugia2453, Luminum, Mahdisney, Marek Koudelka, MarnetteD, Materialscientist, MatthewChown, Melanie9992, MelbourneStar, Mezigue, Mike hayes, Mogism, Mr. Granger, Narnian1950, Necrothesp, NiamhBurns10, Nikg91, NinjaTazzyDevil, Njorent, Noneofyourbusiness, Ntsimp, Official herve, Omgfucku, Onealyako, Optakeover, Patrick Rogel, Pborri, Peach114, PinkFreak91, Pioneer47, Plau, Purple Meat, QuasyBoy, Queenelsa, Quenhitran, Quentin X, Renee2302i9123, Rexwei, Ritzy101, Roadbound, Robsinden, Rodriguezandres789, Ruffnerr, Ruhilgoyal, Rusted AutoParts, SNAAAAKE!!, STATicVapor, Saintfighteraqua, Saltine, Sapphirewhirlwind, Sausboss, Sb1990, Shallowgravy, Shoewax, SimonPerera, Slightsmile, SlimJimmyBRabbit, Smartalic34, Sock, Soy Hermoso, Spencer Maverick, Spike harrison, Spinc5, SpiritedMichelle, Spshu, Ss112, Status, Steveprutz, Sundios, SurfingTiger, TFunk, Takkyon, Tenebrae, Tfixguy, TheMovieBuff, Tim Week, Tokyogirl179, Tomica, Toniposadas, Trillfendi, Trivialist, TropicAces, Tutelary, Varunga, Vranak, Whatsitnow, Widr, WikiKing14, Wikicontributor12, Wikipeef, Wilsonandrewc, Zacharydclark, Zarcadia, ZeroProfileZ, Zuko Halliwell, 588 anonymous edits

West Coast (song) *Source*: http://en.wikipedia.org/w/index.php?oldid=619423238 *Contributors*: (CA)Giacobbe, Acalamari, Afri123, Airmantx, Andrzejbanas, Another Believer, Arjann, Bleff, Burgermeister77, Canadaolympic989, Caseymary, ChrisCarss Former24.108.99.31, Creationul, Diy09, Dkisnis, Easy4me, EditorE, Ellis.o22, Esquelet, Eternal baby, Greenock125, Holiday56, IPadPerson, Javiereq, Jonesey95, Kieranmcdermott1, KirrVlad, Kirtap92, Leo Mercury, Littlecarmen, Lzrbiim, Magioladitis, Matt723star, Michsonicfan, Nxtgenration, R3troguy420, Richhoncho, Shooky123, Sjr 14, SkitChuk, Solidest, Splarks, Ss112, Status, Surah elle, TheDarkKnight180, Thomasamuse, Vinokurov Demis, Werldwayd, WikiRedactor, Wikihelpermusc, Y2kcrazyjoker4, 79 anonymous edits

Shades of Cool *Source*: http://en.wikipedia.org/w/index.php?oldid=617047694 *Contributors*: 2Flows, Abydo, Airmantx, Another Believer, Bleff, Canadaolympic989, Caseymary, Deansfa, I just wanna edit stuff, Iain Robb, Jim1138, Kieranmcdermott1, Kirtap92, Leonmichels, Littlecarmen, Martinelcondo, Michsonicfan, MisterPolitics, QuasyBoy, Shooky123, Status, Vinokurov Demis, Werldwayd, WikiRedactor, Xxvid, 22 anonymous edits

Brooklyn Baby *Source*: http://en.wikipedia.org/w/index.php?oldid=619423475 *Contributors*: Airmantx, Another Believer, Cxleb, EditorE, IPadPerson, KirrVlad, Ldaleback, Leonmichels, Littlecarmen, Status, TheDarkKnight180, Vinokurov Demis, WikiRedactor, 25 anonymous edits

License

Printed in Great Britain
by Amazon.co.uk, Ltd.,
Marston Gate.